W9-BYK-281

Learning Vue.js 2

Learn how to build amazing and complex reactive web applications easily with Vue.js

Olga Filipova

BIRMINGHAM - MUMBAI

Learning Vue.js 2

Copyright © 2016 Packt Publishing

All rights reserved. No part of this book may be reproduced, stored in a retrieval system, or transmitted in any form or by any means, without the prior written permission of the publisher, except in the case of brief quotations embedded in critical articles or reviews.

Every effort has been made in the preparation of this book to ensure the accuracy of the information presented. However, the information contained in this book is sold without warranty, either express or implied. Neither the author, nor Packt Publishing, and its dealers and distributors will be held liable for any damages caused or alleged to be caused directly or indirectly by this book.

Packt Publishing has endeavored to provide trademark information about all of the companies and products mentioned in this book by the appropriate use of capitals. However, Packt Publishing cannot guarantee the accuracy of this information.

First published: December 2016

Production reference: 1071216

Published by Packt Publishing Ltd.
Livery Place
35 Livery Street
Birmingham
B3 2PB, UK.

ISBN 978-1-78646-994-6

www.packtpub.com

Credits

Author

Olga Filipova

Reviewer

Bogdan-Alin Bâlc

Commissioning Editor

Wilson D'souza

Acquisition Editor

Chaitanya Nair

Content Development Editor

Divij Kotian

Technical Editor

Prajakta Mhatre

Copy Editor

Sameen Siddiqui

Project Coordinator

Sheejal Shah

Proofreader

Safis Editing

Indexer

Tejal Daruwale Soni

Production Coordinator

Melwyn D'sa

About the Author

Olga Filipova was born in Ukraine, in Kyiv. She grew up in a family of physicists, scientists, and professors. She studied system analysis at the National University of Ukraine Kyiv Polytechnic Institute. At the age of 20, she moved to Portugal where she did her bachelor's and master's degrees in computer science in the University of Coimbra. During her studies, she participated in research and development of European projects and became an assistant teacher of operating systems and computer graphics. After obtaining her master's degree, she started to work at Feedzai. At that time, it was a small team of four who developed a product from scratch, and now it is one of the most successful Portuguese startups. At some point, her main responsibility became to develop a library written in JavaScript whose purpose was to bring data from the engine to the web interface. This marked Olga's main direction in tech—web development. At the same time, she continued her teaching practice in a course of professional web development in the local professional education center in Coimbra.

In 2013, along with her brother and her husband, she started an educational project based in Ukraine. This project's name is EdEra and it has grown from a small platform of online courses into a big player in the Ukrainian educational system. Currently, EdEra is pointing in an the international direction and preparing an awesome online course about IT. Don't miss it!

In 2014, Olga, with her husband and daughter, moved from Portugal to Berlin, where she started working at Meetrics as a frontend engineer, and after a year she became the lead of an amazing team of frontend software developers.

Olga is happily married to an awesome guy called Rui, who is also a software engineer. Rui studied with Olga at the University of Coimbra and worked with her at Feedzai. Olga has a smart and beautiful daughter called Taissa, a fluffy cat called Patusca, and two fluffiest chinchillas called Barabashka and Cheburashka.

Acknowledgments

I am grateful to Packt Publishing for offering me the possibility to write this book. You are great and so is your team. Thank you Divij, Chaitanya, Prajakta, and the whole Packt team for being awesome and supporting me through all this journey in such a friendly and warm way.

Quality is something that is difficult to achieve when working on something on your own. Thank you, Packt team, you've been awesome. And a big special gratitude goes to Romania, to Bogdan, who thoroughly reviewed the book, ran all the code snippets, tests, and lint. Bogdan's attention to even the most tiny details is astonishing. The book was rewritten after Bogdan's comments, and it became so much cleaner. Thank you very much, Bogdan and Alex, for the recommendation.

Time. Support. Love. When you have these three things you are happy and any challenge in the world can scare you. When you have these three things you know that you are capable of everything. When you have these three things you have power. But you can never have these things alone. That is why you must be eternally grateful to those who provide time, support, and love to you.

That is why my big thanks goes to my company where I am currently working—Meetrics. Meetrics provided me with time to write the book. They trusted me and allowed me to use a fraction of my working time for writing the book. Thank you very much!

I want to thank to all my friends and colleagues who supported me during this journey. Every time I come to Meetrics my team asks me how the book is going. Every time we're going to Portugal or Ukraine, our friends and family ask. Every day my friends from Berlin ask me how is it going. Thank you, people, you are awesome! Thank you, EdEra team, for being amazing and postponing important tasks because of my book.

I would love to express gratitude to my parents for educating me with so much love that I know that I am capable of anything. I know that I will not fail. Thank you for all your love and support. Thank you for giving me this confidence in myself. I want to thank to my lovely daughter, whose love and help keeps me going and continuing what I'm doing, knowing that all this is not for nothing. I want to thank to my brother for all the fun we share even and mostly while we're working.

And I want to address a special thanks with love to my husband. Along this writing journey Rui has given me time, support, and love. Rui did everything at home so I could have all the time for writing. Rui felt every slight change in my mood and provided support during all of them so I could feel comfortable again and write. If I would stay up the whole night writing and needed someone to be nearby, Rui would stay up the whole night. For every chapter in the book, Rui was the first person to review them. This was invaluable feedback. Rui gave me chapters back full of corrections and I felt sad. But then he would say something like: Oh my god, Olga, this chapter is amazing! I understood everything! I am looking forward for the next chapter to see what's next! When someone who you love very much tells you this, you just want to move on and continue your amazing writing. Thank you very much for this!

About the Reviewer

Bogdan-Alin Bâlc is a team lead with a passion for frontend technologies. He has worked with JavaScript for the past 8 years, from the emergence of jQuery and Ajax to modern full-fledged MVC frameworks. When he's not looking into some new JS challenge, he spends time with his friends, playing games and watching sports.

www.PacktPub.com

For support files and downloads related to your book, please visit www.PacktPub.com.

Did you know that Packt offers eBook versions of every book published, with PDF and ePub files available? You can upgrade to the eBook version at www.PacktPub.com and as a print book customer, you are entitled to a discount on the eBook copy. Get in touch with us at service@packtpub.com for more details.

At www.PacktPub.com, you can also read a collection of free technical articles, sign up for a range of free newsletters and receive exclusive discounts and offers on Packt books and eBooks.

https://www.packtpub.com/mapt

Get the most in-demand software skills with Mapt. Mapt gives you full access to all Packt books and video courses, as well as industry-leading tools to help you plan your personal development and advance your career.

Why subscribe?

- Fully searchable across every book published by Packt
- Copy and paste, print, and bookmark content
- On demand and accessible via a web browser

I devote this book to my daughter, Taissa.

Table of Contents

Preface

This book is about Vue.js. We will start our journey trying to understand what Vue.js is, how it compares to other frameworks, and what it allows us to do. We will learn different aspects of Vue.js while building small funny applications on top of it and applying these aspects in practice. In the end, we will look back to see what've we learned and have a look into the future to see what we can still learn and do. So, you will learn the following:

- What is Vue.js and how it works
- Reactivity and data binding with Vue.js
- Reusable components with Vue.js
- Plugins for Vue.js
- Testing and deploying applications written in Vue.js

All the examples in this book are built on top of the recently released Vue 2.0 version. The book also contains references to the previous version regarding deprecated or changed aspects of the framework.

I am sure you will enjoy the process of building applications using Vue.js with this book.

What this book covers

Chapter 1, *Going Shopping with Vue.js*, contains an introduction to Vue.js, to the terminology used through the book, and first basic examples.

Chapter 2, *Fundamentals – Installing and Using*, explains the behind the scenes of Vue.js, provides theoretical insights into the architectural pattern, touches nearly all the main Vue.js concepts, and bootstraps the applications that will be developed through the book.

Chapter 3, *Components – Understanding and Using*, goes deep into components and explains how to rewrite applications using a simple component system and single-file components.

Chapter 4, *Reactivity – Binding Data to Your Application*, contains a detailed explanations of the usage of data binding mechanisms in Vue.js.

Chapter 5, *Vuex – Managing State in Your Application*, contains detailed introduction to Vuex, a state management system for Vue.js, and explains how to use it in your application in order to achieve a nice, maintainable architecture.

Chapter 6, *Plugins – Building Your House with Your Own Bricks*, shows how to use plugins in Vue applications and explains how to use an existing plugin in an application and explains how to build our own plugin and then use it.

Chapter 7, *Testing – Time to Test What We Have Done So Far*, contains an introduction to the testing techniques that can be used in Vue applications to bring them to the needed level of quality. We tackle it by showing how to write unit tests and how to develop end-to-end tests for the applications in the book.

Chapter 8, *Deploying – Time to Go Live!*, shows how to bring your Vue application to the world, guaranteeing its quality with continuous integration tools. It explains how to connect a GitHub repository to the Travis continuous integration system and to the Heroku cloud deployment platform.

Chapter 9, *What Is Next*, wraps up everything that has been done so far and leaves the reader with the follow up steps.

Appendix, *Solutions to Exercises*, provides solutions to the exercises for first three chapters.

What you need for this book

The requirements for this book are the following:

- Computer with an Internet connection
- Text editor/IDE
- Node.js

Who this book is for

This book is for web developers or for people who want to become web developers. Whether you have just started to work with web technologies or you are already a guru of frameworks and languages in the vast ocean of web technologies, this book might show you something new in the world of reactive web applications. If you are a Vue developer and have used Vue 1.0, this book might be a useful guide for you to migrate to Vue 2.0, since all the examples of the book are based on Vue 2.0. Even if you are already using Vue 2.0, this book might be a nice exercise of building an application from scratch, applying all Vue and software engineering concepts and taking it to the deployment stage.

At least some technical background is required. If you can already write code in JavaScript, it is a huge plus.

Conventions

In this book, you will find a number of text styles that distinguish between different kinds of information. Here are some examples of these styles and an explanation of their meaning.

Code words in text, database table names, folder names, filenames, file extensions, pathnames, dummy URLs, user input, and Twitter handles are shown as follows: "Your plugin must provide an `install` method."

A block of code is set as follows:

```
export default {
  components: {
    ShoppingListComponent,
    ShoppingListTitleComponent
  },
  computed: mapGetters({
    shoppinglists: 'getLists'
  })
}
```

When we wish to draw your attention to a particular part of a code block, the relevant lines or items are set in bold:

```
export default {
  components: {
    ShoppingListComponent,
    ShoppingListTitleComponent
  },
  computed: mapGetters({
    shoppinglists: 'getLists'
  }),
  methods: mapActions(['populateShoppingLists']),
  store,
  mounted () {
    this.populateShoppingLists()
  }
}
```

Any command-line input or output is written as follows:

```
cd shopping-list
npm install vue-resource --save-dev
```

New terms and **important words** are shown in bold. Words that you see on the screen, for example, in menus or dialog boxes, appear in the text like this: "Check the **Developer mode** checkbox."

Warnings or important notes appear in a box like this.

Tips and tricks appear like this.

Reader feedback

Feedback from our readers is always welcome. Let us know what you think about this book-what you liked or disliked. Reader feedback is important for us as it helps us develop titles that you will really get the most out of. To send us general feedback, simply e-mail feedback@packtpub.com, and mention the book's title in the subject of your message. If there is a topic that you have expertise in and you are interested in either writing or contributing to a book, see our author guide at www.packtpub.com/authors.

Customer support

Now that you are the proud owner of a Packt book, we have a number of things to help you to get the most from your purchase.

Downloading the example code

You can download the example code files for this book from your account at `http://www.p acktpub.com`. If you purchased this book elsewhere, you can visit `http://www.packtpub.c om/support` and register to have the files e-mailed directly to you.

You can download the code files by following these steps:

1. Log in or register to our website using your e-mail address and password.
2. Hover the mouse pointer on the **SUPPORT** tab at the top.
3. Click on **Code Downloads & Errata**.
4. Enter the name of the book in the **Search** box.
5. Select the book for which you're looking to download the code files.
6. Choose from the drop-down menu where you purchased this book from.
7. Click on **Code Download**.

Once the file is downloaded, please make sure that you unzip or extract the folder using the latest version of:

- WinRAR / 7-Zip for Windows
- Zipeg / iZip / UnRarX for Mac
- 7-Zip / PeaZip for Linux

The code bundle for the book is also hosted on GitHub at `https://github.com/PacktPubl ishing/Learning-Vue.js-2`. We also have other code bundles from our rich catalog of books and videos available at `https://github.com/PacktPublishing/`. Check them out!

Errata

Although we have taken every care to ensure the accuracy of our content, mistakes do happen. If you find a mistake in one of our books-maybe a mistake in the text or the code-we would be grateful if you could report this to us. By doing so, you can save other readers from frustration and help us improve subsequent versions of this book. If you find any errata, please report them by visiting http://www.packtpub.com/submit-errata, selecting your book, clicking on the **Errata Submission Form** link, and entering the details of your errata. Once your errata are verified, your submission will be accepted and the errata will be uploaded to our website or added to any list of existing errata under the Errata section of that title.

To view the previously submitted errata, go to https://www.packtpub.com/books/content/support and enter the name of the book in the search field. The required information will appear under the **Errata** section.

Piracy

Piracy of copyrighted material on the Internet is an ongoing problem across all media. At Packt, we take the protection of our copyright and licenses very seriously. If you come across any illegal copies of our works in any form on the Internet, please provide us with the location address or website name immediately so that we can pursue a remedy.

Please contact us at copyright@packtpub.com with a link to the suspected pirated material.

We appreciate your help in protecting our authors and our ability to bring you valuable content.

Questions

If you have a problem with any aspect of this book, you can contact us at questions@packtpub.com, and we will do our best to address the problem.

1
Going Shopping with Vue.js

"Vue.js is a JavaScript framework for building astonishing web applications.
Vue.js is a JavaScript library for creating web interfaces.
Vue.js is a tool that leverages the use of MVVM architecture."

Simplified JavaScript Jargon suggests that Vue.js is a JavaScript library for creating user interfaces (Views) based on underlying data models (`http://jargon.js.org/_glossary/V UEJS.md`).

The official Vue.js website (`https://vuejs.org/`) just some months ago stated that Vue.js were reactive components for modern web interfaces.

Now it states that Vue.js is a progressive JavaScript framework:

So what is Vue.js after all? Framework? Tool? Library? Should it be used for building full-stack web applications or just for adding some special functionality? Should I switch from my favorite framework to it? If yes, why? Can I use it alongside other tools in my project? What advantages it might bring?

In this chapter, we will try to find the answers to all these questions. We will slightly touch Vue.js and use it within some small and simple examples.

More specifically, we will do the following:

- Learn what Vue.js is, its important parts, and its history
- Learn what projects use Vue.js
- Build a simple shopping list using Vue.js and compare the implementation to the jQuery implementation of the same application
- Build a simple Pomodoro timer using Vue.js
- Enjoy a small and simple exercise

Buzzwords

There will be lots of buzzwords, abbreviations, and other hipster combinations of letters in this book. Please do not be afraid of them. I can tell you more but, for the most part of things you need to do using Vue.js or any other framework, you do not need to know them all by heart! But, in any case, let us leave the thesaurus here so that you become confused with terminology at any point of the book, you can come back here and have a look:

- **Application state**: This is a global centralized state of the application. The data in this state is initialized when the application is started. This data can be accessed by any application's component; however, it cannot be changed easily by them. Each item of the state has an attached mutation that can be dispatched on special events occurring inside the application's components.

- **Bootstrap**: This is a project that provides a set of styles and JavaScript tools for developing a responsive and nice application without having to think a lot about CSS.
- **Content Distribution Network (CDN)**: This is a special server whose aim is to deliver data to the users with high availability and high performance. People and companies who develop frameworks like to distribute them via CDNs because they allow them just to point out the CDN's URL in the installation instructions. Vue.js is hosted in npmcdn (`https://npmcdn.com/`), which is a reliable and global network for the things that are published to the npm.
- **Components**: These are the pieces of the application with their own data and View that can be reused through the application, acting as a brick from which the house is being built.
- **Cascading Style Sheets (CSS)**: This is a set of styles to apply to the HTML document to make it nice and beautiful.
- **Declarative Views**: These are the Views that provide a way of direct data binding between plain JavaScript data models and the representation.
- **Directives**: These are special HTML elements attributes in Vue.js that allow data binding in different ways.
- **Document Object Model (DOM)**: This is a convention for representing nodes in markup languages such as HTML, XML, and XHTML. The nodes of the documents are organized into a DOM tree. When someone says interacting with DOM, it is just their fancy way of saying interacting with HTML elements.
- **npm**: This is a package manager for JavaScript and allows searching, installing, and managing JavaScript packages.
- **Markdown**: This is a human-friendly syntax that allows web writers to write their text without worrying about styles and HTML tags. Markdown files have a `.md` extension.
- **Model View ViewModel (MVVM)**: This is an architectural pattern whose central point is a ViewModel that acts as a bridge between the View and the data model, allowing the data flow between them.
- **Model View Controller (MVC)**: This is an architectural pattern. It allows separating Views from Models and from the way that information flows from Views to Models, and vice versa.
- **One-way data binding**: This is the type of data binding where the changes in the data model are automatically propagated to the View layer, but not vice versa.
- **Rapid prototyping**: In the Web, this is a technique of easily and rapidly building the mockups of the user interface, including some basic user interaction.

- **Reactivity**: In the Web, this is actually the immediate propagation of any changes of data to the View layer.
- **Two-way data binding**: This is the type of data binding where the changes in the data model are automatically propagated to the View layer, and the changes that happen in the View layer are immediately reflected in the data model.
- **User interface** (**UI**): This is a set of visual components that allow the user to communicate with the application.
- **Vuex**: This is an architecture for Vue applications and allows simple management of the application state.

Vue.js history

When, Evan You, Vue.js creator (http://evanyou.me/), was working at Google Creative Labs on one of the projects, they needed to fast prototype a rather big UI interface. Writing a lot of repeated HTML was clearly time- and resource-consuming, and that's why Evan started looking for some already existing tool for this purpose. To his surprise, he discovered that there was no tool, library, or framework that could fit exactly into the purpose of rapid prototyping! At that time, Angular was widely used, React.js was just starting, and frameworks such as Backbone.js were used for large-scale applications with MVC architecture. For the kind of project that needed something really flexible and lightweight just for quick UI prototyping, neither of these complex frameworks were adequate.

When you realize that something cool does not exist and you are able to create it—*just do it*!

 Vue.js was born as a tool for rapid prototyping. Now it can be used to build complex scalable reactive web applications.

That was what Evan did. That is how he came to the idea of creating a library that would help in rapid prototyping by offering an easy and flexible way of reactive data binding and reusable components.

Like every good library, Vue.js has been growing and evolving, thus providing more features than it was promising from the beginning. Currently, it provides an easy way of attaching and creating plugins, writing and using mixins, and overall adding custom behavior. Vue can be used in such a flexible way and is so nonopinionated of the application structuring that it definitely can be considered as a framework capable of supporting the end-to-end building of complex web applications.

The most important thing about Vue.js

Vue.js allows you to simply bind your data models to the representation layer. It also allows you to easily reuse components throughout the application.

You don't need to create special models or collections and to register events object in there. You don't need to follow some special syntax. You don't need to install any of never-ending dependencies.

Your models are plain JavaScript objects. They are being bound to whatever you want in your Views (text, input text, classes, attributes, and so on), and it just works.

You can simply add the `vue.js` file into your project and use it. Alternatively, you can use `vue-cli` with Webpack and Browserify family, which not only bootstraps the whole project but also supports hot reloading and provides developer tools.

You can separate the View layer from styles and JavaScript logic or you can put it alltogether into the same Vue file and build your components' structure and logic in the same place. There is plugin support for all modern and commonly used IDEs.

You can use whatever preprocessors you want, and you can use ES2015. You can use it alongside your favorite framework you have been developing in, or you can use it itself. You can use it just to add a small functionality, or you can use the whole Vue ecosystem to build complex applications.

If you want to check how it compares to other frameworks, such as Angular or React, then please visit `http://vuejs.org/guide/comparison.html`.

If you want to check out all the amazing things about Vue.js, then you are more than welcome to visit `https://github.com/vuejs/awesome-vue`.

Let's go shopping!

I don't know how but I can feel that your weekend is close and that you are starting to think about going shopping to buy the needed groceries for the next week. Unless you are a genius who is able to maintain the whole list in your head or you are a modest person who does not need so much, you probably make a shopping list before going shopping. Maybe you even use some app for that. Now, I ask you: why not use your own app? How do you feel about creating and designing it? Let's do that! Let's create our own shopping list application. Let's start by creating a rapid prototype for it. It's a really easy task—build an interactive prototype for the shopping list.

It should show the list and allow us to add and remove the items. Actually, it's very similar to a ToDo list. Let's start doing it using classic HTML + CSS + JS + jQuery approach. We will also use the Bootstrap framework (http://getbootstrap.com/) to make things a little bit more beautiful without having to write extensive CSS code. (Yes, because our book is not about CSS and because making things with Bootstrap is so crazily easy!)

Implementing a shopping list using jQuery

Probably, your code will end up looking as something like the following:

Here is the HTML code:

```html
<div class="container">
  <h2>My Shopping List</h2>
  <div class="input-group">
    <input placeholder="add shopping list item"
      type="text" class="js-new-item form-control">
    <span class="input-group-btn">
      <button @click="addItem" class="js-add btn btn-default"
        type="button">Add!</button>
    </span>
  </div>
  <ul>
    <li>
      <div class="checkbox">
        <label>
          <input class="js-item" name="list"
            type="checkbox"> Carrot
        </label>
      </div>
    </li>
    <li>
      <div class="checkbox">
        <label>
          <input class="js-item" name="list" type="checkbox"> Book
        </label>
      </div>
    </li>
    <li class="removed">
      <div class="checkbox">
        <label>
          <input class="js-item" name="list" type="checkbox"
            checked> Gift for aunt's birthday
        </label>
      </div>
    </li>
```

```
      </ul>
   </div>
```

Here is the CSS code:

```css
.container {
  width: 40%;
  margin: 20px auto 0px auto;
}

.removed {
  color: gray;
}

.removed label {
  text-decoration: line-through;
}

ul li {
  list-style-type: none;
}
```

Here is the JavaScript/jQuery code:

```javascript
$(document).ready(function () {
  /**
   * Add button click handler
   */
  function onAdd() {
    var $ul, li, $li, $label, $div, value;

    value = $('.js-new-item').val();
    //validate against empty values
    if (value === '') {
      return;
    }
    $ul = $('ul');
    $li = $('<li>').appendTo($ul);
    $div = $('<div>')
        .addClass('checkbox')
        .appendTo($li);
    $label = $('<label>').appendTo($div);
    $('<input>')
        .attr('type', 'checkbox')
        .addClass('item')
        .attr('name', 'list')
        .click(toggleRemoved)
        .appendTo($label);
```

```
     $label
         .append(value);
     $('.js-new-item').val('');
  }

  /**
   * Checkbox click handler -
   * toggles class removed on li parent element
   * @param ev
   */
  function toggleRemoved(ev) {
    var $el;

    $el = $(ev.currentTarget);
    $el.closest('li').toggleClass('removed');
  }

  $('.js-add').click(onAdd);
  $('.js-item').click(toggleRemoved);
});
```

Downloading the example code
Detailed steps to download the code bundle are mentioned in the
Preface of this book.
The code bundle for the book is also hosted on GitHub at https://github
.com/PacktPublishing/Learning-Vue.js-2.
We also have other code bundles from our rich catalog of books and
videos available at https://github.com/PacktPublishing/. Check them
out!

If you open the page in a browser, you will probably see something like the following:

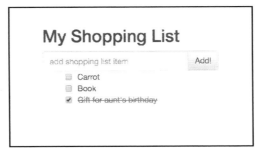

Shopping list implementation using the HTML + CSS + jQuery approach

Please have a look at JSFiddle at `https://jsfiddle.net/chudaol/u5pcnLw9/2/`.

As you can see, it is a very basic piece of HTML code that contains an unordered list of elements, where each element is presented with a checkbox and a text—an input for the user text and the **Add!** button. Each time the **Add!** button is clicked, the content of the text input is transformed into a list entry and appended to the list. When the checkbox of any item is clicked, the state of an entry is toggled from to **to buy** (unchecked) to **bought** (checked).

Let's also add a feature that allows us to change the title of the list (it might become useful if we end up implementing multiple shopping lists in the application).

So, we will end up with some extra markup and some more jQuery event listeners and handlers:

```
<div class="container">
  <h2>My Shopping List</h2>
  <!-- ... -->
  <div class="footer">
    <hr/>
    <em>Change the title of your shopping list here</em>
    <input class="js-change-title" type="text"
      value="My Shopping List"/>
  </div>
</div>

//And javascript code:
function onChangeTitle() {
  $('h2').text($('.js-change-title').val());
}
$('.js-change-title').keyup(onChangeTitle);
```

Check JSFiddle at `https://jsfiddle.net/chudaol/47u38fvh/3/`.

Implementing a shopping list using Vue.js

This was a very simple example. Let's try to implement it step-by-step using Vue.js. There are plenty of ways of including `vue.js` into your project, but in this chapter, we will include it just by adding the JavaScript Vue file from the **CDN**:

```
<script  src="https://cdnjs.cloudflare.com/ajax/libs/vue/2.0.3/vue.js">
</script>
```

So, let's start by rendering a list of elements.

Create the HTML file and add the following markup:

```
<div id="app" class="container">
  <h2>{{ title }}</h2>
  <ul>
    <li>{{ items[0] }}</li>
    <li>{{ items[1] }}</li>
  </ul>
</div>
```

Now add the following JavaScript code:

```
var data = {
  items: ['Bananas', 'Apples'],
  title: 'My Shopping List'
};

new Vue({
  el: '#app',
  data: data
});
```

Open it in the browser. You will see that the list is rendered:

Shopping list implemented using Vue.js

Let's analyze this example. The Vue application code starts with the new Vue keyword. How do we bind the piece of markup to the application data? We pass to the Vue instance the DOM element that must be bound to it. Any other markup in the page will not be affected and will not recognize Vue's magic.

As you can see, our markup is wrapped into the `#app` element and is passed as a first argument in the map of `Vue` options. The `data` argument contains the objects that are being used inside the markup using double curly brackets (`{{}}`) . You will probably find this annotation very easy to understand if you are familiar with templating preprocessors (for example, handlebars; for more information, visit `http://handlebarsjs.com/`).

So what?—you're probably exclaiming. What are you going to teach me? How to use templating preprocessors? Thank you very much, but I would be better off having some beers and watching football.

Stop, dear reader, don't go, just grab your beer and let's continue our example. You'll see that it'll be lots of fun!

Analyzing data binding using developer tools

Let's see data binding in action. Open your browser's developer tools, find your JavaScript code, and add a breakpoint at the start of the script. Now analyze how the data objects look before and after the Vue application is initialized. You see, it changed a lot. Now the `data` object is prepared to the reactive data binding:

The data object before and after the Vue object initialization

Now if we change the `title` property of the `data` object from the developer tools console (we can do it because our `data` is a global object), it will be reflected automatically in the title on the page:

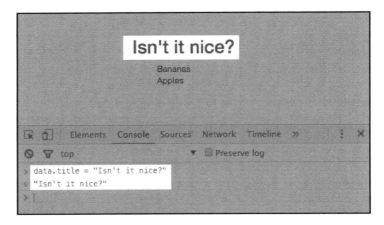

Data binding: changing object properties affects the View immediately

Bringing user input to the data with two-way binding

So, in our example, we were able to bring the data from the plain JavaScript data model to the page. We provided it a sort of a flight from the application code to the page. Don't you think that it would be nice if we could offer a two-way flight to our data?

Let's see now how we can achieve two-way data binding and how we can change the value of a `data` property from the page.

Copy the HTML markup for the title, change the input from the first jQuery example, and add the attribute `v-model="title"` to the `input` element.

Have you already heard about directives in Vue.js? Congratulations, you've just used one! Actually, the `v-model` attribute is a directive of Vue.js that provides two-way data binding. You can read more about it at the official Vue page: `http://vuejs.org/api/#v-model`.

Now, the HTML code for our shopping list application code looks like the following:

```
<div id="app" class="container">
  <h2>{{ title }}</h2>
  <ul>
    <li>{{ items[0] }}</li>
    <li>{{ items[1] }}</li>
  </ul>
  <div class="footer">
    <hr/>
    <em>Change the title of your shopping list here</em>
    <input v-model="title"/>
  </div>
</div>
```

And that's it!

Refresh the page now and modify the input. You'll see the title automatically being updated as you type:

Data binding: changing the text bound to the model's property affects the text bound to the same property immediately

So, everything is nice; however, this example just grabs the two item elements and renders them as list items. We want it to render the list of items independently of the list size.

Rendering the list of items using the v-for directive

So, we need some mechanism to iterate through the `items` array and to render each item in our `<ul>` element.

Fortunately, Vue.js provides us with a nice directive for iterating through iterative JavaScript data structures. It is called `v-for`. We will use it in the list item `<li>` element. Modify the markup of the list so that it looks like the following:

```
<ul>
  <li v-for="item in items">{{ item }}</li>
</ul>
```

 You will learn other nice directives such as `v-if`, `v-else`, `v-show`, `v-on`, `v-bind`, and so on in this book, so keep reading.

Refresh the page and have a look. The page remains the same. Now, try to push an item into the array of `items` from the developer tools console. Try to pop them as well. You will not be surprised to see that the `items` array manipulations are immediately reflected on the page:

Data binding: changing an array affects lists based on it immediately

So, now we have a list of items that is rendered on a page with just one line of the markup. However, we still need these items to have a checkbox that allows us to check the already bought items or uncheck them when needed.

Check and uncheck shopping list items

To achieve this behavior, let's slightly modify our items array by changing our string items and transforming them into the objects with two properties, text and checked (to reflect the state), and let's modify the markup to add a checkbox to each item.

So our JavaScript code for the data declaration will look like the following:

```
var data = {
  items: [{ text: 'Bananas', checked: true },
          { text: 'Apples',  checked: false }],
  title: 'My Shopping List',
  newItem: ''
};
```

And our list markup will look like this:

```
<ul>
  <li v-for="item in items" v-bind:class="{ 'removed':
    item.checked }">
    <div class="checkbox">
      <label>
        <input type="checkbox" v-model="item.checked"> {{
          item.text }}
      </label>
    </div>
  </li>
</ul>
```

Refresh the page and check that the checked property of the items checkbox, and the removed class of each list item, <li>, is bound to the checked Boolean state of the items. Play around and try to click checkboxes to see what happens. Isn't it nice that just with two directives we are able to propagate the state of the items and change the class of the corresponding <li> HTML element?

Adding new shopping list items using the v-on directive

So now we just need a small addition to our code to be able to actually add shopping list items. To achieve that, we will add one more object to our data and call it `newItem`. We'll also add a small method that pushes new item to the `items` array. And we'll call this method from the markup page using the `v:on` directive used on the HTML input element that will be used for the new item and on the button used to click to add a new item.

So our JavaScript code will look like the following:

```
var data = {
  items: [{ text: 'Bananas', checked: true },
          { text: 'Apples', checked: false }],
  title: 'My Shopping List',
  newItem: ''
};
new Vue({
  el: '#app',
  data: data,
  methods: {
    addItem: function () {
      var text;

      text = this.newItem.trim();
      if (text) {
        this.items.push({
          text: text,
          checked: false
        });
        this.newItem = '';
      }
    }
  }
});
```

We added a new property to the `data` object called `newItem`. Then we added a new section called `methods` to our Vue initialization `options` object and added the `addItem` method to this section. All the data properties are accessible in the `methods` section via the `this` keyword. Thus, in this method, we just get `this.newItem` and push it into the `this.items` array. Now we must bind the call to this method to some user action. As it has already been mentioned, we will use the `v-on` directive and apply it to the `enter` keyup on the new item input and to the **Add!** button click.

So add the following markup before our list of items:

```
<div class="input-group">
  <input v-model="newItem" v-on:keyup.enter="addItem"
    placeholder="add shopping list item" type="text" class="form-
    control">
  <span class="input-group-btn">
    <button v-on:click="addItem" class="btn btn-default"
      type="button">Add!</button>
  </span>
</div>
```

 The v-on directive attaches an event listener to the elements. The shortcut is the @ sign. So, instead of writing v-on:keyup="addItem", you can write @keyup="addItem". You can read more about the v-on directive on the official documentation site at http://vuejs.org/api/#v-on.

Let's finalize. The whole code now looks like the following:

Here is the HTML code:

```
<div id="app" class="container">
  <h2>{{ title }}</h2>
  <div class="input-group">
    <input v-model="newItem" @keyup.enter="addItem"
      placeholder="add shopping list item" type="text"
      class="form-control">
  <span class="input-group-btn">
    <button @click="addItem" class="btn btn-default"
      type="button">Add!</button>
  </span>
  </div>
  <ul>
    <li v-for="item in items" :class="{ 'removed': item.checked
      }">
      <div class="checkbox">
        <label>
          <input type="checkbox" v-model="item.checked"> {{
            item.text }}
        </label>
      </div>
    </li>
  </ul>
  <div class="footer hidden">
    <hr/>
    <em>Change the title of your shopping list here</em>
    <input v-model="title"/>
```

```
    </div>
  </div>
```

Here is the JavaScript code:

```javascript
var data = {
  items: [{ text: 'Bananas', checked: true },
          { text: 'Apples', checked: false }],
  title: 'My Shopping List',
  newItem: ''
};

new Vue({
  el: '#app',
  data: data,
  methods: {
    addItem: function () {
      var text;

      text = this.newItem.trim();
      if (text) {
        this.items.push({
          text: text,
          checked: false
        });
        this.newItem = '';
      }
    }
  }
});
```

Here's a link to JSFiddle: `https://jsfiddle.net/chudaol/vxfkxjzk/3/`.

Using Vue.js in an existing project

I can feel now that you have seen how easy is to bind the properties of the model to the presentation layer and you are already starting to think about how it can be used in your existing project. But then you think: hell, no, I need to install some things, run `npm install`, change the project's structure, add directives, and change the code.

And here I can tell you: no! No installs, no npms, just grab the `vue.js` file, insert it into your HTML page, and use it. That's all, no structure changes, no architectural decisions, no discussions. Just use it. I will show you how we used it at EdEra (https://www.ed-era.com) to include a small "check yourself" functionality at the end of a GitBook chapter.

EdEra is a Ukraine-based online educational project whose aim is to transform the whole educational system into something modern, online, interactive, and fun. Actually, I am a co-founder and the chief technical officer of this young nice project, being responsible for the whole technical part of the thing. So, in EdEra, we have some online courses built on top of the open EdX platform (https://open.edx.org/) and some interactive educational books built on top of the great GitBook framework (http://www.gitbook.org). Basically, GitBook is a platform based on top of the Node.js technology stack. It allows someone with basic knowledge of the markdown language and basic Git commands to write books and host them in the GitBook servers. EdEra's books can be found at http://ed-era.com/books (beware, they are all in Ukrainian).

Let's see what we have done in our books using Vue.js.

At some point, I decided to include a small quiz at the end of the chapter about personal pronouns in the book that teaches English. Thus, I've included the `vue.js` JavaScript file, edited the corresponding `.md` file, and included the following HTML code:

```
<div id="pronouns">
    <p><strong>Check yourself :)</strong></p>
    <textarea class="textarea" v-model="text" v-
      on:keyup="checkText">
        {{ text }}
    </textarea><i  v-bind:class="{ 'correct': correct,
      'incorrect': !correct }"></i>
</div>
```

Then I added a custom JavaScript file, where I've included the following code:

```
$(document).ready(function() {
  var initialText, correctText;

  initialText = 'Me is sad because he is more clever than I.';
  correctText = 'I am sad because he is more clever than me.';

  new Vue({
    el: '#pronouns',
    data: {
      text: initialText,
      correct: false
    },
```

```
    methods: {
      checkText: function () {
        var text;
        text = this.text.trim();
        this.correct = text === correctText;
      }
    }
  });
});
```

You can check this code at this GitHub page: `https://github.com/chuda ol/ed-era-book-english`.

Here's a code of a page written in markdown with inserted HTML: `https ://github.com/chudaol/ed-era-book-english/blob/master/2/osobov i_zaimenniki.md`.

And here's a JavaScript code: `https://github.com/chudaol/ed-era-boo k-english/blob/master/custom/js/quiz-vue.js`.

You can even clone the repository and try it locally using `gitbook-cli` (h `ttps://github.com/GitbookIO/gitbook/blob/master/docs/setup.md`).

Let's have a look at this code. You have probably already detected the parts that you have already seen and even tried:

- The `data` object contains two properties:
  - The `string` property text
  - The `Boolean` property correct
- The `checkText` method just grabs the `text` property, compares it with the correct text, and assigns the value to the correct value
- The `v-on` directive calls the `checkText` method on keyup
- The `v-bind` directive binds the class `correct` to the `correct` property

Here is how the code looks in my IDE:

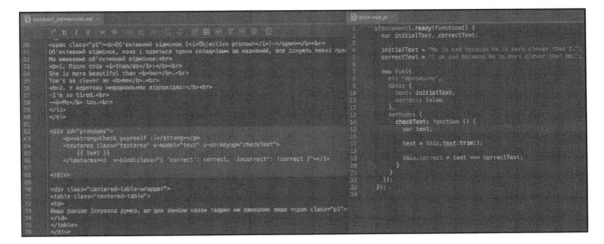

Using Vue in a markdown-driven project

And next is what it looks like in the browser:

Vue.js in action inside the GitBook page

Vue.js in action inside the GitBook page

Check it out at `http://english.ed-era.com/2/osobovi_zaimenniki.html`.

Amazing, right? Pretty simple, pretty reactive!

Vue.js 2.0!

At the time of writing, Vue.js 2.0 was announced (`https://vuejs.org/2016/04/27/announcing-2.0/`). Check the following links in this regard:

- `http://www.infoworld.com/article/3063615/javascript/vuejs-lead-our-javascript-framework-is-faster-than-react.html`
- `https://www.reddit.com/r/vuejs/comments/4gq2r1/announcing_vuejs_20/`

The second version of Vue.js has some considerable differences comparing to its predecessor, starting from the way that data binding is being handled and moving to its API. It uses lightweight virtual DOM implementation for rendering, supports server-side rendering, and is faster and leaner.

At the time of writing, Vue 2.0 was in an early alpha stage. Do not worry, though. All the examples that we will cover in this book are based on the latest stable version of Vue 2.0 and are fully compatible with the both the versions.

Projects using Vue.js

Probably, at this time, you are wondering what projects are out there that are built on top of Vue.js, or use it as a part of their codebase. There are a lot of nice open source, experimental, and enterprise projects using it. The complete and constantly updated list of these projects can be found at `https://github.com/vuejs/awesome-vue#projects-using-vuejs`.

Let's have a look at some of them.

Grammarly

Grammarly (`https://www.grammarly.com/`) is a service that helps you write English correctly. It has several apps, one of them is a simple Chrome extension that just checks any text input that you fill in. Another one is an online editor that you can use to check big chunks of text. This editor is built using Vue.js! The following is a screenshot of this text being edited in the online editor of Grammarly:

Grammarly: a project that is built on top of Vue.js

Optimizely

Optimizely (https://www.optimizely.com/) is a service that helps you test, optimize, and personalize your websites. I've used the Packt site to create an Optimizely experiment and to check out Vue.js in action in this resource. It looks like the following:

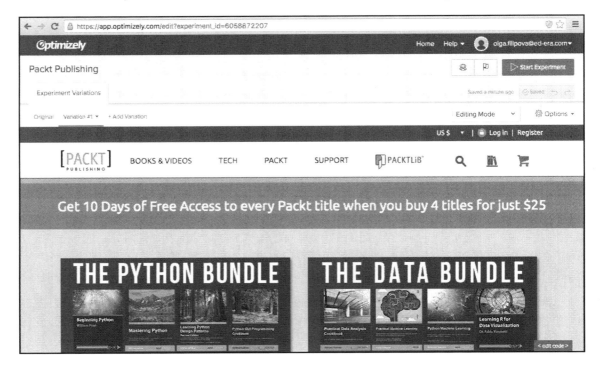

Optimizely: a project that is built on top of Vue.js

Hovering around with the mouse gives us the possibility of opening a context menu that allows different manipulations with the page data, including the simplest one, text editing. Let's try this one:

Using Optimizely and watching Vue.js in action

The text box is opened. When I type in it, the text in the title is reactively changed. We saw and implemented it using Vue.js:

Using Optimizely and watching Vue.js in action

FilterBlend

FilterBlend (`https://github.com/ilyashubin/FilterBlend`) is an open source playground for the CSS background-blend-mode and filter properties.

You can load your images and combine blending with filters.

If you want to give FilterBlend a try, you can install it locally:

1. Clone the repository:

```
git clone https://github.com/ilyashubin/FilterBlend.git
```

2. Enter the `FilterBlend` directory:

```
cd FilterBlend
```

3. Install the dependencies:

```
npm install
```

4. Run the project:

```
gulp
```

Open your browser on `localhost:8000` and play around. You can see that once you change something in the menu on the right, it is immediately propagated to the images on the left side. All this functionality is achieved using Vue.js. Check the code on GitHub.

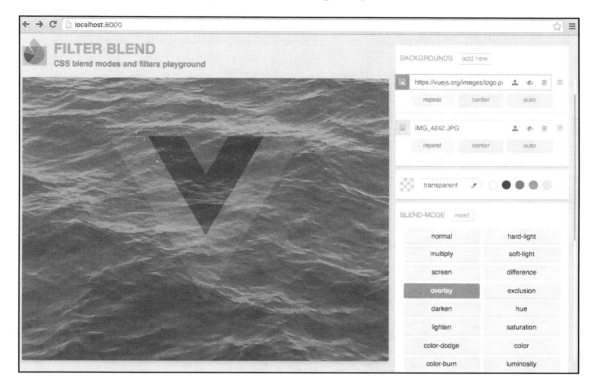

FilterBlend: a project built on top of Vue.js

PushSilver

PushSilver (`https://pushsilver.com`) is a nice and simple service for busy people to create simple invoices. It allows creating invoices, sending and resending them to the clients, and keeping tracking of them. It was created by a developer doing freelance consultancy and being tired of having to create invoices each time for each small project. This tool works well and it was built using Vue.js:

PushSilver: invoice managing application built on top of Vue.js

PushSilver: invoice managing application built on top of Vue.js

Book roadmap

This book, like most part of technical books, is organized in such a way that you do not need to read it from beginning to end. You can choose the parts that interest you the most and skip the rest.

This book is organized as follows:

- If you are reading this, there's no need to specify what is going on in the first chapter.
- Chapter 2, *Fundamentals – Installing and Using,* is pretty theoretical and will explain what's going on behind the scenes of Vue.js and its main parts. So, if you are not into theory and want to put your hands into coding, you are free to skip this part. In this part, we will also go through the installation and setup process.

- From the third to the eighth chapter, we'll explore the main features of Vue.js while building the application:
  - In Chapter 3, *Components – Understanding and Using*, we will introduce Vue components and apply this knowledge to our application.
  - In Chapter 4, *Reactivity – Binding Data to Your Application*, we will use all the data binding mechanisms provided by Vue.
  - In Chapter 5, *Vuex – Managing State in Your Application*, we will introduce the Vuex state management system and explain how to use it in our applications.
  - In Chapter 6, *Plugins – Building Your House with Your Own Bricks*, we will learn how to create and use plugins for Vue applications to enrich their functionality.
  - In Chapter 7, *Testing – Time to Test What We Have Done so Far!*, we will cover and explore custom directives of Vue.js and create some in our application.
  - In Chapter 8, *Deploying – Time to Go Live!*, we will learn how to test and deploy JavaScript application written in Vue.js.
- In Chapter 9, *What Is Next?*, we'll summarize what we've learned and see what we can do next.

Let's manage time!

At this point of time, I already know that you are so, so, so enthusiastic with this book that you want to read it to the end without stopping. But this is not right. We should manage our time and give us some time to work and some time to rest. Let's create a small application that implements a Pomodoro technique timer so that it can help us in our working time management.

 The **Pomodoro** technique is a time management technique named after the kitchen tomato timer (in fact, Pomodoro means tomato in Italian). This technique consists of breaking down the working time into small intervals separated by short breaks. Read more about the Pomodoro technique on the official site: http://pomodorotechnique.com/.

Thus, our goal is very simple. We just have to create a very simple time counter that will decrement untill the end of the working interval and then restart and decrement till the end of the resting time and so on.

Let's do that!

We will introduce two Vue data variables, minute and second, which will be displayed on our page. The main method on each second will decrement second; it will decrement minute when second becomes 0; and when both minute and second variables come to 0, the application should toggle between working and resting interval:

Our JavaScript code will look like the following:

```javascript
const POMODORO_STATES = {
  WORK: 'work',
  REST: 'rest'
};
const WORKING_TIME_LENGTH_IN_MINUTES = 25;
const RESTING_TIME_LENGTH_IN_MINUTES = 5;

new Vue({
  el: '#app',
  data: {
    minute: WORKING_TIME_LENGTH_IN_MINUTES,
    second: 0,
    pomodoroState: POMODORO_STATES.WORK,
    timestamp: 0
  },
  methods: {
    start: function () {
      this._tick();
      this.interval = setInterval(this._tick, 1000);
    },
    _tick: function () {
      //if second is not 0, just decrement second
      if (this.second !== 0) {
        this.second--;
        return;
      }
      //if second is 0 and minute is not 0,
      //decrement minute and set second to 59
      if (this.minute !== 0) {
        this.minute--;
        this.second = 59;
        return;
      }
      //if second is 0 and minute is 0,
      //toggle working/resting intervals
      this.pomodoroState = this.pomodoroState ===
POMODORO_STATES.WORK ? POMODORO_STATES.REST :
POMODORO_STATES.WORK;
```

```
          if (this.pomodoroState === POMODORO_STATES.WORK) {
            this.minute = WORKING_TIME_LENGTH_IN_MINUTES;
          } else {
            this.minute = RESTING_TIME_LENGTH_IN_MINUTES;
          }
        }
      }
    });
```

In our HTML code, let's create two placeholders for `minute` and `second`, and a start button for our Pomodoro timer:

```
<div id="app" class="container">
  <h2>
    <span>Pomodoro</span>
    <button @click="start()">
      <i class="glyphicon glyphicon-play"></i>
    </button>
  </h2>
  <div class="well">
    <div class="pomodoro-timer">
      <span>{{ minute }}</span>:<span>{{ second }}</span>
    </div>
  </div>
</div>
```

Again, we are using Bootstrap for the styling, so our Pomodoro timer looks like the following:

Countdown timer built with Vue.js

Our Pomodoro is nice, but it has some problems:

- First of all, we don't know which state is being toggled. We don't know if we should work or rest. Let's introduce a title that will change each time the Pomodoro state is changed.
- Another problem is inconsistent display of minutes and seconds numbers. For example, for 24 minutes and 5 seconds, we would like to see 24:05 and not 24:5. Let's fix it introducing computed values in our application data and displaying them instead of normal values.

- Yet another problem is that our start button can be clicked over and over again, which creates a timer each time it's clicked. Try to click it several times and see how crazy your timer goes. Let's fix it by introducing start, pause, and stop buttons, apply application states to them, and disable buttons to the state accordingly.

Toggle the title by using computed properties

Let's start by fixing the first problem by creating computed property title and using it in our markup.

 Computed properties are the properties inside the data object that allow us to avoid blowing up the template with some extra logic. You can find more information about computed properties on the official documentation site: http://vuejs.org/guide/computed.html.

Add the computed section in the Vue options object and add the property title there:

```
data: {
  //...
},
computed: {
  title: function () {
    return this.pomodoroState === POMODORO_STATES.WORK ? 'Work!' :
    'Rest!'
  }
},
methods: {
//...
```

And now just use the following property as it was a normal Vue data property in your markup:

```
<h2>
  <span>Pomodoro</span>
  <!--!>
</h2>
<h3>{{ title }}</h3>
<div class="well">
```

And voilà! Now we have a title that changes each time the Pomodoro state is being toggled:

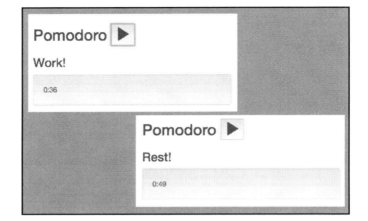

Automatic change of the title based on the state of the timer

Nice, isn't it?

Left-pad time values using computed properties

Now let's apply the same logic for left padding our `minute` and `second` numbers. Let's add two computed properties, `min` and `sec`, in our `computed` section in the `data` options and apply the simple algorithm to pad the numbers with `0` on the left. Of course, we could use a famous left-pad project (`https://github.com/stevemao/left-pad`), but to keep things simple and not to break the whole Internet (`http://www.theregister.co.uk/2016/03/23/npm_left_pad_chaos/`), let's apply a simple logic of our own:

```
computed: {
  title: function () {
    return this.pomodoroState === POMODORO_STATES.WORK ? 'Work!' :
    'Rest!'
  },
  min: function () {
    if (this.minute < 10) {
      return '0' + this.minute;
    }

    return this.minute;
  },
  sec: function () {
    if (this.second < 10) {
      return '0' + this.second;
```

```
    }

    return this.second;
  }
}
```

And let's use these properties instead of `minute` and `second` in our HTML code:

```html
<div class="pomodoro-timer">
 <span>{{ min }}</span>:<span>{{ sec }}</span>
</div>
```

Refresh a page and check how beautiful our numbers are now:

Left padding using computed properties in Vue.js

Keep state with start, pause, and stop buttons

So, to fix the third problem, let's introduce three application states, `started`, `paused`, and `stopped`, and let's have three methods that would allow us to permute over these states. We already have the method that starts the application, so we just add the logic there to change the state to `started`. We also add two additional methods, `pause` and `stop`, which would pause the timer and change to the corresponding application state:

```javascript
const POMODORO_STATES = {
  WORK: 'work',
  REST: 'rest'
};
const STATES = {
  STARTED: 'started',
  STOPPED: 'stopped',
  PAUSED: 'paused'
};
//<...>
new Vue({
  el: '#app',
  data: {
    state: STATES.STOPPED,
```

```
      //<...>
  },
  //<...>
  methods: {
    start: function () {
      this.state = STATES.STARTED;
      this._tick();
      this.interval = setInterval(this._tick, 1000);
    },
    pause: function () {
      this.state = STATES.PAUSED;
      clearInterval(this.interval);
    },
    stop: function () {
      this.state = STATES.STOPPED;
      clearInterval(this.interval);
      this.pomodoroState = POMODORO_STATES.WORK;
      this.minute = WORKING_TIME_LENGTH_IN_MINUTES;
      this.second = 0;
    },
    //<...>
  }
});
```

And, let's add two buttons to our HTML code and add the `click` listeners that call the corresponding methods:

```
<button :disabled="state==='started'"
  @click="start()">
  <i class="glyphicon glyphicon-play"></i>
</button>
<button :disabled="state!=='started'"
  @click="pause()">
  <i class="glyphicon glyphicon-pause"></i>
</button>
<button :disabled="state!=='started' && state !== 'paused'"
  @click="stop()">
  <i class="glyphicon glyphicon-stop"></i>
</button>
```

Now our application looks nice and allows us to start, pause, and stop the timer:

Pomodoro ▶ ❚❚ ■
Work!
00:52

Toggling start, stop, and pause buttons according to the application state

Check what the whole code looks like in JSFiddle at `https://jsfiddle.net/chudaol/b6vm tzq1/1/`.

After so much work and so many of new terms and knowledge, you certainly deserve a kitten! I also love kittens, so here you have a random kitten from the awesome site `http://thecatapi.com/`:

Exercise

At the end of this chapter, I would like to propose a small exercise. The Pomodoro timer that we built earlier in the chapters is, without any doubt, great, but it still lacks some nice features. A really nice thing that it could provide would be showing random kittens from `h ttp://thecatapi.com/` during resting time. Can you implement this? Of course you can! But please do not confuse resting with working time! I am almost sure that your project manager will not like it much if you stare at kittens instead of working.

The solution to this exercise can be found in `Appendix`, *Solutions to Exercises*.

Summary

I am very glad that you have reached this point, this means that you already know what Vue.js is, and if someone asks you whether it is a tool, a library, or a framework, you certainly will find an answer. You also know how to start an application using Vue.js and you know how to use Vue's features in an already existing project. You played around with some really nice projects that are written in Vue.js and you started developing some of your own! Now you do not just go shopping, now you go shopping with a shopping list created by you using Vue.js! Now you don't need to steal your tomato timer from the kitchen to use it as a Pomodoro timer while working; you can use your own digital Pomodoro timer made with Vue.js. And, last but not the least, now you can insert random kittens in your JavaScript application also using Vue.js.

In the next chapter, we will cover the behind the scenes of Vue, how and why does it work, and the architectural patterns it uses. Each of the concepts will be wrapped up with an example to demonstrate it. Then we will be ready to put our hands deep into the code and to improve our applications taking them to the state of awesomeness.

2
Fundamentals – Installing and Using

In the previous chapter, we gained some familiarity with Vue.js. We were able to use it in two different applications that we created from scratch. We learned how to integrate Vue.js into an already existing project. We were able to see Vue's reactive data binding in action.

Now, you are probably asking yourself: how does it work? What does it do to achieve this behavior of fast UI changes when the data model is changed? Probably, you decided to use Vue.js in your project and are now wondering whether it follows some architectural pattern or paradigm so that you should adopt it in your project. In this chapter, we will explore the key concepts of the Vue.js framework to understand all its behind the scenes features. Also in this chapter, we will analyze all the possible ways of installing Vue.js. We will also create a skeleton for our applications, which we will develop and enhance through the next chapters. We will also learn ways of debugging and testing our applications.

So, in this chapter, we are going to learn:

- What the MVVM architecture paradigm is and how it applies to Vue.js
- What declarative Views are
- How Vue.js explores defined properties, getters, and setters
- How reactivity and data binding works in Vue.js
- What dirty checking, DOM, and virtual DOM are
- The main differences between Vue.js 1.0 and Vue.js 2.0
- What reusable components are
- How plugins, directives, custom plugins, and custom directives work in Vue.js
- How to install, start, run, and debug a Vue application

MVVM architectural pattern

Do you remember how we were creating the `Vue` instance in the first chapter? We were instantiating it calling `new Vue({...})`. You also remember that in the options, we were passing the element on the page where this `Vue` instance should be bound and the `data` object that contained the properties we wanted to bind to our View. The `data` object is our Model and the DOM element where the `Vue` instance is bound is our View:

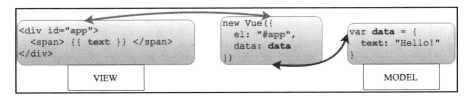

Classic View-Model representation where the Vue instance binds one to another

In the meantime, our `Vue` instance is something that helps to bind our Model to the View and vice versa. Our application thus follows **Model-View-ViewModel (MVVM)** pattern, where the `Vue` instance is a ViewModel:

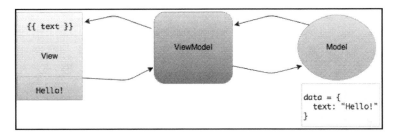

The simplified diagram of the Model-View-ViewModel pattern

Our **Model** contains data and some business logic, and our **View** is responsible for its representation. **ViewModel** handles data binding, ensuring that the data changed in the **Model** is immediately affecting the **View** layer and vice versa.

Our Views thus become completely data driven. **ViewModel** becomes responsible for the control of the data flow, making data binding fully declarative for us.

DefineProperty, getters, and setters

So, what happens with the data once passed to the Vue instance? What are these transformations that Vue applies to it so that it becomes so automatically bound to the View layer?

Let's analyze what would we do if we had, let's say, a string, and every time it changes we would like to apply some transformations to some DOM element. How would we apply the string-changing listener function? To what would we attach it? There is no such thing as `var stringVar='hello';stringVar.onChange(doSomething)`.

So we would probably wrap the string's value setting and getting in some sort of function that would do something, for example, updating the DOM each time the string was updated. How would you implement it? While you're thinking about it, I'll prepare a quick demo of something interesting.

Open the developer tools on your shopping list application. Let's code a little bit. Create an `obj` variable and another `text` variable:

```
var obj = {};
var text = '';
```

Let's store the DOM element `h2` in a variable:

```
var h2 = document.getElementsByTagName('h2')[0];
```

If we assign `text` to the `obj.text` property, how can we achieve that in every change of this property the `innerHTML` of `h2` would change as well?

Let's use the `Object.defineProperty` method (https://developer.mozilla.org/en/docs/Web/JavaScript/Reference/Global_Objects/Object/defineProperty).

This method allows the creation of getter and setter functions, thus specifying what must happen when the property is accessed or changed:

```
Object.defineProperty(obj, 'text', {
  get: function () {
    return text;
  },
  set: function (newVal) {
    text = newVal;
    h2.innerHTML = text;
  }
});
```

Now try to change the `obj.text` property from the console. Look at the title:

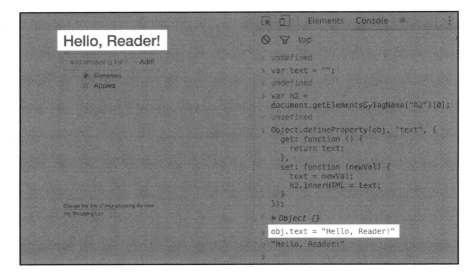

The set method of object.defineProperty is called every time the property changes

This exact mechanism was used by Vue.js. Once the data are passed to the `Vue` instance, all its properties go through the `Object.defineProperty` method, which assigns reactive getters and setters to them. For each directive existing on a page, a watcher is added, which is being notified within the `set` method. Open the `vue.js` code in the console and search for the line that says `set: function reactiveSetter(newVal)`. Add a breakpoint and try to change the title of the shopping list in the input. Now step over until you reach the last call in this function that says `dep.notify()`:

Breakpoint inside the setter function that calls the watchers notify method

Step into the function. You will see that this function is iterating through the watchers of the property and updates them. If you step over this call, you will see that the DOM is not being updated. This is because the updates performed on the same event loop are being put into the queue that is being flushed periodically.

Find the `runBatcherQueue` function and put a breakpoint inside it. Try to change the title again. As you can see, this function iterates through all the watchers that are waiting inside the queue and calls the `run` method on each of them. If you step into this method, you will see that it compares the new value with the previous one:

```
if (value !== this.value ||...
```

It then it calls a callback's execution:

```
this.cb.call(this.vm, value, oldValue);
```

If you step into this callback function, you will see that in the end, it will finally update the DOM value:

```
update: function update(value) {
  this.el[this.attr] = _toString(value);
}
```

Isn't it simple?

In this debugging Vue version 1.0 is used.

So the mechanism behind the Vue.js reactive data binding is very simple. **Watchers** are being assigned to all the directives and data properties. Then, during the set method of Object.defineProperty, the **Watchers** are notified and, in turn, they update the corresponding **DOM** or **data**:

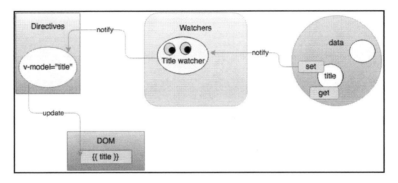

The data flow from the data object to the DOM

DOM elements that have directives have attached listeners that listen to their updates and call the corresponding **data** property setter that, in turn, wakes up its **Watchers**.

Comparing with other frameworks

When you try a new tool, you want to know how it compares with other tools or frameworks. You can find a deep analysis in this regard on the official page of Vue.js: http ://vuejs.org/guide/comparison.html. I will just point to some topics that I find important regarding the mostly used frameworks.

React

React and Vue are really similar. They both use virtual DOM, have reusable components, and are about reactive data. It is worth mentioning, however, that Vue only uses virtual DOM starting from its second major version. Prior to Vue 2.0, it used real DOM. The Vue

2.0 release not only became more performant than Vue 1.0 but it also became more performant than React (`http://vuejs.org/guide/comparison.html#Performance-Profil es`).

The most significant difference is probably the way you create your components in both frameworks. You might already know that in React, everything is JavaScript. Developing everything, even templates, in JavaScript, can actually be good, so programmers are always in the same scope and rendering becomes more flexible.

However, for some designers who want to do rapid prototyping or for developers with not-so-strong programming skills, or for people who simply don't want to learn JSX, it might become really painful to work like this. In Vue components, you can actually also use JSX, but you can still follow a common web development structure: writing CSS inside the `<style>` tags, writing HTML code inside the `<template>` tags, and writing the component's logic in JavaScript inside the `<script>` tags. Compare, for example, the template inside the render function in React and the template that you can write inside the Vue component. In this example, I will show how to render the list of items of the shopping list that we have seen before. So in React, you will end up with the JSX code similar to this one:

```
render () {
  return (
    <ul>
    {items.map(item =>
    <li className={item.checked && 'removed'}>
      <div className='checkbox'>
        <input type='checkbox' checked={item.checked}>
        { item.text }
      </div>
    </li>
    )}
    </ul>
  )
});
```

Using Vue, you will just write the following HTML code inside the `template` tag:

```
<template>
<ul>
  <li v-for="item in items" :class="{ 'removed': item.checked }">
    <div class="checkbox">
    <label>
    <input type="checkbox" v-model="item.checked"> {{ item.text }}
    </label>
    </div>
  </li>
```

```
    </ul>
    </template>
```

I, personally, like to have these things separated, thus I find it nice that Vue offers this possibility.

Another nice thing about Vue is that it allows to scope style within the components using the `scoped` attribute attached to the `style` tag:

```
<style scoped>
</style>
```

Within this style, in case you use preprocessors, you still have access to all globally defined variables and can create or redefine styles that will be only accessible by this component.

It's also worth to mention the learning curve for both frameworks. To be able to start developing applications using React, you would probably have to learn JSX and ES2105 syntax, since most examples in official React documentation use it. With Vue, you can start out of the blue. Just include it in the page, like you would do with jQuery, and you can already use Vue models and data binding using pretty simple and easy to understand syntax, and any JavaScript version you like to use. After that, you can scale up in your learning and in your applications style.

In case you want to perform a deeper analysis of both frameworks, have a look at the documentation, try to elaborate similar examples, and check what suits your needs more.

Angular

There is a huge difference between Angular 1 and Angular 2. We all know that the second version of Angular is completely different from its predecessor. It offers more performance, the API is different, and the underlying implementation has been rewritten.

These two versions are so different that in Vue official documentation, you will find the comparison between both the Angular versions as it was between two different frameworks. However, the learning curve and the way in which each of the frameworks forces you to structure the application are transversal for both the Angular versions. It turns out that Vue is much less opinionated than Angular 1 as well as Angular 2. Just compare Angular's quick start guide and Vue's hello world applications at `https://angular.io/doc s/js/latest/quickstart.html`and `http://vuejs.org/guide/index.html#Hello-World`.

"Even without TypeScript, Angular's Quickstart guide starts out with an app that uses ES2015 JavaScript, NPM with 18 dependencies, 4 files, and over 3,000 words to explain it all – just to say Hello World."

– http://vuejs.org/guide/comparison.html#Learning-Curve

If you still use Angular 1, it's worth to mention that the big difference between this framework and Vue is that in this version of Angular, each time the scope changed, re-evaluated all the watchers, thus performing dirty checking, hence reducing the performance when the amount of watchers became considerably high. Hence, in Vue, when something in the scope changes, only this property's watcher is being re-evaluated. All others are sitting idle and waiting for their respective calls.

Vue

No, it is not a typo. It is also worth comparing Vue with Vue. Vue has also recently launched its second version, which is faster and cleaner than its predecessor. If you still use Vue 1.0, it is worth to upgrade. If you don't know anything about Vue versions, it is worth to check how it evolved and what does the new version allow. Check the Vue blog post that announced Vue 2.0 in April 2016 at `https://vuejs.org/2016/04/27/announcing-2.0/`.

Vue.js fundamentals

Before putting our hands into the code and starting to enhance our applications with components, plugins, mixins, templates, and other things, let's overview the main Vue features. Let's analyze what are reusable components and how the application state can be managed, and also talk about plugins, filters, and mixins. In this section, we will have just a slight overview of these features. We will learn them deeply in the next chapters.

Reusable components

Now that you know not only what data binding in Vue.js is and how to use it, but also how it works, it is time to introduce another powerful Vue.js feature. Components created with Vue.js can be used and reused in the application as bricks you build your house of. Each component has its own scope of styles and bindings, being completely isolated from the other components.

The component creation syntax is very similar to the `Vue` instance creation that we already know, and you should only use `Vue.extend` instead of just `Vue`:

```
var CustomComponent = Vue.extend({...})
```

Custom components in Vue.js

Let's, for example, try to divide our shopping list code into components. As you remember, our shopping list consists essentially of three parts: the part that contains the shopping list item, another part that contains the input for adding new items, and the third part that allows changing the title of the shopping list:

Three essential parts of the shopping list application

Let's change the code of the application so that it uses three components, one for each part.

Our code was looking like the following:

```
var data = {
  items: [{ text: 'Bananas', checked: true },
          { text: 'Apples', checked: false }],
  title: 'My Shopping List',
  newItem: ''
};

new Vue({
  el: '#app',
  data: data,
  methods: {
    addItem: function () {
      var text;

      text = this.newItem.trim();
      if (text) {
        this.items.push({
          text: text,
          checked: false
        });
        this.newItem = '';
      }
    }
  }
});
```

Now we will create three components: `ItemsComponent`, `ChangeTitleComponent`, and `AddItemComponent`. All of them will have the `data` property with the `data` object. The `addItem` method will jump from the main `Vue` instance to `ChangeTitleComponent`. All the necessary HTML will go from our `index.html` file to each of the components. So in the end, our main script will look like the following:

```
var data = {
  items: [{ text: 'Bananas', checked: true },
          { text: 'Apples', checked: false }],
  title: 'My Shopping List',
  newItem: ''
};

/**
 * Declaring components
 */
var ItemsComponent = Vue.extend({
```

```
    data: function () {
      return data;
    },
    template: '<ul>' +
    '           <li v-for="item in items"
                :class="{ 'removed': item.checked }">' +
    '             <div class="checkbox">' +
    '               <label>' +
    '                 <input type="checkbox"
                      v-model="item.checked"> {{ item.text }}' +
    '               </label>' +
    '             </div>' +
    '           </li>' +
    '         </ul>'
});
var ChangeTitleComponent = Vue.extend({
  data: function () {
    return data;
  },
  template: '<input v-model="title"/>'
});
var AddItemComponent = Vue.extend({
  data: function () {
    return data;
  },
  methods: {
    addItem: function () {
      var text;

      text = this.newItem.trim();
      if (text) {
        this.items.push({
          text: text,
          checked: false
        });
        this.newItem = "";
      }
    }
  },
  template:
  '<div class="input-group">' +
    '<input v-model="newItem" @keyup.enter="addItem"
     placeholder="add shopping list item" type="text"
     class="form-control">' +
    '<span class="input-group-btn">' +
    '  <button @click="addItem" class="btn btn-default"
      type="button">Add!</button>' +
    '</span>' +
```

```
    '</div>'
});

/**
 * Registering components
 */
Vue.component('items-component', ItemsComponent);
Vue.component('change-title-component', ChangeTitleComponent);
Vue.component('add-item-component', AddItemComponent);
/**
 * Instantiating a Vue instance
 */
new Vue({
  el: '#app',
  data: data
});
```

How do we use these components inside the View? We should just replace the corresponding markup with the tag of the registered component. Our markup looked like the following:

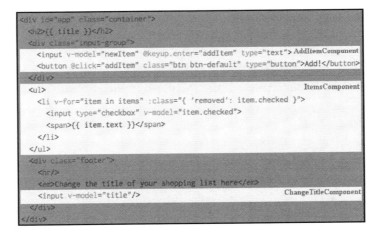

The shopping list application markup with defined components

So, the first highlighted area we will replace with the `<add-item-component></add-item-component>` tag, the second one with the `<items-component></items-component>` tag, and the third one with the `<change-title-component></change-title-component>` tag. Thus, our previously huge markup now looks like the following:

```
<div id="app" class="container">
  <h2>{{ title }}</h2>
  <add-item-component></add-item-component>
```

```
<items-component></items-component>
<div class="footer">
  <hr/>
  <em>Change the title of your shopping list here</em>
  <change-title-component></change-title-component>
</div>
</div>
```

We will go deeply into components in the next chapter and will learn an even nicer way of structuring them. Stay tuned!

Vue.js directives

You have already learned in the previous chapter what directives are and how they are used to enhance the application's behavior.

You've already used some directives that allow data binding in different ways to the View layer (v-model, v-if, v-show, and so on). Besides these default directives, Vue.js allows you to create custom directives. Custom directives provide a mechanism to enable custom behavior of DOM to data mapping.

When registering a custom directive, you can provide three functions: bind, update, and unbind. Inside the bind function, you can attach an event listener to the element and do whatever needs to be done there. Inside the update function that receives old and new values as parameters, you can define a custom behavior of what should happen when data changes. The unbind method provides all the cleaning operations needed (for example, detach event listeners).

 In Vue 2.0, directives have significantly reduced the scope of responsibility—now they are only used to apply low-level direct DOM manipulations. Vue's changing guide suggests to prefer using components over custom directives (https://github.com/vuejs/vue/issues/2873).

Thus, the full version of the custom directive would look like the following:

```
Vue.directive('my-directive', {
  bind: function () {
    // do the preparation work on element binding
  },
  update: function (newValue, oldValue) {
    // do something based on the updated value
  },
  unbind: function () {
    // do the clean-up work
```

```
    }
  })
```

The simplified version, in case you just need to do something on the value update, can only have the `update` method that can be passed directly as the second parameter of the directive function:

```
Vue.directive('my-directive', function (el, binding) {
  // do something with binding.value
})
```

The theory is nice, but without a small example, it turns out boring. So let's have a look at a very simple example, which will show the square of the number each time its value is updated.

Our custom directive will look like the following:

```
Vue.directive('square', function (el, binding) {
  el.innerHTML = Math.pow(binding.value, 2);
});
```

Use this directive in your template file using the v- prefix:

```
<div v-square="item"></div>
```

Instantiate the `Vue` instance with `item` in its data and try to change the value of `item`. You will see that the value inside the `div` element will immediately display the square number of the changed value. The complete code for this custom directive can be found in the JSFiddle at `https://jsfiddle.net/chudaol/we07oxbd/`.

Plugins in Vue.js

Vue's core functionality, as we have already analyzed, provides declarative data binding and components composing. This core behavior is enhanced with plugins that provide a rich set of functionality. There are several types of plugins:

- Plugins that add some global property or method (`vue-element`)
- Plugins that add some global assets (`vue-touch`)
- Plugins that add `Vue` instance methods attaching them to Vue's prototype
- Plugins that provide some external functionality or API (`vue-router`)

Plugins must provide an `install` method that has access to the global `Vue` object that can enhance and modify it. In order to use this plugin, Vue provides the `use` method that receives plugins instances (`Vue.use(SomePlugin)`).

> You can also write a Vue plugin of your own to enable custom behavior for your `Vue` instance.

Let's use the previous custom directives example and create a minimalistic plugin that implements mathematical square and square root directives. Create a file named `VueMathPlugin.js` and add the following code:

```
export default {
    install: function (Vue) {
        Vue.directive('square', function (el, binding) {
            el.innerHTML = Math.pow(binding.value, 2);
        });
        Vue.directive('sqrt', function (el, binding) {
            el.innerHTML = Math.sqrt(binding.value);
        });
    }
};
```

Now create a file called `script.js`. Let's add the main script to this file. In this script, we will import both `Vue` and `VueMathPlugin`, and will call Vue's `use` method in order to tell it to use the plugin and call the plugin's `install` method. Then we'll just initiate a `Vue` instance as we always do:

```
import Vue from 'vue/dist/vue.js';
import VueMathPlugin from './VueMathPlugin.js';

Vue.use(VueMathPlugin);

new Vue({
    el: '#app',
    data: { item: 49 }
});
```

Now create an `index.html` file that includes the `main.js` file (we will build it with Browserify and Babelify). In this file, let's add an input using the `v-model` directive that will be used to change the value of the item. Create two spans using `v-square` and `v-sqrt` directives as well:

```
<body>
  <div id="app">
    <input v-model="item"/>
    <hr>
    <div>Square: <span v-square="item"></span></div>
    <div>Root: <span v-sqrt="item"></span></div>
  </div>
  <script src="main.js"></script>
</body>
```

Create a `package.json` file to include the needed dependencies for building the project and add a script for building the `main.js` file:

```
{
  "name": "vue-custom-plugin",
  "scripts": {
    "build": "browserify script.js -o main.js -t
        [ babelify --presets [ es2015 ] ]"
  },
  "version": "0.0.1",
  "devDependencies": {
    "babel-preset-es2015": "^6.9.0",
    "babelify": "^7.3.0",
    "browserify": "^13.0.1",
    "vue": "^2.0.3"
  }
}
```

Now install the dependencies and build the project from the following command line:

```
npm install
npm run build
```

Open `index.html` in the browser. Try to change the number in the input box. Both square and square root values change immediately:

The changes in the data are applied immediately to the directives created as a part of custom plugin

Exercise

Enhance MathPlugin with trigonometrical functions (sine, cosine, and tangent).

A possible solution to this exercise can be found in the *Annexes*.

Application state and Vuex

When an application reaches a considerable size, it might become necessary for us to manage the global application state somehow. Inspired from Flux (https://facebook.gith ub.io/flux/), there is a Vuex module that allows us to manage and share the global application state among Vue components.

 Do not think about the application state as something complex and difficult to understand. In fact, it is no more than just data. Each component has its own data, and "application state" is data that can be easily shared between all the components!

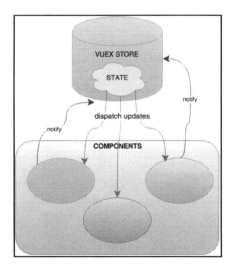

How Vuex store manages applications state updates

Like the other plugins, in order to be able to use and to instantiate the Vuex store, you need to instruct Vue to use it:

```
import Vuex from 'vuex';
import Vue from 'vue';

Vue.use(Vuex);
```

```
var store = new Vuex.Store({
  state: { <...> },
  mutations: { <...> }
});
```

Then, when initializing the main component, assign the store instance to it:

```
new Vue({
  components: components,
  store: store
});
```

Now the main application and all its components are aware about the store, have access to the data inside it, and are able to trigger actions on it at any time of the application's life cycle. We will dig deeply into the application state in the next chapters.

vue-cli

Yes, Vue has its own command-line interface. It allows us to initialize a Vue application with whatever configuration we want. You can initialize it with Webpack boilerplate, with Browserify boilerplate, or just with a simple boilerplate that just creates an HTML file and prepares everything for you to start working with Vue.js.

Install it with npm:

```
npm install -g vue-cli
```

The different ways of initializing an application are as follows:

```
vue init webpack
vue init webpack-simple
vue init browserify
vue init browserify-simple
vue init simple
```

To see the difference, let's run `vue init` with the simple template and with the Webpack template, and look at the differences in the generated structure. Following is how the output differs from both commands:

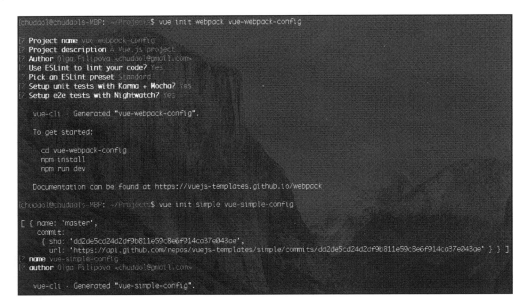

The output from the commands vue init webpack and vue init simple

The following is how the application structure differs:

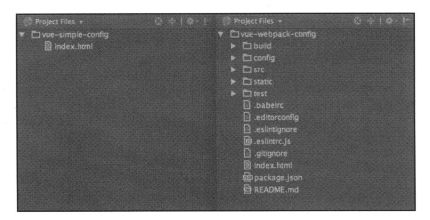

The difference in structure in application scaffolded with vue init simple and vue init webpack

The `index.html` file in the simple configuration already contains Vue.js from the CDN, so if you just need to do something really simple such as quick prototyping, use this one.

But if you are about to start a complex **Single Page Application** (**SPA**) project that will require testing and hot reloading during development, use the Webpack or Browserify configuration.

Vue plugins for IDEs

There are plugins for Vue syntax highlighting for some major IDEs. I will leave you with the links to the fanciest of them:

IDE	Link to the Vue plugin
Sublime	https://github.com/vuejs/vue-syntax-highlight
Webstorm	https://github.com/postalservice14/vuejs-plugin
Atom	https://github.com/hedefalk/atom-vue
Visual Studio Code	https://github.com/LiuJi-Jim/vscode-vue
vim	https://github.com/posva/vim-vue
Brackets	https://github.com/pandao/brackets-vue

Installing, using, and debugging a Vue.js application

In this section, we will analyze all the possible ways of installing Vue.js. We will also create a skeleton for our applications that we will develop and enhance through the next chapters. We will also learn the ways of debugging and testing our applications.

Installing Vue.js

There are a number of ways to install Vue.js. Starting from classic, including the downloaded script into HTML within the `<script>` tags, using tools like bower, npm, or Vue's command-line interface (`vue-cli`), to bootstrap the whole application.

Let's have a look at all these methods and choose our favorite. In all these examples, we will just show a header on a page saying **Learning Vue.js**.

Standalone

Download the `vue.js` file. There are two versions, minified and developer version. The development version is at `https://vuejs.org/js/vue.js`. The minified version is at `https://vuejs.org/js/vue.min.js`.

> If you are developing, make sure you use the development non-minified version of Vue. You will love the nice tips and warnings on the console.

Then just include `vue.js` in the `<script>` tags, as follows:

```
<script src="vue.js"></script>
```

Vue is registered in the global variable. You are ready to use it.

Our example will then look as simple as the following:

```
<div id="app">
  <h1>{{ message }}</h1>
</div>
<script src="vue.js"></script>
<script>
  var data = {
    message: 'Learning Vue.js'
  };

  new Vue({
    el: '#app',
    data: data
  });
</script>
```

CDN

Vue.js is available in the following CDNs:

- **jsdelivr**: `https://cdn.jsdelivr.net/vue/2.0.3/vue.js`
- **cdnjs**: `https://cdnjs.cloudflare.com/ajax/libs/vue/2.0.3/vue.js`
- **unpkg**: `https://unpkg.com/vue@2.0.3/dist/vue.js`(recommended)

Just put the URL in source in the `script` tag and you are ready to use Vue!

```
<script src="
https://cdnjs.cloudflare.com/ajax/libs/vue/2.0.3/vue.js"></script>
```

 Beware the CDN version might not be synchronized with the latest available version of Vue.

Thus, the example will look exactly the same as in the standalone version, but instead of using downloaded file in the <script> tags, we are using a CDN URL.

Bower

If you are already managing your application with Bower and don't want to use other tools, there's also a Bower distribution of Vue. Just call `bower install`:

```
# latest stable release
bower install vue
```

Our example will look exactly like the two previous examples, but it will include the file from the `bower` folder:

```
<script src="bower_components/vue/dist/vue.js"></script>
```

CSP-compliant

Content Security Policy (CSP) is a security standard that provides a set of rules that must be obeyed by the application in order to prevent security attacks. If you are developing applications for browsers, you are likely familiar with this policy!

For the environments that require CSP-compliant scripts, there's a special version of Vue.js at `https://github.com/vuejs/vue/tree/csp/dist`.

Let's do our example as a Chrome application to see the CSP-compliant Vue.js in action!

Start by creating a folder for our application example. The most important thing in a Chrome application is the `manifest.json` file, which describes your application. Let's create it. It should look like the following:

```json
{
  "manifest_version": 2,
  "name": "Learning Vue.js",
  "version": "1.0",
  "minimum_chrome_version": "23",
  "icons": {
    "16": "icon_16.png",
    "128": "icon_128.png"
  },
  "app": {
    "background": {
      "scripts": ["main.js"]
    }
  }
}
```

The next step is to create our `main.js` file, which will be the entry point for the Chrome application. The script should listen for the application launching and open a new window with given sizes. Let's create a window of 500 x 300 size and open it with `index.html`:

```js
chrome.app.runtime.onLaunched.addListener(function() {
  // Center the window on the screen.
  var screenWidth = screen.availWidth;
  var screenHeight = screen.availHeight;
  var width = 500;
  var height = 300;

  chrome.app.window.create("index.html", {
    id: "learningVueID",
    outerBounds: {
      width: width,
      height: height,
      left: Math.round((screenWidth-width)/2),
      top: Math.round((screenHeight-height)/2)
    }
  });
});
```

At this point, the Chrome-specific application magic is over and now we shall just create our index.html file that will do the same thing as in the previous examples. It will include the vue.js file and our script, where we will initialize our Vue application:

```
<html lang="en">
<head>
    <meta charset="UTF-8">
    <title>Vue.js - CSP-compliant</title>
</head>
<body>
<div id="app">
    <h1>{{ message }}</h1>
</div>
<script src="assets/vue.js"></script>
<script src="assets/app.js"></script>
</body>
</html>
```

Download the CSP-compliant version of Vue.js and add it to the assets folder.

Now let's create the app.js file and add the code that we already wrote added several times:

```
var data = {
  message: "Learning Vue.js"
};

new Vue({
  el: "#app",
  data: data
});
```

Add it to the assets folder.

Do not forget to create two icons of 16 and 128 pixels and call them icon_16.png and icon_128.png, respectively.

Your code and structure in the end should look more or less like the following:

Structure and code for the sample Chrome application using vue.js

And now the most important thing. Let's check if it works! It is very, very simple:

1. Go to `chrome://extensions/` url in your Chrome browser.
2. Check the **Developer mode** checkbox.
3. Click on **Load unpacked extension…** and check the folder that we've just created.
4. Your app will appear in the list! Now just open a new tab, click on apps, and check that your app is there. Click on it!

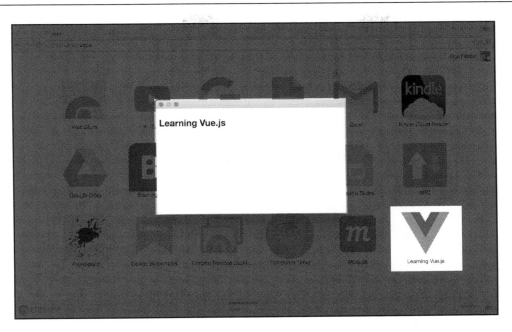

Sample Chrome application using vue.js in the list of Chrome apps

Congratulations! You have just created a Chrome application!

npm

The npm installation method is recommended for large-scale applications. Just run npm install vue as follows:

```
# latest stable release
npm install vue
# latest stable CSP-compliant release
npm install vue@csp
```

Then require it:

```
var Vue = require("vue");
```

Or, for ES2015 lovers, run the following:

```
import Vue from "vue";
```

Our HTML will look exactly like in the previous examples:

```html
<html lang="en">
<head>
  <meta charset="UTF-8">
  <title>Vue.js - NPM Installation</title>
</head>
<body>
  <div id="app">
    <h1>{{ message }}</h1>
  </div>
  <script src="main.js"></script>
</body>
</html>
```

Now let's create a `script.js` file that will look almost exactly the same as in a standalone or CDN version, with the only difference being that it will require `vue.js`:

```js
var Vue = require('vue/dist/vue.js');

var data = {
  message: 'Learning Vue.js'
};

new Vue({
  el: '#app',
  data: data
});
```

Let's install Vue and Browserify in order to be able to compile our `script.js` file into the `main.js` file:

```
npm install vue --save-dev
npm install browserify --save-dev
```

In the `package.json` file, add a script for build as well that will execute Browserify on `script.js` transpiling it into `main.js`. So our `package.json` file will look like the following:

```json
{
  "name": "learningVue",
  "scripts": {
    "build": "browserify script.js -o main.js"
  },
  "version": "0.0.1",
  "devDependencies": {
    "browserify": "^13.0.1",
    "vue": "^2.0.3"
```

```
    }
  }
```

Now run the following command:

```
npm run build
```

And open `index.html` in the browser.

I have a friend that at this point would say something like: really? So many steps, installations, commands, explanations… Just to output some header? I'm out!

If you are also thinking this, wait. Yes, this is true, now we've done something really simple in a rather complex way, but if you stay with me a bit longer, you will see how complex things become easy to implement if we use the proper tools. Also, do not forget to check your Pomodoro timer, maybe it's time to take a rest!

vue-cli

As we have already mentioned in the previous chapter, Vue provides its own command-line interface that allows bootstrapping single-page applications using whatever workflows you want. It immediately provides hot reloading and structure for a test-driven environment. After installing `vue-cli`, just run `vue init <desired boilerplate> <project-name>` and then just install and run:

```
# install vue-cli
$ npm install -g vue-cli
# create a new project
$ vue init webpack learn-vue
# install and run
$ cd learn-vue
$ npm install
$ npm run dev
```

Now open your browser on `localhost:8080`. You just used `vue-cli` to scaffold your application. Let's adapt it to our example. Open a source folder. In the `src` folder, you will find an `App.vue` file. Do you remember we talked about Vue components that are like bricks from which you build your application? Do you remember that we were creating and registering them inside our main script file, and I mentioned that we will learn to build components in a more elegant way? Congratulations, you are looking at the component built in a fancy way!

Find the line that says `import Hello from './components/Hello'`. This is exactly how the components are being reused inside other components. Have a look at the template at the top of the component file. At some point, it contains the `<hello></hello>` tag. This is exactly where in our HTML file the `hello` component will appear. Have a look at this component; it is in the `src/components` folder. As you can see, it contains a template with `{{ msg }}` and a script that exports data with defined `msg`. This is exactly the same as we were doing in our previous examples without using components. Let's slightly modify the code to make it the same as in the previous examples. In the `Hello.vue` file, change `msg` in the `data` object:

```
<script>
export default {
  data () {
    return {
    msg: "Learning Vue.js"
    }
  }
}
</script>
```

In the `App.vue` component, remove everything from the template except the `hello` tag so that the template looks like the following:

```
<template>
  <div id="app">
    <hello></hello>
  </div>
</template>
```

Now if you rerun the application, you will see our example with beautiful styles that we didn't touch:

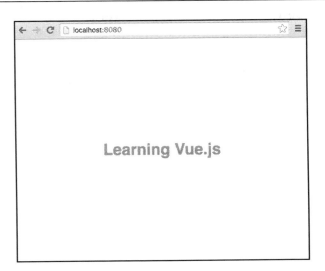

Vue application bootstrapped using vue-cli

 Besides Webpack boilerplate template, you can use the following configurations with your `vue-cli`:

- `webpack-simple`: A simple Webpack + vue-loader setup for quick prototyping
- `browserify`: A full-featured Browserify + Vueify setup with hot-reload, linting, and unit testing
- `browserify-simple`: A simple Browserify + Vueify setup for quick prototyping
- `simple`: The simplest possible Vue setup in a single HTML file

Dev build

My dear reader, I can see your shining eyes and I can read your mind. Now that you know how to install and use Vue.js and how it works, you definitely want to put your hands deeply into the core code and contribute!

I understand you. For this, you need to use the development version of Vue.js, which you have to download from GitHub and compile yourself.

Let's build our example with this development version of Vue. Create a new folder, for example, `dev-build`, and copy all the files from the npm example to this folder.

Do not forget to copy the `node_modules` folder. You should `cd` into it and download files from GitHub to it, and then run `npm install` and `npm run build`:

```
cd <APP-PATH>/node_modules
rm -rf vue
git clone https://github.com/vuejs/vue.git
cd vue
npm install
npm run build
```

Now build our example application:

```
cd <APP-PATH>
npm run build
```

Open `index.html` in the browser; you will see the usual **Learning Vue.js** header.

Let's now try to change something in `vue.js` source! Go to the `node_modules/vue/src/compiler/parser` folder and open the `text-parser.js` file. Find the line that says the following:

```
const defaultTagRE = /\{\{((?:.|\n)+?)\}\}/g
```

Actually, this regular expression defines default delimiters used in the HTML templates. The things inside these delimiters are recognized as a Vue data or as a JavaScript code. Let's change them! Let's replace { and } with double percentage signs! Go on and edit the file:

```
const defaultTagRE = /\%\%((?:.|\n)+?)\%\%/g
```

Now rebuild both Vue source and our application and refresh the browser. What do you see?

After changing the Vue source and replacing delimiters, {{ }} delimiters do not work anymore!

The message inside {{ }} is no longer recognized as data that we passed to Vue. In fact, it is being rendered as part of HTML.

Now go to the `index.html` file and replace our curly brackets delimiters with double percentage, as follows:

```
<div id="app">
  <h1>%% message %%</h1>
</div>
```

Rebuild our application and refresh the browser! What about now? You see how easy it is to change the framework's code and to try out your changes. I'm sure you have plenty of ideas about how to improve or add some functionality to Vue.js. So change it, rebuild, test, deploy! Happy pull requests!

Debugging your Vue application

You can debug your Vue application the same way you debug any other web application. Use your developer tools (firebug), breakpoints, debugger statements, and so on. If you want to dive deep inside the Chrome debugging tools, check Chrome's documentation at `https://developer.chrome.com/devtools`.

Vue also provides *Vue.js devtools*, so it gets easier to debug Vue applications. You can download and install it from the Chrome web store at `https://chrome.google.com/webstore/detail/vuejs-devtools/nhdogjmejiglipccpnnnanhbledajbpd`.

Unfortunately, it doesn't work with locally opened files, so use some simple HTTP server in order to serve our examples as a web page (for example, `https://www.npmjs.com/package/http-server`).

After installing it, open, for example, our shopping list application. Open developer tools. You will see the **Vue** tab has automatically appeared:

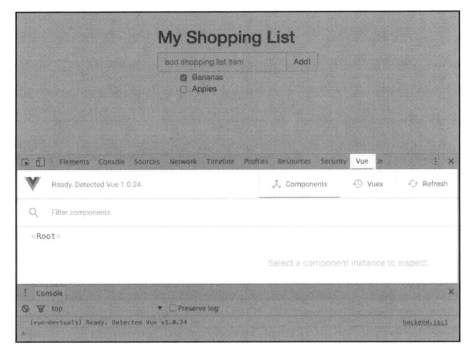

Vue devtools

In our case, we only have one component—**<Root>**. As you can imagine, once we start working with components and having lots of them, they will all appear in the left part of the Vue devtools palette. Click on the **<Root>** component and inspect it. You'll see all the data attached to this component. If you try to change something, for example, add a shopping list item, check or uncheck a checkbox, change the title, and so on, all these changes will be immediately propagated to the data in the Vue devtools. You will immediately see the changes on the right-hand side of it. Let's try, for example, to add a shopping list item. Once you start typing, you see on the right how newItem changes accordingly:

The changes in the Models are immediately propagated to the Vue devtools data

When we start adding more components and introduce complexity to our Vue applications, the debugging will certainly become more fun!

Scaffolding our applications

Do you remember the two applications that we started to work on in the first chapter, the shopping list application and the Pomodoro one? In this section, we will scaffold these applications using the `vue-cli` tool in order for them to be ready to contain reusable components, be tested, and be deployed. Once we bootstrap these applications, we will work on them until the end of this book. So let's do it carefully and with lots of love!

Scaffolding the shopping list application

We will scaffold the shopping list application using `vue-cli` Webpack configuration.

In case you have ignored all previous practical exercises related to `vue-cli`, do not forget to install it before proceeding to the next steps:
npm install -g vue-cli

If you already have `vue-cli` installed, go to the directory where you want to bootstrap the application and run the following:

```
vue init webpack shopping-list
```

Answer yes to all the questions (just click enter) and voilà! You have the application bootstrapped:

```
$ vue init webpack shopping-list
? Project name shopping-list
? Project description Shopping List application
? Author Olga Filipova <chudaol@gmail.com>
? Use ESLint to lint your code? Yes
? Pick an ESLint preset Standard
? Setup unit tests with Karma + Mocha? Yes
? Setup e2e tests with Nightwatch? Yes

   vue-cli · Generated "shopping-list".

   To get started:

     cd shopping-list
     npm install
     npm run dev
```

Bootstraping the shopping list application with vue-cli

Switch to the shopping list directory and run `npm install` and `npm run dev`. Open your browser at `localhost:8080`. You will see the **Hello World** page of the newly created Vue application:

The Hello World view of the newly bootstrapped application

Let's clean the bootstrapped code so that the application gets ready to be populated with our application-specific code. Go to the `App.vue` file and remove everything, leaving just the tags that define the application structure:

- `<template>` with the main `<div>` inside
- The `<script>` tag
- The `<style>` tag

So, in the end, your `App.vue` file looks like the following:

```
<template>
  <div id="app">
  </div>
</template>
<script>
</script>
<style>
</style>
```

Have a look at the page opened in the browser. Funny, you haven't done anything, but the page now doesn't contain the default **Hello World**. The page is empty! It has changed automatically!

Try adding something inside the `<template>` tags. Look at the page; it automatically reloads once you introduce changes. This works because of the `vue-hot-reload` plugin that detects changes in your Vue components and automatically rebuilds the project and reloads the browser page. Try to write some JavaScript code inside the `<script>` tags that doesn't correspond to lint standards, for example, using `notDefinedVariable`:

```
<script>
  notDefinedVariable = 5;
</script>
```

The page in the browser is not refreshed. Look at your shell console. It shows the *lint* errors and "refuses" to build your application:

Each time the application is changed the lint rules are checked

This happens, thanks to the ESLint plugin, which checks the code against the lint rules each time the application changes.

With that, we can be sure that our code will follow the best quality standards.

Speaking of quality, we should also prepare our application to be able to run unit tests. Luckily for us, `vue-cli` with Webpack has already done it for us. Run `npm run unit` to run unit tests and `npm run e2e` to run end-to-end nightwatch tests. End-to-end tests will not run in parallel with your running application since both are using the same port. So, if you want to run tests during development, you should change the port in the `config/index.js` configuration file or simply stop the application between running tests. After running tests, you will see the end-to-end tests fail. This is because they are checking for the application's specific elements that we have removed. Open the file `test.js` from the `test/e2e/specs/` directory and clean all the assertions that we don't need anymore. Now it should look like the following:

```
module.exports = {
  'default e2e tests': function (browser) {
    browser
    .url('http://localhost:8080')
      .waitForElementVisible('#app', 5000)
      .end()
  }
}
```

Rerun the tests. Now they should be passing. From now on, as we will add code to our application, we will add unit and end-to-end tests.

Bootstraping your Pomodoro application

For the Pomodoro application, do the same as for the shopping list application. Run `vue init webpack pomodoro` and repeat all the necessary steps to ensure that the structure is ready to be populated with the Pomodoro application code!

Exercise

Implement our Pomodoro application as a Chrome app! You just need to use it with a CSP-compliant version of Vue.js and add a `manifest.json` file.

Summary

In this chapter, we have analyzed the behind-the-scenes of Vue.js. You learned how data reactivity is achieved. You saw how Vue.js leverages `Object.defineProperty` getters and setters to propagate changes in the data. You saw an overview of the key Vue.js concepts, such as reusable components, plugins system, and state management with Vuex. We have bootstrapped the applications that we will develop during the next chapters.

In the next chapter, we will have a deeper look into the Vue's components system. We will use components in our applications.

3
Components – Understanding and Using

In the previous chapter, you learned how Vue.js works. You saw behind the scenes and even made a slight debug of the core Vue.js code. You learned some of Vue's key concepts. You also learned and tried different ways of installing Vue.js. We have bootstrapped the applications; we will develop and enhance from this chapter on. We have also seen how to debug and to test our applications.

In the first chapter, we talked about components and even created some. In this chapter, we will use components in our applications and see some interesting directives in action. That being said, in this chapter, we are going to do the following:

- Revisit the components topic and review what components are
- Create components for our applications
- Learn what single-file components are
- Learn how to achieve reactive CSS transitions with special attributes

Revisiting components

As you surely remember from the previous chapters, components are special parts of the Vue application that have their own scope of data and methods. Components can be used and reused throughout the application. In the previous chapter, you learned that a component is created by using the `Vue.extend({...})` method and registered using the `Vue.component()` syntax. So, in order to create and use a component, we would write the following JavaScript code:

```
//creating component
var HelloComponent = Vue.extend({
  template: '<h1>Hello</h1>'
});
//registering component
Vue.component('hello-component', HelloComponent);

//initializing the Vue application
new Vue({
  el: '#app'
});
```

Then, we will use `hello-component` inside the HTML:

```
<div id='app'>
  <hello-component></hello-component>
</div>
```

Both initialization and registration can be written as a single `Vue.component` invocation with corresponding options:

`Vue.component('hello-component', { template: '<h1>Hello</h1>' });`

Benefits of using components

There are some things that we need to learn before going deep into the components and rewrite our applications using them. In this section, we will cover things such as handling `data` and `el` properties inside a component, component templates, scope, and preprocessors.

Declaring templates in HTML

In our previous example, we created a Vue component with a template written as a string. It's actually easy and nice because we have everything we need inside our component. Now imagine our component with a more complex HTML structure. Writing a complex HTML string template is error-prone, ugly, and against best practices.

 By best practices, I mean clean and maintainable code. Complex HTML written as a string is anything but maintainable.

Vue allows declaring templates inside an HTML file within a special `<template>` tag!

So, to rewrite our example, we will declare an HTML tag template with the corresponding markup inside:

```
<template id="hello">
  <h1>Hello</h1>
</template>
```

And then, inside our component, instead of the HTML string, we will just use the ID of the template:

```
Vue.component('hello-component', {
  template: '#hello'
});
```

Our whole code will look like the following:

```
<body>
  <template id="hello">
    <h1>Hello</h1>
  </template>

  <div id="app">
    <hello-component></hello-component>
  </div>

  <script src="vue.js"></script>
  <script>
    Vue.component('hello-component', {
      template: '#hello'
    });

    new Vue({
      el: '#app'
```

```
    });
  </script>
</body>
```

In the preceding example, we had only used the `template` attribute for the component. Let's move on and see how the `data` and `el` attributes should be treated inside a component.

Handling data and el properties inside a component

As already mentioned, the component's syntax is the same as the Vue instance's syntax, but it must extend the Vue instead of calling it directly. With this premise, it seems correct to create a component like the following:

```
var HelloComponent = Vue.extend({
  el: '#hello',
  data: { msg: 'Hello' }
});
```

But this would lead to a scope leak. Every instance of `HelloComponent` would share the same `data` and `el`. And this is not exactly what we want. That is why Vue explicitly demands to declare these properties as functions:

```
var HelloComponent = Vue.component('hello-component', {
  el: function () {
    return '#hello';
  },
  data: function () {
    return {
      msg: 'Hello'
    }
  }
});
```

Even if you make a mistake and declare the `data` or the `el` properties as an object or an element, Vue will kindly warn you:

Vue's warning when using data as an object instead of a function inside of a Vue component

Scope of the components

As already mentioned, all components have their own scope that is inaccessible by other components. Nevertheless, the global application scope is accessible by all the registered components. You can see the components' scope as local and the application scope as global scopes. It's the same. However, using the parent's data inside a component is not straightforward. You have to explicitly indicate inside a component which parent's data properties should be accessed using the `prop` attribute and bind them to the component instance using the `v-bind` syntax. Let's see how it works on our `HelloComponent` example.

Let's start by declaring `HelloComponent` with data that contains the attribute `msg`:

```
Vue.component('hello-component', {
  data: function () {
    return {
      msg: 'Hello'
    }
  }
});
```

Now, let's create a `Vue` instance with some data inside it:

```
new Vue({
  el: '#app',
  data: {
    user: 'hero'
  }
});
```

Inside our HTML, let's create a template and apply it to the component using the template's ID:

```
//template declaration
<template id="hello">
  <h1>{{msg}} {{user}}</h1>
</template>

//using template in component
Vue.component('hello-component', {
  template: '#hello',
  data: function () {
    return {
      msg: 'Hello'
    }
  }
});
```

In order to see the component on the page, we should invoke it inside the HTML of our `app` container:

```
<div id="app">
  <hello-component></hello-component>
</div>
```

If you open the page in the browser, you will only see **Hello**; the `user` data property is still not bound to the component:

The parent's data property is not yet bound to our Vue component

In order to bind the data from the parent Vue application, we have to do the following two things:

- Indicate this property inside of the `prop` attribute of a component
- Bind it to the `hello-component` invocation:

```
//calling parent's data attributes in the component
Vue.component('hello-component', {
  template: '#hello',
  data: function () {
    return {
      msg: 'Hello'
    }
  },
  props: ['user']
});

//binding a user data property to the component
<div id="app">
  <hello-component v-bind:user="user"></hello-component>
</div>
```

Refresh the page and you will see how it now presents you with a greeting:

Hello hero

After the correct binding of the parent's `data` property to the component, everything works as expected.

Actually, the `v-bind:user` syntax can be shortcut just by using the
following:

`:user<hello-component :user="user"></hello-component>`

Components inside other components

The beauty of the components is that they can be used and reused inside other components
as Lego bricks and blocks! Let's build another component; let's call it **greetings,** which will
be composed of two sub-components: the form asking for the user's name and our `hello`
component.

In order to do this, let's declare the template for the form and our already familiar `hello`
template:

```
<!--template for the form-->
<template id="form">
  <div>
    <label for="name">What's your name?</label>
    <input v-model="user" type="text" id="name">
  </div>
</template>

//template for saying hello
<template id="hello">
  <h1>{{msg}} {{user}}</h1>
</template>
```

Now we will register two Vue components based on these templates:

```
//register form component
Vue.component('form-component', {
  template: '#form',
  props: ['user']
});
//register hello component
Vue.component('hello-component', {
  template: '#hello',
  data: function () {
    return {
      msg: 'Hello'
    }
  },
  props: ['user']
});
```

Finally, we will create our greetings template that will use both `form` and `hello` components. Do not forget that we have to bind the `user` property on the components invocation:

```
<template id="greetings">
  <div>
    <form-component :user="user"></form-component>
    <hello-component :user="user"></hello-component>
  </div>
</template>
```

At this point, we can create our greetings component and use the greetings template inside it. Let's initialize, which `data` function with the name of the user in this component:

```
//create greetings component based on the greetings template
Vue.component('greetings-component', {
  template: '#greetings',
  data: function () {
    return {
      user: 'hero'
    }
  }
});
```

Inside our main application container, we will now invoke the greetings component:

```
<div id="app">
  <greetings-component></greetings-component>
</div>
```

Do not forget to initialize the Vue application:

```
new Vue({
  el: '#app'
});
```

Open the page in the browser. You should see something like the following:

The page built from various Vue components

Try to change the name in the input. You are expecting it to change also in the greetings header because we bound it to it. But strangely, it doesn't change. Well, this is actually the normal behavior. By default, all props follow one-way data binding. This means that if the data changes within the parent's scope, these changes are propagated to the child component, but not vice versa. It is done this way in order to prevent children components from accidentally mutating the parent state. It is, however, possible to force children components to communicate with their parents by invoking events. Check the Vue documentation at https://vuejs.org/guide/components.html#Custom-Events.

In our case, we can bind a user model to our form `input` component and emit the `input` event every time the user types in the input box. We achieve it by using the `v-on:input` modifier, just like it is described in this section at https://vuejs.org/guide/components. html#Form-Input-Components-using-Custom-Events.

Thus, we have to pass `v-model:user` to `form-component`:

```
<form-component v-model="user"></form-component>
```

Then, `form-component` should accept the `value` prop and emit the `input` event:

```
Vue.component('form-component', {
  template: '#form',
  props: ['value'],
  methods: {
    onInput: function (event) {
      this.$emit('input', event.target.value)
    }
  }
});
```

The input box inside the `form-component` template should bind the `v-on:input` and the `onInput` method to the `v-on:input` modifier:

```
<input v-bind:value="value" type="text" id="name" v-on:input="onInput">
```

Actually, prior to Vue 2.0, this kind of two-way synchronization between components and their parents was possible by explicitly telling the property being bound to **sync** using the `.sync` modifier: `<form-component :user.sync="user"></form-component>`

Refresh the page. Now you can change the name inside the input and it is immediately propagated to the parent's scope, and thus to other children components that rely on this property:

What's your name? Vue

Hello Vue

Binding properties with the .sync modifier allows two-way data binding between parent and children components

You can find the complete code for this example in the JSFiddle at `https://jsfiddle.net/chudaol/1mzzo8yn/`.

Before the Vue 2.0 release, there was one more data-binding modifier, `.once`. With this modifier, the data would be bound only once, and any other changes would not affect the state of components. Compare the following:

```
<form-component :user="user"></form-component>
<form-component :user.sync="user"></form-component>
<form-component :user.once="user"></form-component>
```

Rewriting the shopping list with simple components

Now that we already know a lot about components, let's rewrite our shopping list application using them.

For the rewriting of the application, we will use this version of the shopping list application as a base: `https://jsfiddle.net/chudaol/vxfkxjzk/3/`.

We have already done it previously, when we started talking about components. But at that time, we used string templates inside the components' options. Let's do it now using templates as we have just learned to do. Let's just have a look at the interface and identify the components again:

My Shopping List

add shopping list item   1   Add!

☑ Bananas ³
☐ Apples ²

Change the title of your shopping list here My Shopping List   ⁴

Our shopping list application will have four components

Thus, I suggest that our shopping list application consists of the following four components:

- `AddItemComponent`: The component responsible for adding a new item to the shopping list
- `ItemComponent`: The component responsible for the rendering of the new item in the shopping list
- `ItemsComponent`: The component responsible for rendering and managing the list of `ItemComponent`
- `ChangeTitleComponent`: The component responsible for changing the title of the list

Defining templates for all the components

Let's create templates for these components assuming that the components themselves are already defined and registered.

CamelCase VS kebab-case
You have probably noticed that while we declare variables describing components in CamelCase (`var HelloComponent=Vue.extend({...})`), we name them in kebab-case: `Vue.component('hello-component', {...})`. We do this because of the case-insensitive HTML attribute nature. Thus, our components for the shopping list application will be called as follows:
```
add-item-component
item-component
items-component
change-title-component
```

Have a look at how our markup was previously (`https://jsfiddle.net/chudaol/vxfkxjzk/3/`).

Let's rewrite it using templates and components' names. In this part, we will just worry about the presentation layer, leaving the data binding and actions handling for a future implementation. We just copy and paste the HTML part of the application and distribute it over our components. Our four templates will look something like the following:

```html
<!--add new item template-->
<template id="add-item-template">
  <div class="input-group">
    <input @keyup.enter="addItem" v-model="newItem"
      placeholder="add shopping list item" type="text"
      class="form-control">
    <span class="input-group-btn">
      <button @click="addItem" class="btn btn-default"
        type="button">Add!</button>
    </span>
  </div>
</template>

<!--list item template-->
<template id="item-template">
  <li :class="{ 'removed': item.checked }">
    <div class="checkbox">
      <label>
        <input type="checkbox" v-model="item.checked"> {{ item.text }}
      </label>
    </div>
  </li>
</template>

<!--items list template-->
```

```
<template id="items-template">
  <ul>
    <item-component v-for="item in items" :item="item">
    </item-component>
  </ul>
</template>

<!--change title template-->
<template id="change-title-template">
  <div>
    <em>Change the title of your shopping list here</em>
    <input v-bind:value="value" v-on:input="onInput"/>
  </div>
</template>
```

Thus, our main components' markup will consist of some components:

```
<div id="app" class="container">
  <h2>{{ title }}</h2>
  <add-item-component></add-item-component>
  <items-component :items="items"></items-component>
  <div class="footer">
    <hr/>
    <change-title-component v-model="title"</change-title-component>
  </div>
</div>
```

As you can see, the majority of each template is a plain copy and paste of the corresponding HTML code.

However, there are some significant differences. The list item template, for example, is slightly changed. You have already learned and used the v-for directive previously. In the previous examples, we used this directive with HTML elements such as <li>. Now you see that it can also be used with Vue custom components.

You might have also noticed a small difference in the change title template. Now it has a value bound to it and emits the onInput method bound to the v-on:input modifier. As you have learned in the previous section, children components cannot directly affect directly a parent's data, which is why we have to use the events system.

Defining and registering all the components

Have a look at the JavaScript code in our previous shopping list application: `https://jsfiddle.net/chudaol/c8LjyenL/`. Let's add the code that creates Vue components. We will use the IDs of already defined templates for their `template` attribute. Also, do not forget about the `props` attribute to pass the properties from the parent application. Thus, we add the following code:

```
//add item component
Vue.component('add-item-component', {
  template: '#add-item-template',
  data: function () {
    return {
      newItem: ''
    }
  }
});
//item component
Vue.component('item-component', {
  template: '#item-template',
  props: ['item']
});
//items component
Vue.component('items-component', {
  template: '#items-template',
  props: ['items']
});
//change title component
Vue.component('change-title-component', {
  template: '#change-title-template',
  props: ['value'],
  methods: {
    onInput: function (event) {
      this.$emit('input', event.target.value)
    }
  }
});
```

As you can see, in `props` of each component, we have passed different data attributes—only those that specifically concern the component. We have also moved the `newItem` attribute to the `data` attribute of `add-item-component`. In `change-title-component`, we have added the `onInput` method that emits the input event, so the title in the parent component is affected by whatever the user types in the input box.

Open the HTML file in the browser. The interface is exactly the same as it was earlier! The complete code of what we have done in this section can be found in the JSFiddle at `https://jsfiddle.net/chudaol/xkhum2ck/1/`.

Exercise

Although our application looks exactly as it was looking earlier, its functionality was lost. Not only does it not add items, but it also shows the ugly error in the devtools console.

Please use the events emitting system to bring the adding items functionality back.

A possible solution for this exercise can be found in the `Appendix`, *Solutions to Exercises*.

Single-file components

We know from the old best practices that it is always good to separate HTML from CSS and JavaScript files. Some modern frameworks such as React are relaxing and gradually wiping out this rule. Nowadays, you will not be shocked by looking at the small file or the component that contains its own markup, style, and application code inside it. Actually, for small components, we even find it more convenient to have such architecture. Vue also allows defining everything related to the same component in the same file. This kind of component is known as a single-file component.

A single-file Vue component is a file with a `.vue` extension. The application that contains such components can be built using the `webpack` `vue` configuration. To scaffold an app with such a configuration, the easiest way is to use `vue-cli` (`https://github.com/vuejs-templates/webpack`).

A Vue component can have up to three sections in it:

- `<script>`
- `<template>`
- `<style>`

Each of these sections is responsible for exactly what you are thinking. Put into the `<template>` tag whatever the HTML template should be responsible for, put into the `<script>` tag the JavaScript code responsible for the Vue component, methods, data, props, and so on. The `<style>` tag shall contain the CSS style for the given component.

Do you remember our `hello-component`? Have a look at it in the JSFiddle at `https://jsfiddle.net/chudaol/mf82ts9a/2/`.

Start by scaffolding the app using the `webpack-simple` configuration with `vue-cli`:

```
npm install -g vue-cli vue init webpack-simple hello
```

To rewrite it as a Vue component, we create our `HelloComponent.vue` file and add the following code:

```
<template>
  <h1>{{ msg }}</h1>
</template>

<script>
export default {
  data () {
    return {
      msg: 'Hello!'
    }
  }
}
</script>
```

Note that we do not need to specify the template in our JavaScript component definition. Being a single-file component, it is implicit that the template that should be used is the one defined in this file. You might also have noticed that we use ES6 style in here. Also, do not forget that the `data` attribute should be a function and not an object.

In our main script, we have to create the Vue app and instruct it to use `HelloComponent`:

```
import Vue from 'vue'
import HelloComponent from './HelloComponent.vue'

new Vue({
  el: '#app',
  components: { HelloComponent }
});
```

Our `index.html` markup will not change. It will still invoke `hello-component`:

```
<body>
  <div id="app">
    <hello-component></hello-component>
  </div>
  <script src="./dist/build.js"></script>
</body>
```

Now we just need to install `npm` dependencies (if you still haven't done so) and build the application:

```
npm install
npm run dev
```

Once you do it, your browser will automatically open the `localhost:8080` page!

Check the complete code in the `chapter3/hello` folder.

You can also test, modify, retest, and check the `hello` component in the webpackbin at `http://www.webpackbin.com/N1LbBIsLb`.

Webpackbin is a nice service to run and test applications built with Webpack. It is a very nice tool even though it's still in beta. As it's still young, it still has some minor issues. For instance, if you try to download the package of the entire project, it will not build.

Plugins for IDEs

Vue creators and contributors thought about developers and developed plugins for a large set of modern IDEs. You can find them at `https://github.com/vuejs/awesome-vue#syntax-highlighting`. If you are like me and use WebStorm IDE by IntelliJ, follow these instructions to install the Vue support plugin:

1. Go to **Preferences** | **Plugins**.
2. Click on **Browse repositories**.

3. Type `vue` in the search box.
4. Select **Vue.js** and click on the **Install** button:

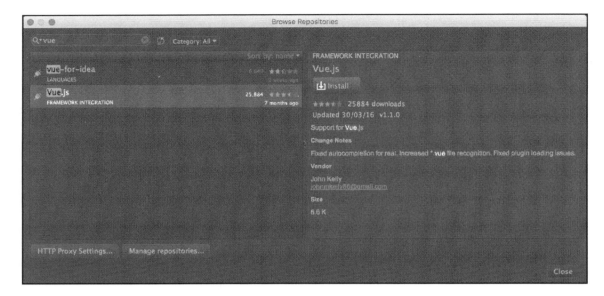

Installing the Vue plugin for webstorm IDE

Style and scope

It is pretty obvious that the template and the script of the component belong only to it. However, the same does not apply to style. Try, for example, to add a `style` tag to our `hello` component and add the CSS rule for the `<h1>` tag to have the red color:

```
<style>
  h1 {
    color: red;
  }
</style>
```

Now, when the page is refreshed, it is quite expected that the color of the **Hello!** header changes to red. Now try to add the `<h1>` tag to the main `index.html` file. You might be surprised, but it will also be red:

```
<div id="app">
  <h1>This is a single file component demo</h1>
  <hello-component></hello-component>
</div>
```

> This is a single file component demo
>
> Hello!

All the <h1> tags have the style that we defined inside a component

To make the style be attached only to the scope of the component, we need to indicate the attribute `scoped` to the `<style>` tag:

```
<style scoped>
  h1 {
    color: red;
  }
</style>
```

Look at the page and you'll see that only the **Hello!** text is red, the other h1 has its default style.

Hot-reloading

You might have noticed that now I no longer ask you to refresh the page but to look at the page. This is because the page is automatically refreshed on each change when the application is bootstrapped using `vue-cli` Webpack scaffolding approach. The magic happens thanks to the `vue-hot-reload` API that watches the application's files and tells the browser to automatically reload every time something has changed! Yay!

Preprocessors

If you are into preprocessors, you are more than welcome to use them in your `.vue` components. This is possible due to `vue-loader` that allows using Webpack loaders.

> You can find more about `vue-loaders` and preprocessors in the tutorial at `http://vue-loader.vuejs.org/en/`.

HTML preprocessors

In order to be able to use a preprocessor in a single-file Vue components, just add the `lang` attribute to the `<template>` tag! Do not forget to install the corresponding node module:

```
npm install jade --save-dev
```

Using `jade`, for example, in our `hello` component's template, would be as easy as follows:

```
<template lang="jade">
  h1 {{ msg }}
</template>
```

CSS preprocessors

The same logic applies to the CSS preprocessors. Let's see how to use, for example, a sass preprocessor:

```
<style lang="sass" scoped>
  $red: red;
  h1 {
    color: $red;
  }
</style>
```

> Like in the previous example, do not forget to install the corresponding loader for this to work:
> npm install sass-loader node-sass --save-dev

JavaScript preprocessors

It is also possible to use any JavaScript preprocessors. Like in the two previous examples, just use the `lang` attribute to specify the preprocessor to use. And do not forget to install it via npm!

```
> npm install coffee-loader coffee-script --save-dev
<script lang="coffee">
  exports.default = data: ->
  { msg: 'Hello!' }
</script>
```

Rewriting our shopping list application with single-file components

Now that we already know so much about components and how to use them, and also know nice techniques to make our code easier to write, let's get back to our shopping list and rewrite it as single-file component's Vue application. To have an easy setup, we can use vue-cli with Webpack configuration. Actually, we've already done it in Chapter 2, *Fundamentals – Installing and Using*. So, just find this application and be prepared to start working on it. If you cannot find it, you can easily create it:

```
#install vue-cli if you still hadn't installed it
$ npm install vue-cli -g
#bootstrap the application
$ vue init webpack shopping-list
$ cd shopping-list
$ npm install
$ npm run dev
```

Ensure that your index.html file looks like the following:

```html
<!DOCTYPE html>
<html>
  <head>
    <meta charset="utf-8">
    <title>shopping-list</title>
    <link rel="stylesheet"
      href="https://maxcdn.bootstrapcdn.com/bootstrap/
      3.3.6/css/bootstrap.min.css">
  </head>
  <body>
    <app></app>
  </body>
</html>
```

And your main.js file should look like the following:

```js
import Vue from 'vue'
import App from './App'

new Vue({
  el: 'app',
  components: { App }
})
```

We are now ready to create our components and to populate our application with them. Of course, you remember that our shopping list has essentially four components:

- `AddItemComponent`: The component responsible for adding a new item to the shopping list
- `ItemComponent`: The component responsible for the rendering of the new item in the shopping list items list
- `ItemsComponent`: The component responsible for the rendering and managing the list of `ItemComponent`
- `ChangeTitleComponent`: The component responsible for changing the title of the list

Let's create all of them in the `components` folder. To start with, just include three empty sections (`<template>`, `<script>`, and `<style>`) in each of them and invoke them in the correct places within the main `App.vue` component. Please put something into the template that will allow us to visibly identify the different components on the page. So, the code of all our four components will look like the following:

```
1   <template>
2     <div>
3       add items
4     </div>
5   </template>
6
7   <script>
8     export default {}
9   </script>
10
11  <style scoped>
12  </style>
13
```
```
1   <template>
2     <div>
3       item
4     </div>
5   </template>
6
7   <script>
8     export default {}
9   </script>
10
11  <style scoped>
12  </style>
13
```
```
1   <template>
2     <div>
3       items
4     </div>
5   </template>
6
7   <script>
8     export default {}
9   </script>
10
11  <style scoped>
12  </style>
13
```
```
1   <template>
2     <div>
3       change title
4     </div>
5   </template>
6
7   <script>
8     export default {}
9   </script>
10
11  <style scoped>
12  </style>
13
```

The code for all four components of the shopping list application

Now open the `App.vue` component. This is our main component that will assemble all the components together.

Remove everything from the `<template>`, `<script>`, and `<style>` tags. We will now start to build our application.

First of all, we must import the components that will be used by `App.vue` (in this case, all of them).

> Do not forget that, as we are using ES2015 in this application, we can use import/export and all the other beautiful ES2015 things.

Inside the `<script>` tag, let's import the components and export the object that will contain the imported components and data function that returns the shopping list's items:

```
<script>
  import AddItemComponent from './components/AddItemComponent'
  import ItemsComponent from './components/ItemsComponent'
  import ChangeTitleComponent from './components/ChangeTitleComponent'

  export default {
    components: {
      AddItemComponent,
      ItemsComponent,
      ChangeTitleComponent
    },
    data () {
      return {
        items: [{ text: 'Bananas', checked: true },
                { text: 'Apples', checked: false }]
      }
    },
    methods: {
      addItem (text) {
        this.items.push({
          text: text,
          checked: false
        })
      }
    }
  }
</script>
```

Our template can basically be the same as the template that we have built in the shopping list application using simple components. Let's just remove everything concerning the models and data binding for now. First, insert the component responsible for adding items, then the component containing all the items, and then, in the footer, the component responsible for changing the title.

Our template will then look like the following:

```
<template>
  <div id="app" class="container">
```

```
      <h2>{{ title }}</h2>
      <add-item-component></add-item-component>
      <items-component></items-component>
      <div class="footer">
        <hr/>
        <change-title-component></change-title-component>
      </div>
    </div>
  </template>
```

You still remember that the names of the components' variables are CamelCased, and when they are used inside the template, they should be invoked using kebab-case, right? Good, let's see how it looks in the browser:

add items
items

change title

Shopping list application built of single-file components

Doesn't seem that beautiful, right? Let's fill each of the components with their templates.

We will continue using Bootstrap's CSS style for this application. Include it globally in the `index.html` file:
```
<link rel="stylesheet"
href=" https://maxcdn.bootstrapcdn.com/bootstrap/3.3.6/cs
s/bootstrap.min.css">
```

AddItemComponent

Open `AddItemComponent.vue`. Let's fill its `<template>`. It will look like the following:

```
<template>
  <div>
    <div class="input-group">
      <input type="text" class="input form-control"
        placeholder="add shopping list item">
      <span class="input-group-btn">
        <button class="btn btn-default" type="button">Add!</button>
      </span>
```

```
    </div>
  </div>
</template>
```

If you look at the page in your browser, you can already see that it changed and became more recognizable as our shopping list application.

Configuring ItemComponent and ItemsComponent

Let's now move to the ItemComponent. We will just copy and paste the HTML from the simple component example:

```
//ItemComponent.vue
<template>
  <li :class="{ 'removed': item.checked }">
    <div class="checkbox">
      <label>
        <input type="checkbox" v-model="item.checked"> {{ item.text }}
      </label>
    </div>
  </li>
</template>
```

Let's also add some scoped style for this component. This component's specific style is the style that has to do with the <li>, <span>, and class .removed. Let's copy and paste them into this component:

```
//ItemComponent.vue
<style scoped>
  .removed {
    color: gray;
  }
  .removed span {
    text-decoration: line-through;
  }
  li {
    list-style-type: none;
  }
  li span {
    margin-left: 5px;
  }
</style>
```

Now open `ItemsComponents`. As you remember, it is a list of the `ItemComponent` elements. Even if you do not remember, I guess that the plural characteristics of the name of this component suggests this. In order for it to be able to use the `ItemComponent`, it must import it and register in the `components` property. So, let's modify the script first:

```
//ItemsComponent.vue
<script>
  import ItemComponent from './ItemComponent'

  export default {
    components: {
      ItemComponent
    }
  }
</script>
```

Now you can use `item-component` in `<template>`! Do you still remember how to iterate with `vue.js`? Of course you do! That is why you are opening the `<template>` tag right now and writing the following code:

```
//temsComponent.vue
<template>
  <div>
    <item-component v-for="item in items" :item="item">
    </item-component>
  </div>
</template>
```

If you check the page now, you'll be surprised to see that things actually do not work. The web console is full of errors. Can you figure out why?

Do you remember that when children components want to have access to the parent's data, they must declare "props" on the component initialization? This is exactly what we've forgotten about on the declaration of both `ItemsComponent` and `ItemComponent`.

First of all, within `App.vue`, bind items to the `items-component` invocation:

```
//App.vue
<items-component :items="items"></items-component>
```

Then add the `props` attribute to `ItemsComponent`:

```
//ItemsComponent.vue
<script>
  import ItemComponent from './ItemComponent'

  export default {
```

```
    components: {
      ItemComponent
    },
    props: ['items']
  }
</script>
```

Now go back to `ItemComponent` and add the `props` property:

```
//temComponent.vue
<script>
  export default {
    props: ['item']
  }
</script>
```

Check the page now. Now it indeed contains the list of items and has a look and feel almost the same as it had when we first created it. Check the full code for this section in the `chapter3/shopping-list` folder.

Exercise

Finish the shopping list application so that it has the same functionality as before.

There's not so much left and I'm sure you will be done with it in less than half an hour. The possible solution to this exercise can be found in the `Appendix`, *Solutions to Exercises*.

Rewriting the Pomodoro application with single-file components

I hope you still remember and possibly even use the Pomodoro application that we developed in the first chapter of this book.

I would like to revisit it now and to do the same exercise we did in the previous section—define the components of the application and rewrite it using these components.

Let's have a look at our Pomodoro application. And now I am going to spoil you: I'll include a screenshot that already contains the kittens that are being shown during the resting time using `http://thecatapi.com/api`:

The Pomodoro application in its Rest! state

There are some easily identifiable components:

- The component of the controls (start, pause, end), let's name it `ControlsComponent`
- The component of the time countdown, `CowntdownComponent`
- The component of the title of the current state (**Work!/Rest!**), `StateTitleComponent`
- The component of the kittens rendering that depends on the state (working or resting), `KittensComponent` (this is my favorite one!)

Now, please stop staring at the kitten and let's start implementing our Pomodoro application using single-file components! Some first steps to scaffold the application are as follows:

1. Start by opening the scaffolded Pomodoro application from the previous chapter or create a new application based on the Webpack template.

2. Run `npm install` and `npm run dev` in the `application` folder.

3. Ensure that your `index.html` looks like the following:

```html
<!DOCTYPE html>
<html>
  <head>
    <meta charset="utf-8">
    <title>pomodoro</title>
  </head>
  <body>
    <app></app>
  </body>
</html>
```

4. Ensure that your `main.js` file looks like the following:

```javascript
import Vue from 'vue'
import App from './App'

/* eslint-disable no-new */
new Vue({
  el: 'app',
  components: { App }
})
```

5. Open your browser to the page `localhost:8080`.

6. Then, like in the previous example, go to the `components` folder and create all the necessary `.vue` components.

7. Go to `App.vue`, and import and register all the created components.

8. In the `<template>` section of each of the components, put something that will uniquely identify it so that we can easily recognize it when checking the page.

You will almost certainly come to the structure and the initial code, which looks something like the following:

The very initial state of the Pomodoro application implemented with single-file components

Now, let's assume that our components are ready to use and let's place them where they belong into the application's layout, accordingly.

I will just slightly remind you how the whole application's markup looked earlier:

```
<div id="app" class="container">
  <h2>
    <span>Pomodoro</span>
    // Looks like our ControlsComponent
    <button >
      <i class="glyphicon glyphicon-play"></i>
    </button>
    <button >
      <i class="glyphicon glyphicon-pause"></i>
    </button>
    <button >
      <i class="glyphicon glyphicon-stop"></i>
    </button>
  </h2>
```

```
// Looks like our StateTitleComponent
<h3>{{ title }}</h3>
// Looks like our CountdownComponent
<div class="well">
  <div class="pomodoro-timer">
    <span>{{ min }}</span>:<span>{{ sec }}</span>
  </div>
</div>
// Looks like our KittensComponent
<div class="well">
  <img :src="catImgSrc" />
</div>
</div>
```

You've probably noticed that I removed some parts that are responsible for the class bindings or actions handlers. Do not worry. Remember Scarlett O'Hara in *Gone with the Wind*? She used to say,

> *"I can't think about that right now. I'll think about that tomorrow."*

(http://goo.gl/InYm8e). Scarlett O'Hara was a wise woman. Be like Scarlett O'Hara. For now, we will focus merely on the <template> tag for our App.vue. Everything else will come later and we will think about it then. Now we can basically copy and paste this HTML snippet and replace the sections that we identify, such as the components with their kebab-case names. So, the template in App.vue will look like the following:

```
//App.vue
<template>
  <div id="app" class="container">
    <h2>
      <span>Pomodoro</span>
      <controls-component></controls-component>
    </h2>
    <state-title-component></state-title-component>
    <countdown-component></countdown-component>
    <kittens-component></kittens-component>
  </div>
</template>
```

A bit smaller, huh? Check your browser with your app opened. Not very beautiful and for sure has nothing to do with our Pomodoro application, but… it works!

Pomodoro Controls

state title
Countdown
Kittens

Pomodoro application bootstrapped as a single-file components application

What should we do now? Copy the corresponding markup to their component's `<template>` sections. Please do this tiny copy and paste by yourself, let it be a small home exercise. However, if you want to check yourself, take a look at the `chapter3/pomodoro` folder. That's it for now! All the data bindings and interesting stuff will come in the next chapter. So do not close the book. However, do not forget to take some Pomodoro pauses.

Reactive binding of CSS transitions

Just before the *transition* to the next chapter, which will talk a lot about different types of data binding, I would like to give you just a tiny flavor of something interesting that is possible to bind. I know that you pay a lot of attention to the words, my dear reader. So, you've already found the word transition two times until now, and you have probably guessed that we can actually bind CSS transitions to the data changes.

So, imagine that you have an element that should only be shown if the `data` attribute `show` is `true`. This is easy, right? You already know the `v-if` directive:

```
<div v-if="show">hello</div>
```

Thus, whenever the `show` attribute is changed, this `<div>` behaves accordingly. Imagine that on hiding/showing, you would like to apply some CSS transition. With Vue you can use the special `transition` wrapper component to specify the transition to use on data changing:

```
<transition name="fade">
  <div v-if="show" transition="my">hello</div>
</transition>
```

After that, you just have to define CSS rules for the `fade-enter`, `fade-leave`, `fade-enter-active`, and `fade-leave-active` classes. Check the official Vue documentation page regarding these classes at `https://vuejs.org/v2/guide/transitions.html#Transition-Classes`.

Let's see how it works in our `kittens` component example. Let's start by adding the `v-if` directive to the `kittens-component` inside `App.vue`:

```
<template>
  <...>
  <kittens-component v-if="kittens"></kittens-component>
  <...>
</template>
```

Also, we should add the `data` function in the `<script>` tag of `App.vue` (let's also make it global so that we can modify it from the devtools console):

```
<script>
// ... //
window.data = {
  kittens: true
};

export default {
  //.....//
  data () {
    return window.data
  }
}
</script>
```

Look at the browser: everything seems unchanged. Open the devtools console and type the following:

```
data.kittens = false
```

You'll see that the `kittens` component will disappear from the page. If you type the following, it will appear again:

```
data.kittens = true
```

I hope you haven't forgotten to include Bootstrap's CSS in the main `index.html` file. Without it, you'll see no appearing/disappearing at all because our `<div>` tag has no information nor any class applied to it:
`<link rel="stylesheet"`
`href="https://maxcdn.bootstrapcdn.com/bootstrap/3.3.6/css`
`/bootstrap.min.css">`

However, we are talking about the *CSS transitions* and not about simply hiding/showing stuff. Now let's apply the CSS `fade` transition to our `kittens` component. Just add a wrapper component `transition` with a name attribute `fade`:

```
<template>
  <...>
  <transition name="fade">
    <kittens-component v-if="kittens"></kittens-component>
  </transition>
  <...>
</template>
```

Now if we define nice rules to the correct classes, we'll see a nice CSS transition. Let's do it. Add the following CSS rules inside the `<style>` tag:

```
<style scoped>
  .fade-enter-active, .fade-leave-active {
    transition: opacity .5s
  }
  .fade-enter, .fade-leave-active {
    opacity: 0
  }
</style>
```

Look at the page again. Open the console and type `data.kittens = false` and `data.kittens = true` again. Now you can see a nice `fade` transition happening on each data change. In the next chapter, we will talk more about transitions in Vue.js and apply them to our applications.

Summary

In this chapter, you learned about Vue components and how to use them. You saw how to create and register them using a classic approach (application that uses HTML, CSS, and JavaScript) and you also saw how easy it is to create and manipulate them using a single-file components approach. Things to retain:

- While variables are created using CamelCased format, in order to be able to use components inside templates, you must apply the corresponding kebab-cased format, for example, `MyBeautifulComponent` -> `my-beautiful-component`
- Attributes `data` and `el` inside the component must be functions and not objects: `{data: function () {}}`
- If you want the style of the component not to leak to the global scope, add a `scoped` attribute to it: `<style scoped></style>`

We have also rewritten our applications using single-file components and touched on the data binding to the CSS transitions slightly.

In the next chapter, we will dive deeply into all the types of data binding, including CSS and JavaScript transitions. We will bring our applications back to life using data binding. Last but not least, we will see more cats!

4
Reactivity – Binding Data to Your Application

In the previous chapter, you learned one of the most important concepts of Vue.js: components. You saw how to create components, how to register, how to invoke, and how to use and reuse them. You also learned the concept of single-file components and even used them in the shopping list and Pomodoro applications.

In this chapter, we will go deeper into the concept of data binding. We have already talked about it earlier, so you are already familiar with it. We will bind data in all possible ways in our components.

Summing it up, in this chapter, we are going to:

- Revisit the data binding syntax
- Apply data binding in our applications
- Iterate over the array of elements and render each element using the same template with different data
- Revisit and apply the shorthands of data and events binding in our applications

Revisiting data binding

We have been talking about data binding and reactivity starting from the very first chapter. So, you already know that data binding is a mechanism of propagating changes from the data to the visible layer and vice versa. In this chapter, we will carefully revisit all the different ways of data binding and apply them in our applications.

Interpolating data

Let's imagine the following piece of HTML code:

```html
<div id="hello"></div>
```

Also, imagine the following JavaScript object:

```javascript
var data = {
  msg: 'Hello'
};
```

How can we render the values of data entries on the page? How can we access them so that we can use them inside our HTML? Actually, we have been doing this a lot with Vue.js during the last two chapters. There is no problem in understanding and doing it again and again.

> *"Repetitio est mater studiorum"*

If you are already a professional of data interpolation, just skip this section and proceed to the expressions and filters.

So, what should we do to populate the `<div>` with the value of `msg`? If we go the old-fashioned jQuery way, we would probably do something like the following:

```javascript
$("#hello").text(data.msg);
```

But then, during runtime, if you change the value of `msg` and if you want this change to be propagated to the DOM, you must do it manually. By simply changing the `data.msg` value, nothing will happen.

For example, let's write the following code:

```javascript
var data = {
  msg: 'Hello'
};
$('#hello').text(data.msg);
data.msg = 'Bye';
```

Then the text that will appear in the `<div>` will, of course, be `Hello`. Check this JSFiddle at `https://jsfiddle.net/chudaol/uevnd0e4/`.

With Vue, the simplest interpolation is done with `{{ }}` (handlebars annotation). In our example, we would write the following HTML code:

```html
<div id="hello">{{ msg }}</div>
```

The content of the `<div>` thus becomes bound to the `msg` data. Each time `msg` changes, the content of the `div` changes automatically following its content. Have a look at the jsfiddle example at `https://jsfiddle.net/chudaol/xuvqotmq/1/`. `data.msg` is also changed after the Vue instantiation. The value that appears on the screen is the new one!

It is still one-way binding interpolation. If we change the value in the DOM, nothing will happen to data. Still, if we only need the values of the data to appear in the DOM and to be changed accordingly, it is a perfect and valid approach.

At this moment, it should be really clear that if we want to use the values of the `data` object inside the template, we should surround them with `{{}}`.

Let's add the missing interpolations to our Pomodoro application. Please check the current situation in the `chapter4/pomodoro` folder. If you run `npm run dev` and have a look at the opened page, you will see that the page looks like the following:

Missing interpolations in our Pomodoro application

From the very first glance at the page, we are able to identify what is missing there.

The page is missing the timer, the kittens, the title of the Pomodoro state (the one that displays **Work!** or **Rest!**), and the logic that shows or hides the kittens' placeholder according to the Pomodoro state. Let's start by adding the title of the Pomodoro state and the minutes and seconds of the Pomodoro timer.

Adding title of the Pomodoro state

First of all, we should decide what component this element should belong to. Have a look at our four components. It is more than obvious that it should belong to `StateTitleComponent`. If you look at the following code, you will see that it actually already interpolates the title in its template:

```
//StateTitleComponent.vue
<template>
  <h3>{{ title }}</h3>
</template>
```

```
<style scoped>
</style>

<script>
</script>
```

Good! In the previous chapter, we've already done most of the work. Now we just have to add the data that must be interpolated. In the `<script>` tag of this component, let's add the `data` object with the `title` attribute inside. For now, let's hardcode it to one of the possible values and then decide how to change it. What do you prefer? **Work!** or **Rest!**? I think I know the answer, so let's add the following code to our `script` tag:

```
//StateTitleComponent.vue
<script>
  export default {
    data () {
      return {
        title: 'Learning Vue.js!'
      }
    }
  }
</script>
```

Let's leave it like this for now. We will come back to this later in the methods and event handling section.

Exercise

In the same way in which we added the title of the Pomodoro state, please add the minutes and seconds timer counters to the `CountDownComponent`. They can be hardcoded for now.

Using expressions and filters

In the previous example, we have used simple property keys inside the {{ }} interpolations. Actually, Vue supports a lot more inside these nice curly brackets. Let's see what it is possible to do there.

Expressions

It might sound unexpected, but Vue supports full JavaScript expressions inside the data binding brackets! Let's go to any of the Pomodoro application components and add any JavaScript expression to the template. You can do some experiments in the `chapter4/pomodoro2` folder.

Try, for example, to open the `StateTitleComponent.vue` file. Let's add some JavaScript expression interpolation to its template, for example:

```
{{ Math.pow(5, 2) }}
```

Actually, you just need to uncomment the following lines:

```
//StateTitleComponent.vue
<!--<p>-->
  <!--{{ Math.pow(5, 2) }}-->
<!--</p>-->
```

You will see number **25** on the page. Nice, isn't it? Let's replace some of our data bindings in the Pomodoro application with a JavaScript expression. For example, in the `CountdownComponent` component's template, two directives, each for `min` and `sec`, can be replaced by one expression. Currently it looks as follows:

```
//CountdownComponent.vue
<template>
  <div class="well">
    <div class="pomodoro-timer">
      <span>{{ min }}</span>:<span>{{ sec }}</span>
    </div>
  </div>
</template>
```

We can replace it with the following code:

```
//CountdownComponent.vue
<template>
  <div class="well">
    <div class="pomodoro-timer">
      <span>{{ min + ':' + sec }}</span>
    </div>
  </div>
</template>
```

Where else can we add some expressions? Let's have a look at StateTitleComponent. At this moment, we use the hardcoded title. We know, however, that somehow it should depend on the Pomodoro state. If it is in the *working* state, it should display **Work!**, otherwise it should display **Rest!**. Let's create this attribute and call it isworking, and let's assign it to the main App.vue component because it seems to belong to the global application state. Then we will reuse it inside the StateTitleComponent component's props attribute. Thus, open App.vue, and add the Boolean property isworking and set it to true:

```
//App.vue
<...>
window.data = {
  kittens: true,
  isworking: true
};

export default {
  <...>
  data () {
    return window.data
  }
}
```

Let's now reuse this property in StateTitleComponent, add two string properties for each of the possible titles, and, finally, add the expression in the template that will conditionally render one title or another accordingly to the current state. Thus, the script of the component will look like the following:

```
//StateTitleComponent.vue
<script>
  export default {
    data () {
      return {
        workingtitle: 'Work!',
        restingtitle: 'Rest!'
      }
    },
    props: ['isworking']
  }
</script>
```

Now we can conditionally render one title or another based on the `isworking` property. Thus, the template of `StateTitleComponent` will look like the following:

```
<template>
  <div>
    <h3>
      {{ isworking ? workingtitle : restingtitle }}
    </h3>
  </div>
</template>
```

Look at the refreshed page. Strangely, it shows **Rest!** as the title. How did this happen if the `isworking` property is set to `true` in `App.vue`? We simply forgot to bind this property on the component invocation in the `App.vue` template! Open the `App.vue` component and add the following code on the `state-title-component` invocation:

```
<state-title-component v-bind:isworking="isworking"></state-title-
component>
```

Now, if you look at the page, the correct title appears as **Work!** If you open the devtools console and type `data.isworking = false`, you will see the title changing.

If the `isworking` attribute is `false`, the title is **Rest!**, as shown in the following screenshot:

If the `isworking` attribute is `true`, the title is **Work!**, as shown in the following screenshot:

Filters

Besides expressions inside the curly interpolation brackets, it is also possible to use filters that are applied to the result of the expression. Filters are just functions. They are created by us and applied by using the pipe symbol: `|`. If you create a filter that makes letters uppercase and call it uppercase, in order to apply it, just use it after the pipe symbol inside the mustache interpolation:

```
<h3> {{ title | lowercase }} </h3>
```

You can chain as many filters as you want, for example, if you have filter A, B, C, you can do something like `{{ key | A | B | C }}`. Filters are created using `Vue.filter` syntax. Let's create our `lowercase` filter:

```
//main.js
Vue.filter('lowercase', (key) => {
  return key.toLowerCase()
})
```

Let's apply it to the Pomodoro title in the main `App.vue` component. In order to be able to use the filter, we should pass the `'Pomodoro'` string inside the handlebars interpolation notation. We should pass it as a JavaScript string expression and apply a filter using the pipe symbol:

```
<template>
  <...>
    <h2>
      <span>{{ 'Pomodoro' | lowercase }}</span>
      <controls-component></controls-component>
    </h2>
  <...>
</template>
```

Check the page; the **Pomodoro** title will actually appear written in the lowercase syntax.

Let's revisit our `CountdownTimer` component and have a look at the timer. For now, there are only hardcoded values, right? But when the application is fully functional, the values will come from some computation. The range of values will be from 0 to 60. It is okay if the timer shows **20:40**, but it is not okay for fewer than ten values. For example, when it is only 1 minute and 5 seconds, it will be **1:5**, which is not good. We are expecting to see something like **01:05**. So, we need the `leftpad` filter! Let's create it.

Go to the `main.js` file and add a `leftpad` filter after the uppercase filter definition:

```
//main.js
Vue.filter('leftpad', (value) => {
  if (value >= 10) {
    return value
  }
  return '0' + value
})
```

Open the `CountdownComponent` component and let's again split `min` and `sec` to the different interpolation brackets and add filters to each of them:

```
//CountdownComponent.vue
<template>
  <div class="well">
    <div class="pomodoro-timer">
      <span>{{ min | leftpad }}:{{ sec | leftpad }}</span>
    </div>
  </div>
</template>
```

Replace `min` and `sec` in data with 1 and 5, respectively, and have a look. The numbers appear with a preceding "0"!

Exercise

Create two filters, `uppercase` and `addspace`, and apply them to the title **Pomodoro**:

- The `uppercase` filter must do exactly what it says it does
- The `addspace` filter must add a space on the right of the given string value

Do not forget that **Pomodoro** is not a key, so inside the interpolation brackets, it should be treated as a string! The title before and after this exercise would look something like the following:

The title of the Pomodoro application before and after applying filters uppercase and addspace

Check yourself: have a look at the `chapter4/pomodoro3` folder.

Revisiting and applying directives

In the previous section, we saw how to interpolate the application's data and how to bind it to the visual layer. Though the syntax is pretty powerful and offers a high possibility of data modification (using filters and expressions), it has some limitations. Try, for example, to implement the following using `{{}}` notation:

- Use the interpolated data in the user input and apply the changes to the corresponding data when the user types in the input
- Bind a specific element's attribute (for example, `src`) to the data
- Render some element conditionally
- Iterate through an array and render some component with the elements of the array
- Create event listeners on the elements

Let's try at least the first one. Open, for example, the shopping list application (it's in the `chapter4/shopping-list` folder). Create an `input` element in the `App.vue` template and set its value to `{{ title }}`:

```
<template>
  <div id="app" class="container">
    <h2>{{ title }}</h2>
    <input type="text" value="{{ title }}">
```

```
    <add-item-component></add-item-component>
    <...>
  </div>
</template>
```

Oh no! Errors, errors everywhere. **Interpolation inside attributes has been removed,** it says. Does it mean that prior to Vue 2.0 you could easily use the interpolation inside attributes? Yes, and no. You would not get an error if you'd use interpolations inside attributes, but changing the title inside the input would result in nothing. In Vue 2.0, as well as in the prior versions, to achieve this kind of behavior, we must use directives.

 Directives are special attributes of the elements that have a v- prefix. Why v-? Because Vue! Directives provide a tiny syntax that provides a richer set of possibilities than simple text interpolation. They have the power to reactively apply some special behavior to the visual layer on each data change.

Two-way binding using the v-model directive

Two-way binding is a type of binding where not only data changes are propagated to the DOM layer, but also the changes that occur to the bound data in the DOM are propagated to the data. To bind the data in such a way to the DOM, we can use the v-model directive.

I am sure you still remember from the first chapter that the v-model directive is used as follows:

```
<input type="text" v-model="title">
```

In this way, the value of the title will appear in the input, and if you type something in this input, the corresponding change will be immediately applied to the data and reflected in all interpolated values on the page.

Just replace the handlebars notation with v-model and open the page.

Try to type something in the input. You will see how the title is immediately changed!

Just remember, this directive can only be used with the following elements:

- <input>
- <select>
- <textarea>

Try all of them and then delete this code. Our main purpose is to be able to change the title using the change title component.

Two-way binding between components

Remember from the previous chapter that two-way binding between components cannot be easily achieved using the `v-model` directive. Due to architectural reasons, Vue just prevents children from easily changing the parents' scope.

That's why we used the events system in the previous chapter to be able to change the title of the shopping list from the child component.

We will do it again in this chapter. Just wait couple of paragraphs until we reach the section on `v-on` directives.

Binding attributes using the v-bind directive

The `v-bind` directive allows us to bind an element's `attribute` or a `component` property to an expression. In order to apply it to the specific attribute, we use a colon delimiter:

```
v-bind:attribute
```

For example:

- `v-bind:src="src"`
- `v-bind:class="className"`

Any expression can be written inside the `""`. The data properties can be used as well, just like in the previous examples. Let's add the kitten image to `KittenComponent` in our Pomodoro application using `thecatapi` as the source. Open our Pomodoro application from the `chapter4/pomodoro3` folder.

Open `KittenComponent`, add `catimgsrc` to the component's data, and bind it to the image template using `v-bind` syntax with the `src` attribute:

```
<template>
  <div class="well">
    <img v-bind:src="catImgSrc" />
  </div>
</template>

<style scoped>
```

```
    </style>

    <script>
      export default {
        data () {
          return {
            catimgsrc: "http://thecatapi.com/api/images/get?size=med"
          }
        }
      }
    </script>
```

Open the page. Enjoy the kitten!

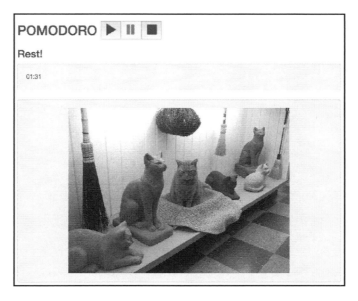

Pomodoro KittenComponent with applied source attribute

Conditional rendering using v-if and v-show directives

If you have paid enough attention in the earlier sections, and if I ask you to conditionally render something, you might be actually able to do it using JavaScript expressions inside the interpolation brackets {{ }}.

However, try to conditionally render some element or the whole component. It might not be as simple as applying an expression inside the brackets.

The v-if directive allows to conditionally render the whole element, which might also be a component element depending on some condition. The condition can be any expression and it can use the data properties as well. For example, we can do the following:

```
<div v-if="1 < 5">hello</div>
```

Or:

```
<div v-if="Math.random() * 10 < 6">hello</div>
```

Or even:

```
<div v-if="new Date().getHours() >= 16">Beer Time!</div>
```

Or using the component's data:

```
<template>
  <div>
    <h1 v-if="!isadmin">Beer Time!</h1>
  </div>
</template>
<script>
  export default {
    data () {
      return {
        isadmin: false
      }
    }
  }
</script>
```

The v-show attribute does the same job. The only difference is that v-if will or will not render the element to the condition accordingly, whereas the v-show attribute will always render the element, just applying display:none CSS property when the result of the condition is false. Let's see the difference. Open the beer-time project in the chapter4/beer-time folder. Run npm install and npm run dev. Open the App.vue component and play with true/false values, and try to replace v-if with v-show. Open devtools and check the **elements** tab.

Let's first check how it looks when we switch between true and false in the isadmin property value using v-if.

When the condition is met, everything appears as expected; the element is rendered and appears on the page:

Conditional rendering using the v-if directive. Condition is met.

When the condition is not met, the element is not rendered:

Conditional rendering using the v-if directive. Condition is not met.

Note that when the condition is not fulfilled, the corresponding element is not rendered at all!

Let's play with the condition result value using the `v-show` directive. When the condition is met, it appears in exactly the same way as it was in the previous case using `v-if`:

Conditional rendering using the v-show directive. Condition is met.

Now let's check what will happen with the element using the `v-show` directive when the right condition is not met:

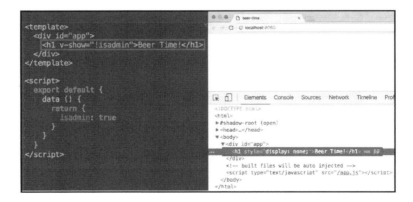

Conditional rendering using the v-show directive. Condition is not met.

In this case, everything is the same when the condition is met, but when the condition is not fulfilled, the element is rendered as well with the `display:none` CSS property.

How do you decide which one is better to use? On the first render, if the condition is not met, the `v-if` directive will not render the element at all, hence reducing the computation costs on the initial rendering. But, if the property changes frequently during runtime, the cost of rendering/removing an element is higher than just to apply the `display:none` property. Thus, use `v-show` with frequently changing properties and `v-if` if the condition will not change too much during runtime.

Let's come back to our Pomodoro application. `KittensComponent` should be conditionally rendered when Pomodoro is not in its working state. So, open your Pomodoro application code in the `chapter4/pomodoro4` folder.

What do you think should be used? `v-if` or `v-show`? Let's analyze. Independently from what we use, should this element be visible on the initial render? The answer is no, because on the initial render, the user starts her working day and starts the Pomodoro timer. It might be better to use `v-if` to not have the cost of initial rendering when there is no need. But, let's analyze another factor—the frequency of toggling the state that will make the kittens component visible/invisible. This will happen at each Pomodoro interval, right? After 15-20 minutes of work and then after 5 minutes of rest interval, which is, actually, not so frequent and will not affect the cost of rendering that much. In this case, in my opinion, it doesn't matter which one you use. Let's use `v-show`. Open the `App.vue` file and apply the `v-show` directive to the `kittens-component` invocation:

```
<template>
  <div id="app" class="container">
    <...>
    <transition name="fade">
      <kittens-component v-show="!isworking"></kittens-component>
    </transition>
  </div>
</template>
```

Open the page and try to toggle the value of `data.isworking` in the devtools console. You will see how the **kittens** container appears and disappears.

Array iteration using the v-for directive

You probably remember that array iteration is done using the `v-for` directive with the following syntax:

```
<div v-for item in items>
  item
</div>
```

Or with components:

```
<component v-for item in items v-bind:componentitem="item"></component>
```

For each item in the array, this will render a component and bind the component's `item` property to the value of the item. Of course, you remember that inside the `""` of the binding syntax you can use whatever JavaScript expression you want. So, just be creative!

 Do not forget that the property we use in the binding syntax (`componentitem`) should be present in the component's data!

Have a look, for example, at our shopping list application (The `chapter4/shopping-list` folder). It already uses the `v-for` syntax in `ItemsComponent` to render the list of items:

```
<template>
  <ul>
    <item-component v-for="item in items" :item="item"></item-component>
  </ul>
</template>
```

`ItemComponent`, in turn, has the `item` property declared using `props`:

```
<script>
  export default {
    props: ['item']
  }
</script>
```

Now, let's do something interesting with our shopping list application. Until now we were dealing only with one shopping list. Imagine that you want to have a different shopping list for different kind of shopping. For example, you might have a regular shopping list for the normal groceries shopping day. You might have a different shopping list for the holidays. You might also want to have a different shopping list when you buy a new house. Let's use the power of the reusability of the Vue components and transform our shopping list application into the list of shopping lists! We will display them using Bootstrap's tab panel; for more information, refer to `http://getbootstrap.com/javascript/#tabs`.

Open your shopping list application in the IDE (the `chapter4/shopping-list` folder).

First of all, we should add Bootstrap's JavaScript file and jQuery, because bootstrap relies on it for doing its amazing magic. Go on and just add them manually to the `index.html` file:

```
<body>
  <...>
  <script src="https://code.jquery.com/jquery-3.1.0.js"></script>
  <script
src="https://maxcdn.bootstrapcdn.com/bootstrap/3.3.7/js/bootstrap.min.js">
  </script>
  <...>
</body>
```

Now, let's establish a step-by-step overview of what we should do in order to transform our application into the list of shopping lists:

1. First of all, we must create a new component. Let's call it `ShoppingListComponent` and move the content of our current `App.vue` to there.
2. Our new `ShoppingListComponent` should contain the `props` attribute with `title` and `items` that it will receive from `App.vue`.
3. `ItemsComponent` should receive `items` from the `props` attribute rather than having it hardcoded.
4. In `App` component's `data`, let's declare and hardcode (for now) an array of `shoppinglists`, each of the items should have a title, an array of items, and an ID.
5. `App.vue` should import `ShoppingListComponent`, and in the template, iterate over the `shoppinglists` array, and for each of them, build the `html/jade` structure of the tabs panel for each of the shopping lists.

Okay, then, let's start!

Creating ShoppingListComponent and modifying ItemsComponent

Inside the `components` folder, create a new `ShoppingListComponent.vue`. Copy and paste the `App.vue` file's content into this new file. Do not forget to declare `props` that will contain `title` and `items` and bind `items` to the `items-component` invocation inside the template. Your final code for this component should look something like the following:

```
//ShoppingListComponent.vue
<template>
  <div>
    <h2>{{ title }}</h2>
    <add-item-component></add-item-component>
    <items-component v-bind:items="items"></items-component>
```

```
      <div class="footer">
        <hr />
        <change-title-component></change-title-component>
      </div>
    </div>
  </template>

  <script>
    import AddItemComponent from './AddItemComponent'
    import ItemsComponent from './ItemsComponent'
    import ChangeTitleComponent from './ChangeTitleComponent'

    export default {
      components: {
        AddItemComponent,
        ItemsComponent,
        ChangeTitleComponent
      }
      props: ['title', 'items']
    }
  </script>

  <style scoped>
    .footer {
      font-size: 0.7em;
      margin-top: 20vh;
    }
  </style>
```

Note that we removed the styling for the container and the container's `class` from the parent `div`. This part of the code should stay in `App.vue` because it defines the global application's container styling. Do not forget about the `props` attribute and binding `props` to `items-component`!

Open `ItemsComponent.vue` and ensure that it contains the `props` attribute with `items`:

```
  <script>
    <...>
    export default {
      props: ['items'],
      <...>
    }
  </script>
```

Modifying App.vue

Now go to `App.vue`. Remove all the code inside the `<script>` and `<template>` tags. In the `script` tag, import `ShoppingListComponent` and invoke it inside the `components` property:

```
//App.vue
<script>
  import ShoppingListComponent from './components/ShoppingListComponent'

  export default {
    components: {
      ShoppingListComponent
    }
  }
</script>
```

Add a `data` attribute and create a `shoppinglists` array there. Add arbitrary data for this array. Each of the objects of the array should have `id`, `title`, and `items` attributes. `items`, as you remember, must contain the `checked` and `text` properties. For example, your `data` property might look like the following:

```
//App.vue
<script>
  import ShoppingListComponent from './components/ShoppingListComponent'

  export default {
    components: {
      ShoppingListComponent
    },
    data () {
      return {
        shoppinglists: [
          {
            id: 'groceries',
            title: 'Groceries',
            items: [{ text: 'Bananas', checked: true },
                    { text: 'Apples', checked: false }]
          },
          {
            id: 'clothes',
            title: 'Clothes',
            items: [{ text: 'black dress', checked: false },
                    { text: 'all stars', checked: false }]
          }
        ]
      }
```

```
      }
    }
  </script>
```

Be more creative than me: add more lists, more items, something nice and interesting!

Let's now create a structure for composing the bootstrap tab panel based on iteration over the shopping list! Let's start by defining a basic structure needed for tabs to work. Let's add all the necessary classes and jade structure pretending that we have only one element. Let's also write in Caps Lock all the unknowns that will be reused from our shopping list array:

```
//App.vue
<template>
  <div id="app" class="container">
    <ul class="nav nav-tabs" role="tablist">
      <li role="presentation">
        <a href="ID" aria-controls="ID" role="tab" data-
toggle="tab">TITLE</a>
      </li>
    </ul>
    <div class="tab-content">
      <div class="tab-pane" role="tabpanel" id="ID">
        SHOPPING LIST COMPONENT
      </div>
    </div>
  </div>
</template>
```

There are two elements where we need to iterate over the shopping lists array—the `<li>` tag that contains an `<a>` attribute and the `tab-pane` div. In the first case, we must bind the ID of each shopping list to the `href` and `aria-controls` attribute and interpolate the title. In the second case, we need to bind the `id` attribute to the `id` property and render the shopping list item and bind the `items` array and `title` to it. Easy! Let's go. Start by adding the `v-for` directive to each of the elements (to the `<li>` and to the `tab-pane div` element):

```
//App.vue
<template>
  <div id="app" class="container">
    <ul class="nav nav-tabs" role="tablist">
      <li v-for="list in shoppinglists" role="presentation">
        <a href="ID" aria-controls="ID" role="tab" data-
          toggle="tab">TITLE</a>
      </li>
    </ul>
    <div class="tab-content">
```

```
        <div v-for="list in shoppinglists" class="tab-pane"
          role="tabpanel"
          id="ID">
          SHOPPING LIST COMPONENT
        </div>
      </div>
    </div>
  </template>
```

Now replace the parts in Caps Lock with the proper bindings. Remember that to the `bind` attribute, we use the `v-bind:<corresponding_attribute>`="expression" syntax.

For the `href` attribute of the anchor element, we have to define an expression that appends the ID selector # to `id`: `v-bind:href="'#' + list.id"`. The `aria-controls` attribute should be bound to the value of the ID. `title` can be bound using the simple `{{ }}` notation interpolation.

For `shopping-list-component`, we must bind `title` and `items` to the corresponding values of the list item. Do you remember that we defined the `title` and `items` properties inside the `props` of the `ShoppingListComponent`? The bindings, thus, should look like `v-bind:title=list.title` and `v-bind:items=list.items`.

So after the proper binding attribution, the template will look like the following:

```
//App.vue
<template>
  <div id="app" class="container">
    <ul class="nav nav-tabs" role="tablist">
      <li v-for="list in shoppinglists" role="presentation">
        <a v-bind:href="'#' + list.id" v-bind:aria-controls="list.id"
          role="tab" data-toggle="tab">{{ list.title }}</a>
      </li>
    </ul>
    <div class="tab-content">
      <div v-for="list in shoppinglists" class="tab-pane" role="tabpanel"
        v-bind:id="list.id">
        <shopping-list-component v-bind:
          v-bind:items="list.items"></shopping-list-component>
      </div>
    </div>
  </div>
</template>
```

We're almost done! If you open the page now, you will see both of the titles of the tabs appearing on the page:

Tab titles as seen on the screen after the modification

If you start clicking on the tabs titles, the corresponding tab panes will open. But this is not what we were expecting to see, right? What we were expecting is for the first tab to be visible (active) by default. For this to happen, we should add the active class to the first li and to the first tab-pane div. But how can we do it if the code is the same for all the tabs as long as we are iterating through the array?

Fortunately, for us, Vue allows us to provide not only the *iteration item* inside the v-for loop, but also index, and then reuse this index variable inside the expressions used in the templates. Thus, we can use it to conditionally render the active class if the index is "0". Using the index variable inside the v-for loop is as easy as the following:

```
v-for="(list, index) in shoppinglists"
```

The syntax for class binding is the same as for everything else (class is also an attribute):

```
v-bind:class= "active"
```

Do you remember that we can write any JavaScript expression inside the quotes? In this case, we want to write a condition that evaluates the value of index, and in case it is "0", the value of class is active:

```
v-bind:class= "index===0 ? 'active' : ''"
```

Add the index variable to the v-for modifiers and the class bindings to the li and to the tab-pane element, so that the final template code looks like following:

```
<template>
  <div id="app" class="container">
    <ul class="nav nav-tabs" role="tablist">
      <li v-bind:class= "index===0 ? 'active' :
      ''" v-for="(list, index) in shoppinglists" role="presentation">
        <a v-bind:href="'#' + list.id" v-bind:aria-controls="list.id"
          role="tab" data-toggle="tab">{{ list.title }}</a>
      </li>
    </ul>
    <div class="tab-content">
```

```
    <div v-bind:class= "index===0 ? 'active' : ''"
      v-for="(list,index) in shoppinglists" class="tab-pane"
      role="tabpanel" v-bind:id="list.id">
      <shopping-list-component v-bind:
        v-bind:items="list.items"></shopping-list-component>
    </div>
  </div>
  </div>
</template>
```

Look at the page. Now you should see nice tabs that display the content by default:

The look and feel of the shopping list application after the correct class binding

The final shopping list application code after these modifications can be found in the `chapter4/shopping-list2` folder.

Event listeners using the v-on directive

It is very easy to listen to the events and call callbacks using Vue.js. Event listening is also done using a special directive with specific modifiers for each of the event types. The directive is `v-on`. The modifiers are applied after the colon:

```
v-on:click="myMethod"
```

Ok, you say, and where do I declare this method? You will probably not believe me, but all the component's methods are declared inside the `methods` property! So, to declare the method called `myMethod`, you should do the following:

```
<script>
  export default {
    methods: {
      myMethod () {
        //do something nice
      }
    }
```

```
    }
  </script>
```

All the `data` and `props` attributes are accessible inside the methods using the `this` keyword.

Let's add a method to add a new item to the `items` array. We have actually done it already in the previous chapter, when we learned how to pass data between parent and children components using the events emitting system. We will just recap this part here.

In order to be able to add new items within `AddItemComponent` to the shopping list that belongs to `ShoppingListComponent`, we should do the following:

- Ensure that `AddItemComponent` has a `data` property called `newItem`.
- Create an `addItem` method inside the `AddItemComponent` that pushes the `newItem` and emits the event `add`.
- Apply an event listener to the **Add!** button using the `v-on:click` directive. This event listener should call the defined `addItem` method.
- Create an `addItem` method inside the `ShoppingListComponent` that will receive the `text` as a parameter and push it to the `items` array.
- Bind the `v-on` directive with a custom `add` modifier to the `add-item-component` invocation inside the `ShoppingListComponent`. This listener will call the `addItem` method defined in this component.

Let's go then! Use the shopping list application from the `chapter4/shopping-list2` folder and play with it.

Start by opening `AddItemComponent` and add the missing `v-on` directive to the **Add!** button and the `addItem` method:

```
//AddItemComponent.vue
<template>
  <div class="input-group">
    <input type="text" v-model="newItem"
      placeholder="add shopping list item" class="form-control">
    <span class="input-group-btn">
      <button v-on:click="addItem" class="btn btn-default"
        type="button">Add!</button>
    </span>
  </div>
</template>

<script>
  export default {
```

```
      data () {
        return {
          newItem: ''
        }
      },
      methods: {
        addItem () {
          var text

          text = this.newItem.trim()
          if (text) {
            this.$emit('add', this.newItem)
            this.newItem = ''
          }
        }
      }
    }
  }
</script>
```

Switch to `ShoppingListComponent` and bind the `v-on:add` directive to the invocation of `add-item-component` inside the `template` tag:

```
//ShoppingListComponent.vue
<template>
  <div>
    <h2>{{ title }}</h2>
    <add-item-component v-on:add="addItem"></add-item-component>
    <items-component v-bind:items="items"></items-component>
    <div class="footer">
      <hr />
      <change-title-component></change-title-component>
    </div>
  </div>
</template>
```

Now create the `addItem` method inside the `ShoppingListComponent`. It should receive the text and just push it into the `this.items` array:

```
//ShoppingListComponent.vue
<script>
  import AddItemComponent from './AddItemComponent'
  import ItemsComponent from './ItemsComponent'
  import ChangeTitleComponent from './ChangeTitleComponent'

  export default {
    components: {
      AddItemComponent,
      ItemsComponent,
```

```
      ChangeTitleComponent
    },
    props: ['title', 'items'],
    methods: {
      addItem (text) {
        this.items.push({
          text: text,
          checked: false
        })
      }
    }
  }
</script>
```

Open the page and try to add the items to the list by typing in the input box and clicking the button afterward. It works!

Now, I would like to ask you to switch your role from the application's developer to its user. Type the new item in the input box. What is the obvious user action after the item has been introduced? Aren't you trying to hit the *Enter* button? I bet you are! When nothing is happening, it is a little bit frustrating, isn't it? Don't worry, my friend, we just have to add one more event listener to the input box and call the same method as we did with the **Add!** button.

Sounds easy, right? What event is fired when we're hitting the *Enter* button? Right, it is the keyup event. So, we just have to use the v-on directive with the keyup method after the delimiter colon: v-on:keyup. The problem is that this event is fired when any keyboard button is hit, which means that while we're typing the new shopping list item, each time the new letter is being introduced, the method will be called. This is not what we want. Of course, we could add a condition inside our addItem method that would check for the event.code attribute and, only in case it's 13 (which corresponds to the *Enter* key), we would call the rest of the method. Fortunately, for us, Vue provides a mechanism to provide keystroke modifiers to this method that allows us to only call a method if a certain key code was hit. It should be implemented using the dot (.) modifier. In our case, it is as follows:

```
v-on:keyup.enter
```

Let's add it to our input box. Go to `AddItemComponent` and add the `v-on:keyup.enter` directive to the input as follows:

```
<template>
  <div class="input-group">
    <input type="text" v-on:keyup.enter="addItem" v-model="newItem"
      placeholder="add shopping list item" class="form-control">
    <span class="input-group-btn">
      <button v-on:click="addItem" class="btn btn-default"
        type="button">Add!</button>
    </span>
  </div>
</template>
```

Open the page and try to add the item to the shopping list using the *Enter* button. It works!

Let's do the same for title changing. The only difference is that the adding items, we used a custom `add` event and here we will use the native input event. We have already done it. We just have to perform the following steps:

1. Bind the model title using the `v-model` directive to `change-title-component` in the template of the `ShoppingListComponent`.
2. Export `value` in the `props` attribute of the `ChangeTitleComponent`.
3. Create an `onInput` method inside the `ChangeTitleComponent` that will emit the native `input` method with the value of the event target.
4. Bind `value` to `input` inside the `ChangeTitleComponent` component's template and the `v-on` directive with the `onInput` modifier.

Thus, the `change-title-component` invocation inside the `ShoppingListComponent` template will look like the following:

```
//ShoppingListComponent.vue
<change-title-component v-model="title"></change-title-component>
```

`ChangeTitleComponent` will look like the following:

```
//ChangeTitleComponent.vue
<template>
  <div>
    <em>Change the title of your shopping list here</em>
    <input v-bind:value="value" v-on:input="onInput"/>
  </div>
</template>

<script>
```

```
export default {
  props: ['value'],
  methods: {
    onInput (event) {
      this.$emit('input', event.target.value)
    }
  }
}
</script>
```

The final code for this part can be found in the `chapter4/shopping-list3` folder.

Shorthands

Of course, it is not time consuming to write the `v-bind` or `v-on` directive in the code each time. Developers tend to think that each time we decrease the amount of code, we win. Vue.js allows us to win! Just remember that the shorthand for the `v-bind` directive is a colon (`:`) and the shorthand for the `v-on` directive is the @ symbol. This means that the following code does the same thing:

```
v-bind:items="items"   :items="items"
v-bind:class=' $index === 0 ? "active" : ""'
:class=' $index===0 ? "active" : ""'
v-on:keyup.enter="addItem"   @keyup.enter="addItem"
```

Exercise

Rewrite all the `v-bind` and `v-on` directives in the shopping list application using the shortcuts we just learned.

Check yourself by looking at the `chapter4/shopping-list4` folder.

Kittens

In this chapter, we haven't touched a lot on our Pomodoro application with its nice kittens. I promise you that we'll do a lot of it in the next chapter. In the meantime, I hope that this kitten will make you happy:

Kitten asking "What's next?"

Summary

In this chapter, we had an extensive overview of all the possible ways of binding data to our presentation layer. You learned how to simply interpolate data using handlebars brackets ({{ }}). You also learned how to use JavaScript expressions and filters in such an interpolation. You learned and applied directives such as v-bind, v-model, v-for, v-if, and v-show.

We modified our applications so that they use richer and more efficient data-binding syntax.

In the next chapter, we will talk about Vuex, the state management architecture inspired by Flux and Redux but with simplified concepts.

We will create global application state management stores for both of our applications and explore their potential by working with it.

5
Vuex – Managing State in Your Application

In the previous chapter, you learned one of the most important concepts of Vue.js: data binding. You learned and applied a lot of ways of binding data to our application. You also learned how to use directives, how to listen to events, and how to create and invoke methods. In this chapter, you will see how to manage the data that represents a global application state. We will talk about Vuex, a special architecture for centralized states in Vue applications. You will learn how to create a global data store and how to retrieve and change it inside the components. We will define what data is local and what should be global in our applications, and we will use the Vuex store to work with a global state in them.

Summing it up, in this chapter, we are going to:

- Understand the difference between local and global application states
- Understand what Vuex is and how it works
- Learn how to use data from the global store
- Learn about store getters, mutations, and actions
- Install and use the Vuex store in the shopping list and Pomodoro applications

Parent-child components' communication, events, and brain teaser

Remember our shopping list application? Do you remember our `ChangeTitleComponent` and how we ensured that typing in its input box would affect the title of the shopping list that belongs to the parent component? You remember that each component has its own scope, and the scope of the parent component cannot be affected by children components. Thus, in order to be able to propagate the changes from inside the children components to the parent components, we used events. Putting it very simply, you can call the `$emit` method from the child component with the name of the event being dispatched and listen to this event within the `v-on` directive on the parent component.

If it is a native event, such as `input`, it's even more simple. Just bind the needed attribute to the child component as a `v-model` and then call the `$emit` method with the name of the event (for example, `input`) from the child component.

Actually, this is exactly what we have done with `ChangeTitleComponent`.

Open the code inside the `chapter5/shopping-list` folder and check if I'm right. (You might also want to run `npm install` and `npm run dev` if you want to check the application's behavior in your browser.)

We bound the title using the `v-model` directive to `ChangeTitleComponent` inside the `ShoppingListComponent` template:

```
//ShoppingListComponent.vue
<template>
  <div>
    <...>
    <div class="footer">
      <hr />
      <change-title-component v-model="title"></change-title-component>
    </div>
  </div>
</template>
```

After that, we declare the value of the title model inside the `props` attribute of the `ChangeTitleComponent` and emit the `input` event on the `input` action:

```
<template>
  <div>
    <em>Change the title of your shopping list here</em>
    <input :value="value" @input="onInput"/>
  </div>
```

```
</template>

<script>
  export default {
    props: ['value'],
    methods: {
      onInput (event) {
        this.$emit('input', event.target.value)
      }
    }
  }
</script>
```

Seems pretty straightforward, right?

If we try to change the title in the input box, the title of our shopping list changes accordingly:

After establishing events-based communication between the parent and child components, we are able to change the title

Looks like we were actually able to achieve our purpose. However, if you open your devtools, you will see an ugly error:

> [Vue warn]: Avoid mutating a prop directly since the value will be overwritten whenever the parent component rerenders. Instead, use a data or computed property based on the prop's value. Prop being mutated: "title"

Ouch! Vue is actually right, we are mutating the data that is contained inside the ShoppingList component's props attribute. This attribute comes from the main parent component, App.vue, which is, in turn, the parent of our ShoppingListComponent. And we already know that we cannot mutate the parent's data from the child component. If the title belonged directly to the ShoppingListComponent, we were all good, but in this case, we are definitely doing something wrong.

Also, if you are paying enough attention, you probably noticed that there's one more place that contains the same piece of data that doesn't change despite our effort. Look at the tab's title. It continues to display the word **Groceries**. But we want it to change as well!

Small side note: I've added a new component, `ShoppingListTitleComponent`. It represents the tab's title. Do you remember computed properties? Note that this component contains one that just prepends `#` to the ID imported through the `props` attribute to generate an anchor:

```
<template>
  <a :href="href" :aria-controls="id" role="tab" data-toggle="tab">
  {{ title }}</a>
</template>
<script>
  export default{
    props: ['id', 'title'],
    computed: {
      href () {
        return '#' + this.id
      }
    }
  }
</script>
```

The anchor that displays the tab's title contains an `href` binding directive that relies on this computed property.

So, back to the title changing. What can we do to change the title of this component when the title inside the `ChangeTitleComponent` changes? If we could propagate the event to the main `App.vue` component, we could actually solve both problems. Whenever the data in the parent component changes, it affects all the children components.

So, we need to somehow make the event flow from `ChangeTitleComponent` until the main `App` component. Sounds difficult, but actually, we just need to register our custom event in both `ChangeTitleComponent` and its parent and emit it until it reaches the `App` component. The `App` component should handle this event by applying the change to the corresponding title. In order for `App.vue` to know exactly which shopping list is being changed, its child `ShoppingListComponent` should also pass the ID of the shopping list that it represents. For this to happen, `App.vue` should pass the `id` property to the component, and the shopping list component should register it in its `props` attribute.

So, we will do the following:

1. Bind the `id` property to `ShoppingListComponent` on its creation inside the `App` component's template.
2. Bind property `title` instead of `v-model` to the `change-title-component` from within the `ShoppingList` component.
3. Attach the custom event (let's call it `changeTitle`) to `input` inside the `ChangeTitleComponent`.
4. Tell `ShoppingListComponent` to listen to the custom `changeTitle` event coming from the `change-title-component` using the `v-on` directive and handle it by emitting another event (it can also be called `changeTitle`) that should be caught by the `App` component.
5. Attach listener to the `changeTitle` event to the `shopping-list-component` inside `App.vue` and handle it by actually changing the title of the corresponding shopping list.

Let's start by modifying the `App.vue` file's template and binding the shopping list's ID to `shopping-list-component`:

```
//App.vue
<template>
  <div id="app" class="container">
    <...>
        <shopping-list-component :id="list.id" :
          :items="list.items"></shopping-list-component>
    <...>
  </div>
</template>
```

Now register the `id` attribute inside the `ShoppingListComponent` component's `props`:

```
//ShoppingListComponent.vue
<script>
  <...>
  export default {
    <...>
    props: ['id', 'title', 'items'],
    <...>
  }
</script>
```

Bind the `title` data property instead of the `v-model` directive to the `change-title-component`:

```
//ShoppingListComponent.vue
<template>
  <...>
      <change-title-component :></change-title-component>
  <...>
</template>

//ChangeTitleComponent.vue
<template>
  <div>
    <em>Change the title of your shopping list here</em>
    <input :value="title" @input="onInput"/>
  </div>
</template>

<script>
  export default {
    props: ['value', 'title'],
    <...>
  }
</script>
```

Emit a custom event instead of `input` from the `ChangeTitleComponent` and listen to this event in its parent component:

```
//ChangeTitleComponent.vue
<script>
  export default {
    <...>
    methods: {
      onInput (event) {
        this.$emit('changeTitle', event.target.value)
      }
    }
  }
</script>

//ShoppingListComponent.vue
<template>
  <...>
      <change-title-component :
        v-on:changeTitle="onChangeTitle"></change-title-component>
  <...>
</template>
```

Create the `onChangeTitle` method in `ShoppingListComponent` that will emit its own `changeTitle` event. Listen to this event in the `App.vue` component using the `v-on` directive. Note that the `onChangeTitle` method of the shopping list component should send its ID in order for `App.vue` to know which shopping list's title is being changed. So, the `onChangeTitle` method and its handling will look as follows:

```
//ShoppingListComponent.vue
<script>
  <...>

  export default {
    <...>
    methods: {
      <...>
      onChangeTitle (text) {
        this.$emit('changeTitle', this.id, text)
      }
    }
  }
</script>

//App.vue
<template>
  <...>
  <shopping-list-component :id="list.id" :
    :items="list.items" v-on:changeTitle="onChangeTitle">
  </shopping-list-component>
  <...>
</template>
```

Finally, let's create a `changeTitle` method inside `App.vue` that will find a shopping list in the `shoppinglists` array by its ID and change its title:

```
<script>
  <...>
  import _ from 'underscore'

  export default {
    <...>
    methods: {
      onChangeTitle (id, text) {
        _.findWhere(this.shoppinglists, { id: id }).title = text
      }
    }
  }
</script>
```

Note that we have used the `underscore` class's `findWhere` method (`http://underscorejs.org/#findWhere`) to make our task of finding the shopping list by its ID easier.

And ... we are done! Check the final code for this teaser in the `chapter5/shopping-list2` folder. Check the page in the browser. Try to change the title in the input box. You will see that it changes everywhere!

Admit that this was quite challenging. Try to repeat all the steps by yourself. In the meantime, let me be random and tell you two words: global and local. Think about it.

Why do we need a global state store?

As a developer, you are already familiar with global and local concepts. There are global variables that are accessible by each section of the application, but methods also have their own (local) scope and their scope is not accessible by other methods.

A component-based system also has its local and global states. Each component has its local data, but the application has a global application state that can be accessed by any component of the application. The challenge that we have met in the previous paragraph would be easily solved if we had some kind of a global variables store containing the titles of the shopping lists and each component could access and modify them. Fortunately for us, Vue's creator thought about us and created Vuex architecture. This architecture allows us to create a global application store—the place where the global application state can be stored and managed!

What is Vuex?

As previously mentioned, Vuex is an application architecture for centralized state management. It was inspired by Flux and Redux, but it is a little bit easier to understand and to use:

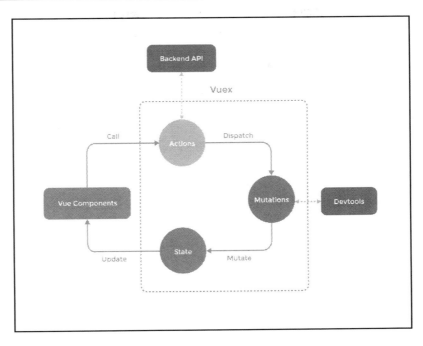

Vuex architecture; the image is taken from the Vuex GitHub page at https://github.com/vuejs/vuex

Look in the mirror (do not forget to smile to yourself). You see a nice pretty human. However, there's a whole complex system inside it. What do you do when you feel cold? And how do you feel when it's hot? How does it feel to be hungry? And very hungry? And how does it feel to touch a fluffy cat? The human can be in various types of states (happy, hungry, smiley, angry, and so on). The human also has a lot of components, such as hands, arms, legs, stomach, face, and so on. Can you imagine how would it be if, let's say, a hand were able to directly influence your stomach, making you feel hungry, without your awareness?

The way we work is very similar to the centralized state management system. Our brain contains an initial state of things (happy, not hungry, satisfied, and so on). It also provides the mechanism that allows pulling the strings in it that can affect the state. For example, *make a smile, feel satisfied, clap your hands,* and so on. Our hands, stomach, mouth, and other components cannot directly affect the state. But they can tell our brain to dispatch certain changes, and these changes, in turn, will affect the state.

For example, when you are hungry, you eat. Your stomach at some certain point tells the brain that it is full. The action dispatches a mutation of the state of being hungry to be satisfied. Your component mouth is bound to this state and it makes it express the smile. Thus, the components are bound to the read-only brain state and can dispatch brain actions that will alter the state. The components are not aware of each other and cannot modify each other's state directly in any way. They also can also not affect directly the brain's initial state. They can only call the actions. Actions belong to the brain, and in their callbacks, the state can be modified. Thus, our brain is a single source of truth.

Single source of truth in information systems is a way of designing the architecture of the application in such a way that every data element is only stored once. This data is read-only to prevent the application's components from corrupting the state that is accessed by other components. The Vuex store is designed in such a way that it is not possible to change its state from any component.

How does the store work and what is so special about it?

The Vuex store contains essentially two things: **state** and **mutations**. State is an object that represents the initial state of the application data. Mutations is also an object containing action functions that affect the state. Vuex store is just a plain JavaScript file that exports these two objects and tells Vue to use Vuex (`Vue.use(Vuex)`). Then it can be imported into any other component. If you import it in the main `App.vue` file and register the store on the `Vue` application initialization, it is passed to the whole children chain and can be accessed through the `this.$store` variable. So, very roughly, in a very simplified way, we would create a store, import it in the main app, and use it in a component in the following way:

```
//CREATE STORE
//initialize state
const state = {
  msg: 'Hello!'
}
//initialize mutations
const mutations = {
  changeMessage(state, msg) {
    state.msg = msg
  }
}
//create store with defined state and mutations
export default new Vuex.Store({
```

```
    state: state
    mutations: mutations
})
```

//CREATE VUE APP
```
<script>
  import store from './vuex/store'
  export default {
    components: {
      SomeComponent
    },
    store: store
  }
</script>
```

//INSIDE SomeComponent
```
<script>
  export default {
    computed: {
      msg () {
        return this.$store.state.msg;
      }
    },
    methods: {
      changeMessage () {
        this.$store.commit('changeMessage', newMsg);
      }
    }
  }
</script>
```

The very logical question might arise: why create a Vuex store instead of just having a shared JavaScript file that imports some state? You can, of course, do that, but then you must make sure that none of the components can mutate the state directly. Being able to change the store attributes directly would, of course, be a lot easier, but then it might lead to errors and inconsistencies. Vuex provide a clean way of implicitly protecting the store's state of direct access. And, it's reactive. Putting all this in statements:

- The Vuex store is reactive. Once components retrieve a state from it, they will reactively update their views every time the state changes.
- Components are not able to directly mutate the store's state. Instead, they have to dispatch mutations declared by the store, which allows easy tracking of changes.
- Our Vuex store thus becomes a single source of truth.

Let's create a simple greetings example to see Vuex in action.

Greetings with store

We will create a very simple Vue application with two components: one of them will contain the greetings message and the other one will contain `input` that will allow us to change this message. Our store will contain the initial state that will represent the initial greeting and the mutation that will be able to change the message. Let's start by creating a Vue application. We will use `vue-cli` and the `webpack-simple` template:

```
vue init webpack-simple simple-store
```

Install the dependencies and run the application as follows:

```
cd simple-store npm install npm run dev
```

The application is started! Open the browser in `localhost:8080`. Actually, the greeting is already there. Let's now add the necessary components:

- `ShowGreetingsComponent` will just display the greetings message
- `ChangeGreetingsComponent` will display the input field that will allow to change the message

In the `src` folder, create a `components` subfolder. Start by adding `ShowGreetingsComponent.vue` to this folder.

It will look as simple as the following:

```
<template>
  <h1>{{ msg }}</h1>
</template>
<script>
  export default {
    props: ['msg']
  }
</script>
```

After that, add `ChangeGreetingsComponent.vue` to this folder. It has to contain the input with the `v-model='msg'` directive:

```
<template>
  <input v-model='msg'>
</template>
<script>
  export default {
    props: ['msg']
  }
</script>
```

Now open the `App.vue` file, import the components, and replace the markup with these two components. Do not forget to bind `msg` to both of them. So, your `App.vue` after the modifications will look like the following:

```
<template>
  <div>
    <show-greetings-component :msg='msg'></show-greetings-component>
    <change-greetings-component :msg='msg'></change-greetings-component>
  <div>
</template>

<script>
import ShowGreetingsComponent from
'./components/ShowGreetingsComponent.vue'
import ChangeGreetingsComponent from
'./components/ChangeGreetingsComponent.vue'

export default {
  components: { ShowGreetingsComponent, ChangeGreetingsComponent },
  data () {
    return {
      msg: 'Hello Vue!'
    }
  }
}
</script>
```

Open the browser. You will see the input box with our greeting; however, typing in it will not change the message in the title. We were already expecting that because we know that components cannot directly affect each other's state. Let's now introduce the store! First of all, we must install `vuex`:

```
npm install vuex --save
```

Create a folder named `vuex` in the `src` folder. Create a JavaScript file named `store.js`. This will be our state management entry. First of all, import both Vue and Vuex and tell Vue that we want to use Vuex in this application:

```
//store.js
import Vue from 'vue'
import Vuex from 'vuex'
Vue.use(Vuex)
```

Now create two constants, `state` and `mutations`. `State` will contain the message `msg` while `mutations` will export the method that will allow us to modify `msg`:

```
const state = {
  msg: 'Hello Vue!'
}

const mutations = {
  changeMessage(state, msg) {
    state.msg = msg
  }
}
```

Now initialize the Vuex store with the already created `state` and `mutations`:

```
export default new Vuex.Store({
  state: state,
  mutations: mutations
})
```

> As we are using ES6, the notation `{state: state, mutations: mutations}` can be replaced with, simply, `{state, mutations}`

Our whole store's code will thus look like the following:

```
//store.js
import Vue from 'vue'
import Vuex from 'vuex'

Vue.use(Vuex)
const state = {
  msg: 'Hello Vue!'
}
const mutations = {
  changeMessage(state, msg) {
    state.msg = msg
  }
}
export default new Vuex.Store({
  state,
  mutations
})
```

We can now import the store in our `App.vue`. By doing this, we tell all the components that they can use the global store, and as a result, we can remove data from `App.vue`. Also, we do not need to bind data to the components anymore:

```
//App.vue
<template>
  <div>
    <show-greetings-component></show-greetings-component>
    <change-greetings-component></change-greetings-component>
  </div>
</template>

<script>
import ShowGreetingsComponent from
'./components/ShowGreetingsComponent.vue'
import ChangeGreetingsComponent from
'./components/ChangeGreetingsComponent.vue'
import store from './vuex/store'

export default {
  components: {ShowGreetingsComponent, ChangeGreetingsComponent},
  store
}
</script>
```

Now let's go back to our components and reuse the data from the store. In order to be able to reuse reactive data from the store's state, we should use computed properties. Vue is so smart that it will do all the work for us to reactively update these properties whenever the state changes. And no, we do not need to import the store inside the components. We have access to it just by using the `this.$store` variable. So, our `ShowGreetingsComponent` will look like the following:

```
//ShowGreetingsComponent.vue
<template>
  <h1>{{ msg }}</h1>
</template>
<style>
</style>
<script>
  export default {
    computed: {
      msg () {
        return this.$store.state.msg
      }
    }
  }
</script>
```

Follow the same logic to reuse the store's `msg` in the `ChangeGreetingsComponent`. Now we just have to dispatch the mutation on each `keyup` event. For this to happen, we just need to create a method that will commit the corresponding store's mutation and that we will call from the input's `keyup` listener:

```
//ChangeGreetingsComponent.vue
<template>
  <input v-model='msg' @keyup='changeMsg'>
</template>
<script>
  export default {
    computed: {
      msg() {
        return this.$store.state.msg
      }
    },
    methods: {
      changeMsg(ev) {
        this.$store.commit('changeMessage', ev.target.value)
      }
    }
  }
</script>
```

Open the page. Try to change the title. Et voilà! It works!

Using the Vuex store to call the mutations and change the store's state propagating it through the components

We don't need to bind the `v-model` directive anymore because all the changes happen due to the calling store's mutation method. Thus, the `msg` property can be bound as the value's attribute to the input box:

```
<template>
  <input :value='msg' @keyup='changeMsg'>
</template>
```

Check the code for this section in the `chapter5/simple-store` folder. In this example, we have used a very simplified version of the store. However, complex **Single-Page Applications (SPAs)** require a more complex and modular structure. We can and should extract the store's getters and actions that dispatch mutations to separated files. We can also group these files according to the corresponding data's responsibilities. In the next sections, we will see how we can achieve such a modular structure by using getters and actions.

Store state and getters

It is, of course, good that we can reuse the `this.$store.state` keyword inside the components. But imagine the following scenarios:

- In a large-scale app where different components access the state of the store using `$this.store.state.somevalue`, we decide to change the name of `somevalue`. This means that we have to change the name of the variable inside each and every component that uses it!
- We want to use a *computed* value of state. For example, let's say we want to have a counter. Its initial state is "0". Each time we use it, we want to increment it. This means that each component has to contain a function that reuses the store's value and increments it, which means having repeated code in each component, which is not good at all!

Sorry for the not-so-good scenarios, guys! Fortunately, there is a nice way not to fall into any of them. Imagine the centralized getter that accesses the store's state and provides a getter function to each of the state's items. If needed, this getter can apply some computation to the state's item. And if we need to change the name of some of the attributes, we only change it in one place, in this getter. It's rather a good practice or a convention than an architectural mandatory system, but I strongly recommend to use it even if you have only a couple of state items.

Let's create such a getter for our simple greetings application. Just create a `getters.js` file inside the `vuex` folder and export a `getMessage` function that will return `state.msg`:

```
//getters.js
export default {
  getMessage(state) {
    return state.msg
  }
}
```

Then it should be imported by the store and exported in the new `Vuex` object, so the store knows what its getters are:

```
//store.js
import Vue from 'vue'
import Vuex from 'vuex'
import getters from './getters'

Vue.use(Vuex)

const state = {
  msg: 'Hello Vue!'
}

const mutations = {
  changeMessage(state, msg) {
    state.msg = msg
  }
}

export default new Vuex.Store({
  state, mutations, getters
})
```

And then, in our components, we use getters instead of directly accessing the store's state. Just replace your `computed` property in both the components with the following:

```
computed: {
  msg () {
    return this.$store.getters.getMessage
  }
},
```

Open the page; everything works like a charm!

Still the `this.$store.getters` notation contains so many letters to write. We, programmers are lazy, right? Vue is nice enough to provide us with an easy way to support our laziness. It provides a `mapGetters` helper that does exactly as its name suggests—provides all the store's getters to our components. Just import it and use it in your `computed` properties as follows:

```
//ShowGreetingsComponent.vue
<template>
  <h1>{{ getMessage }}</h1>
</template>
<script>
  import { mapGetters } from 'vuex'
```

```
   export default {
     computed: mapGetters(['getMessage'])
   }
</script>

//ChangeGreetingsComponent.vue
<template>
   <input :value='getMessage' @keyup='changeMsg'>
</template>
<script>
  import { mapGetters } from 'vuex'

  export default {
    computed: mapGetters(['getMessage']),
    methods: {
      changeMsg(ev) {
        this.$store.commit('changeMessage', ev.target.value)
      }
    }
  }
</script>
```

Note that we've changed the property used inside the template to have the same name as the getter's method name. However, it is also possible to map the corresponding getter method's name to the property name that we want to use in our component:

```
//ShowGreetingsComponent.vue
<template>
   <h1>{{ msg }}</h1>
</template>
<style>
</style>
<script>
  import { mapGetters } from 'vuex'

  export default {
    computed: mapGetters({
      msg: 'getMessage'
    })
  }
</script>

//ChangeGreetingsComponent.vue
<template>
   <input :value='msg' @keyup='changeMsg'>
</template>
<script>
  import { mapGetters } from 'vuex'
```

```
export default {
  computed: mapGetters({
    msg: 'getMessage'
  }),
  methods: {
    changeMsg(ev) {
      this.$store.commit('changeMessage', ev.target.value)
    }
  }
}
</script>
```

So, we were able to extract the getter for the `msg` property to the centralized store's getters file.

Now, if you decide to add some computation to the `msg` property, you only need to do it in one place. Just in one place!

Rick was always changing the code in all the components and just discovered that it is possible to only change it in one place

For example, if we want to reuse the uppercased message in all the components, we can apply the `uppercase` function inside the getter as follows:

```
//getters.js
export default {
  getMessage(state) {
    return (state.msg).toUpperCase()
  }
}
```

From now on, each component that uses the getter to retrieve the state will have an uppercased message:

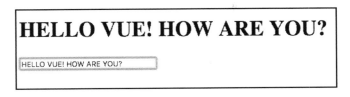

The ShowTitleComponent uppercased message. The toUpperCase function is applied inside the getters

Note also how smoothly the message is being changed to uppercase inside the input box while you're typing in it! Check the final code for this section inside the `chapter5/simple-store2` folder.

If we decide to change the name of the state's attribute, we will only change it inside the getters function. For example, if we want to change the name of `msg` to `message`, we will do it inside our store:

```
const state = {
  message: 'Hello Vue!'
}

const mutations = {
  changeMessage(state, msg) {
    state.message = msg
  }
}
```

And then, we will also change it inside the corresponding getter *function*:

```
export default {
  getMessage(state) {
    return (state.message).toUpperCase()
  }
}
```

That's it! The rest of the application is left completely untouched. This is the power of such architecture. In some very complex applications, we can have more than one getters files that export state for different kind of the application's properties. **Modularity** is a power that drives the maintainability; use it!

Mutations

From the previous example, it should be clear that mutations are no more than simple event handler functions that are defined by **name**. Mutation handler functions receive a `state` as a first argument. Other arguments can be used to pass different parameters to the handler function:

```
const mutations = {
  changeMessage(state, msg) {
    state.message = msg
  },
  incrementCounter(state) {
    state.counter ++;
  }
}
```

A particularity of mutations is that they cannot be called directly. To be able to dispatch a mutation, we should call a method called `commit` with a name of the corresponding mutation and parameters:

```
store.commit('changeMessage', 'newMessage')
store.commit('incrementCounter')
```

Prior to Vue 2.0, a method to dispatch mutation was called "dispatch". So you would call it as follows:
```
store.dispatch('changeMessage', 'newMessage')
```

You can create as many mutations as you wish. They can perform different operations on same-state items. You can go even further and declare mutation names as constants in a separated file. In this way, you can easily import them and use them instead of strings. So, for our example, we would create a file inside the `vuex` directory and call it `mutation_types.js`, and export all the constant names there:

```
//mutation_types.js
export const INCREMENT_COUNTER = 'INCREMENT_COUNTER'
export const CHANGE_MSG = 'CHANGE_MSG'
```

Then, in our store, we will import these constants and reuse them:

```
//store.js
<...>
import { CHANGE_MSG, INCREMENT_COUNTER } from './mutation_types'
   <...>
const mutations = {
  [CHANGE_MSG](state, msg) {
```

```
      state.message = msg
  },
  [INCREMENT_COUNTER](state) {
    state.counter ++
  }
}
```

Inside the components that dispatch mutations, we will import the corresponding mutation type and dispatch it using the variable name:

```
this.$store.commit(CHANGE_MSG, ev.target.value)
```

This kind of structure makes a lot of sense in big applications. Again, you can group your mutation types according to the functionality they provide to the application and import only those mutations in the components that are needed for the specific component. This is, again, about best practices, modularity, and maintainability.

Actions

When we dispatch a mutation, we basically perform an action. Saying that we *commit* a CHANGE_MSG mutation is the same as saying that we *perform an action* of changing the message. For the sake of beauty and total extraction, like we extract the store state's items into getters and mutations names constants to the mutation_types we can also extract the mutations to the actions.

 Thus, action is no more than just a function that dispatches a mutation!

```
function changeMessage(msg) { store.commit(CHANGE_MSG,
msg) }
```

Let's create a simple actions file for our change, message example. But before that, let's create one more item for the store's initial state, counter, and initialize it with a "0" value. So, our store will look like the following:

```
//store.js
import Vue from 'vue'
import Vuex from 'vuex'
import { CHANGE_MSG, INCREMENT_COUNTER } from './mutation_types'

Vue.use(Vuex)

const state = {
  message: 'Hello Vue!',
  counter: 0
```

```
  }

const mutations = {
  [CHANGE_MSG](state, msg) {
    state.message = msg
  },
  [INCREMENT_COUNTER](state) {
    state.counter ++;
  }
}

export default new Vuex.Store({
  state,
  mutations
})
```

Let's also add a counter getter to the getters file, so our `getters.js` file looks like the following:

```
//getters.js
export default {
  getMessage(state) {
    return (state.message).toUpperCase()
  },
  getCounter(state) {
    return (state.counter)
  }
}
```

And, finally, let's use the counter's getter inside `ShowGreetingsComponent` to show the amount of times the message `msg` was changed:

```
<template>
  <div>
    <h1>{{ msg }}</h1>
    <div>the message was changed {{ counter }} times</div>
  </div>
</template>
<script>
  import { mapGetters } from 'vuex'

  export default {
    computed: mapGetters({
      msg: 'getMessage',
      counter: 'getCounter'
    })
  }
</script>
```

Let's now create actions for both the mutations, for the counter and for the change message. Inside a `vuex` folder, create an `actions.js` file and export the `actions` functions:

```
//actions.js
import { CHANGE_MSG, INCREMENT_COUNTER } from './mutation_types'

export const changeMessage = (store, msg) => {
 store.commit(CHANGE_MSG, msg)
}
export const incrementCounter = (store) => {
 store.commit(INCREMENT_COUNTER)
}
```

We can and should use ES2015 arguments destructuring and make our code more elegant. Let's also export all the actions in a single `export default` statement:

```
//actions.js
import { CHANGE_MSG, INCREMENT_COUNTER } from './mutation_types'

export default {
  changeMessage ({ commit }, msg) {
    commit(CHANGE_MSG, msg)
  },
  incrementCounter ({ commit }) {
    commit(INCREMENT_COUNTER)
  }
}
```

Okay, now we have nice and beautiful actions. Let's use them in our `ChangeGreetingsComponent`! To be able to use actions inside components, we should first import them to our store and then export in the new `Vuex` object. Then actions can be dispatched using the `this.$store.dispatch` method inside the components:

```
// ChangeGreetingsComponent.vue
<template>
  <input :value="msg" @keyup="changeMsg">
</template>
<script>
  import { mapGetters } from 'vuex'

  export default {
    computed: mapGetters({
      msg: 'getMessage'
    }),
    methods: {
      changeMsg(ev) {
        this.$store.dispatch('changeMessage', ev.target.value)
```

```
        }
      }
    }
</script>
```

So what's actually the difference? We continue to write `this.$store` code, the only difference is that instead of calling the `commit` method we call `dispatch`. Do you remember how we discovered `mapGetters` helper? Wasn't it nice? Actually Vue also provides a `mapActions` helper that allows us to avoid writing the extensive `this.$store.dispatch` something method. Just import `mapActions` in the same way as we import `mapGetters` and use it inside the component's methods property:

```
//ChangeGreetingsComponent.vue
<template>
  <input :value="msg" @keyup="changeMessage">
</template>
<script>
  import { mapGetters } from 'vuex'
  import { mapActions } from 'vuex'

  export default {
    computed: mapGetters({
      msg: 'getMessage'
    }),
    methods:  mapActions(['changeMessage', 'incrementCounter'])
  }
</script>
```

Note that we changed the handler's function for the `keyup` event, so we don't have to map the events' names to the corresponding actions. However, just like in the case of `mapGetters`, we can also map custom events' names to the corresponding actions names.

We should also change the `changeMessage` invocation because we don't extract any event's target value inside the actions now; thus, we should do it inside the invocation:

```
//ChangeGreetingsComponent.vue
<template>
  <input :value="msg" @keyup="changeMessage($event.target.value)">
</template>
```

Finally, let's bind the `incrementCounter` action to the user's input. Let's, for example, call this action from our input template on the `keyup.enter` event:

```
<template>
  <input :value="msg" @keyup="changeMessage"
  @keyup.enter="incrementCounter">
```

```
</template>
```

If you open the page, and try to change the title and hit the *Enter* button, you will see that the counter will be incremented each time you hit *Enter*:

Using actions to increment the counter on the page

So, you see how easy it is to modularize our application by using actions instead of directly accessing the store. You export actions in your Vuex store, import the `mapActions` in the components, and call them from the event handler directives in the templates.

Do you remember our "human" example in which we were comparing the parts of the human body to the components and the human brain to the store of the application state? Imagine that you are running. It is only *one* action but how many changes are being dispatched and how many components are being affected by those changes? When you run, your heart rate increases, you sweat, your arms move, and your face smiles because you realize how nice it is to run! When you eat, you also smile because it is good to eat. You also smile when you see a kitten. So, different actions can dispatch more than one change, and the same change can be dispatched by more than one action.

The same happens with our Vuex store, and its mutations and actions. Within the same action, more than one mutation can be dispatched. For instance, we could dispatch our mutation for changing a message and increasing the counter within the same action. Let's create this action inside our `action.js` file. Let's call it `handleMessageInputChanges` and make it receive one argument: `event`. It will dispatch the `CHANGE_MSG` mutation with `event.target.value`, and in case `event.keyCode` is `enter`, it will dispatch the `INCREMENT_COUNTER` mutation:

```
//actions.js
handleMessageInputChanges ({ commit }, event) {
  commit(CHANGE_MSG, event.target.value)
  if (event.keyCode === 13) {
    commit(INCREMENT_COUNTER)
  }
}
```

Now let's import this action inside our `ChangeGreetingsComponent` component's `mapActions` object and let's use it calling it with the `$event` parameter:

```
//ChangeGreetingsComponent.vue
<template>
  <input :value="msg" @keyup="handleMessageInputChanges($event)" />
</template>
<script>
  import { mapGetters, mapActions } from 'vuex'

  export default {
    computed: mapGetters({
      msg: 'getMessage'
    }),
    methods:  mapActions(['handleMessageInputChanges'])
  }
</script>
```

Open the page, and try to change the greetings message and increment the counter by hitting the *Enter* button. It works!

The final code for the simple-store example can be found in the `chapter5/simple-store3` folder.

Installing and using the Vuex store in our applications

Now that we know what Vuex is, how to create a store, dispatch mutations, and how to use getters and actions, we can install the store in our applications and use it to finalize their data flow and communication chain.

You can find the applications to work on in the following folders:

- **Pomodoro**: `chapter5/pomodoro`
- **Shopping list**: `chapter5/shopping-list2`

Do not forget to run `npm install` on both applications.

Start by installing `vuex` and define the necessary directory and file structure in both applications.

To install `vuex`, just run the following:

```
npm install vuex --save
```

After installing `vuex`, create a subfolder `vuex` in each of the application's `src` folders. In this folder, create four files: `store.js`, `mutation_types.js`, `actions.js`, and `getters.js`.

Prepare the `store.js` structure:

```
//store.js
import Vue from 'vue'
import Vuex from 'vuex'
import getters from './getters'
import actions from './actions'
import mutations from './mutations'

Vue.use(Vuex)

const state = {
}

export default new Vuex.Store({
  state,
  mutations,
  getters,
  actions
})
```

Import and use the store in the main `App.vue`:

```
//App.vue
<script>
  <...>
  import store from './vuex/store'

  export default {
    store,
    <...>
  }
</script>
```

We will now define which is the global and which is the local state in each of the applications, define what data and binding are missing, divide the data, and add all the missing stuff using what we've just learned.

Using the Vuex store in the shopping list application

I hope you still remember the challenge we were facing at the beginning of this chapter. We would like to establish communication between the components in such a way that it would be easy to change the title of the shopping lists from the ChangeTitleComponent and propagate it to both ShoppingListTitle and ShoppingListComponent. Let's remove the hardcoded array of shopping lists from App.vue and copy it to the store's state:

```
//store.js
<...>
const state = {
  shoppinglists: [
    {
      id: 'groceries',
      title: 'Groceries',
      items: [{ text: 'Bananas', checked: true },
              { text: 'Apples', checked: false }]
    },
    {
      id: 'clothes',
      title: 'Clothes',
      items: [{ text: 'black dress', checked: false },
              { text: 'all-stars', checked: false }]
    }
  ]
}

<...>
```

Let's define getters for the shopping lists:

```
//getters.js
export default {
  getLists: state => state.shoppinglists
}
```

Now, import mapGetters in App.vue and map the shoppinglists value to the getLists method so that the <script> tag inside the App.vue component will look like the following:

```
//App.vue
<script>
  import ShoppingListComponent from './components/ShoppingListComponent'
  import ShoppingListTitleComponent from
```

```
'./components/ShoppingListTitleComponent'
import _ from 'underscore'
import store from './vuex/store'
import { mapGetters } from 'vuex'

export default {
  components: {
    ShoppingListComponent,
    ShoppingListTitleComponent
  },
  computed: mapGetters({
    shoppinglists: 'getLists'
  }),
  methods: {
    onChangeTitle (id, text) {
      _.findWhere(this.shoppinglists, { id: id }).title = text
    }
  },
  store
}
</script>
```

The rest is left untouched!

Now let's define a mutation inside our store that will be responsible for changing the title. It is clear that it should be a function that receives a new title string as a parameter. However, there is some difficulty. We don't know which of the shopping lists title should be changed. If we could pass a list's ID from a component to this function, we could actually write a piece of code that would find a correct list by its ID. Did I just say *if we could*? Of course, we can! Actually, our ShoppingListComponent already receives the ID from its parent App.vue. Let's just pass this ID from ShoppingListComponent to ChangeTitleComponent. In this way, we will be able to invoke the necessary action from the component where the title is actually changed, without having to propagate the event through the parents' chain.

So, just bind the ID to the change-title-component inside the ShoppingListComponent component's template, as follows:

```
//ShoppingListComponent.vue
<template>
  <...>
    <change-title-component : :id="id" v-
      on:changeTitle="onChangeTitle"></change-title-component>
  <...>
</template>
```

Do not forget to add the `id` attribute to the `ChangeTitleComponent` component's `props` attribute:

```
//ChangeTitleComponent.vue
<script>
  export default {
    props: ['title', 'id'],
    <...>
  }
</script>
```

Okay, now our `ChangeTitleComponent` has access to both `title` and `id` of the shopping list. Let's add the corresponding mutation to the store.

We can start by writing a function that finds a shopping list by its ID. For this, I will use the underscore class's `_.findWhere` method, just like we did in the `App.vue` component's `changeTitle` method.

Import underscore inside `mutations.js` and add the `findById` function as follows:

```
//mutations.js
<...>
function findById (state, id) {
  return _.findWhere(state.shoppinglists, { id: id })
}
<...>
```

Let's now add the mutation and let's call it, for example, `CHANGE_TITLE`. This mutation will receive the `data` object as a parameter containing `title` and `id`, and assign the value of the received title to the title of the found shopping list item. First of all, let's declare a constant `CHANGE_TITLE` in `mutation_types.js` and reuse it instead of writing the mutation's name as a string:

```
//mutation_types.js
export const CHANGE_TITLE = 'CHANGE_TITLE'

//mutations.js
import _ from 'underscore'
import * as types from './mutation_types'

function findById (state, id) {
  return _.findWhere(state.shoppinglists, { id: id })
}

export default {
  [types.CHANGE_TITLE] (state, data) {
    findById(state, data.id).title = data.title
```

```
      }
    }
```

We are almost finished. Let's now define a `changeTitle` action inside the `actions.js` file and reuse it in our `ChangeTitleComponent`. Open the `actions.js` file and add the following code:

```
//actions.js
import { CHANGE_TITLE } from './mutation_types'

export default {
  changeTitle: ({ commit }, data) => {
    commit(CHANGE_TITLE, data)
  }
}
```

And, the final touch. Open `ChangeTitleComponent.vue`, import the `mapActions` helper, map the `onInput` method to the `changeTitle` action, and call it inside `template` with the object mapping title to `event.target.value` and ID to the `id` parameter. So, the code of `ChangeTitleComponent` will look like the following:

```
//ChangeTitleComponent.vue
<template>
  <div>
    <em>Change the title of your shopping list here</em>
    <input :value="title" @input="onInput({ title: $event.target.value,
      id: id })"/>
  </div>
</template>

<script>
  import { mapActions } from 'vuex'

  export default {
    props: ['title', 'id'],
    methods: mapActions({
      onInput: 'changeTitle'
    })
  }
</script>
```

You can now remove all the events-handling code from the `ShoppingListComponent` and the main `App` component.

Open the page and try to type in the input box! The title will change in all locations:

Using store, mutations, and actions—all components update their state without the need of events handling mechanism

The final code for the shopping list application after applying the store's functions can be found in the `chapter5/shopping-list3` folder.

Using Vuex store in the Pomodoro application

Finally, we got back to our Pomodoro! When was the last time you took a 5-minute break? Let's build our Pomodoro application with the Vuex architecture and then take a rest look at kittens. Let's start with the base in the `chapter5/pomodoro` folder, where you already included the basic structure of the Vuex store (if not, go to the start of the *Installing and using Vuex store in our applications* section).

Bringing life to start, pause, and stop buttons

Let's start by analyzing what can actually be done with our Pomodoro timer. Look at the page. We have only three buttons: start, pause, and stop. This means that our application can be in one of these three states. Let's define and export them in our `store.js` file:

```
//store.js
<...>
const state = {
```

```
    started: false,
    paused: false,
    stopped: false
  }
  <...>
```

Initially, all these states are set to `false`, which makes sense because the application is not started, it's not paused and, of course, it is not stopped!

Let's now define getters for these states. Open the `getters.js` file and add the getter functions for all three states:

```
//getters.js
export default {
  isStarted: state => state.started,
  isPaused: state => state.paused,
  isStopped: state => state.stopped
}
```

What should happen to our control buttons for each of the defined states:

- The start button should become disabled when the application is started. However, it should be enabled again when the application is paused so that we can use this button to resume the application.
- The pause button can only be enabled when the application is started (because we cannot pause something that has not been started yet). However, it should be disabled if the application is paused (because we cannot pause something that is already paused).
- The stop button can only be enabled when the application is started.

Let's translate this into code by adding the `disabled` class to our control buttons conditionally, depending on the application states.

 Once we apply the `disabled` class, Bootstrap will take care of the buttons' behavior for us by not only applying special styling but also deactivating interactive elements.

In order to be able to use the already defined getters, we must import `mapGetters` into the `<script>` tag of the component. After that, we must tell the component that we want to use them by exporting them within the `computed` property object:

```
//ControlsComponent.vue
<script>
  import { mapGetters } from 'vuex'
```

```
  export default {
    computed: mapGetters(['isStarted', 'isPaused', 'isStopped'])
  }
</script>
```

Now these getters can be used inside the template. So, we will apply the `disabled` class to the following:

- The start button when the application is started and not paused (`isStarted && !isPaused`)
- The pause button when the application is not started or paused (`!isStarted || isPaused`)
- The stop button when the application is not started (`!isStarted`)

Our template will now look like the following:

```
//ControlsComponent.vue
<template>
  <span>
    <button  :disabled='isStarted && !isPaused'>
      <i class="glyphicon glyphicon-play"></i>
    </button>
    <button  :disabled='!isStarted || isPaused'>
      <i class="glyphicon glyphicon-pause"></i>
    </button>
    <button  :disabled='!isStarted'>
      <i class="glyphicon glyphicon-stop"></i>
    </button>
  </span>
</template>
```

You see now that the pause and stop buttons look different! If you mouse hover your mouse over them, the cursor is not changed, which means that they are really disabled! Let's just create a style for the icons that are inside the disabled buttons to highlight the disabled state even more:

```
//ControlsComponent.vue
<style scoped>
 button:disabled i {
   color: gray;
 }
</style>
```

Okay, now that we have beautiful disabled buttons, let's bring a bit of life into them!

Let's think about what should actually happen to the application states when we start, pause, or stop the application:

- When we start the application, the state started should become true and both paused and stopped states should for sure become false.
- When we pause the application, the state paused is true, state stopped is false, and state started is true because a paused application continues to be started.
- When we stop the application, the state stopped becomes true and both the paused and started states become false. Let's translate all this behavior into mutation_types, mutations, and actions!

Open mutation_types.js and add three mutation types as follows:

```
//mutation_types.js
export const START = 'START'
export const PAUSE = 'PAUSE'
export const STOP = 'STOP'
```

Now let's define mutations! Open the mutations.js file and add three mutations for each of the mutation types. So, we have decided that when we:

- **Start the application**: The state started is true, and states paused and stopped are false.
- **Pause the application**: The state started is true, the state paused is true, and stopped are false.
- **Stop the application**: The state stopped is true, and states started and paused are false.

Now let's put it into the code. Import mutation_types to mutations.js and write all three necessary mutations as follows:

```
//mutations.js
import * as types from './mutation_types'

export default {
  [types.START] (state) {
    state.started = true
    state.paused = false
    state.stopped = false
  },
  [types.PAUSE] (state) {
```

```
    state.paused = true
    state.started = true
    state.stopped = false
  },
  [types.STOP] (state) {
    state.stopped = true
    state.paused = false
    state.started = false
  }
}
```

Now let's define our actions! Go to the `actions.js` file, import mutation types, and export three functions:

```
//actions.js
import * as types from './mutation_types'

export default {
  start: ({ commit }) => {
    commit(types.START)
  },
  pause: ({ commit }) => {
    commit(types.PAUSE)
  },
  stop: ({ commit }) => {
    commit(types.STOP)
  }
}
```

The final touch to bring our buttons to life is to import these actions into `ControlsComponent` and call them on the `click` event on each button. Let's do it. Do you still remember how to call the action on some event applied to the HTML element? If we are talking about the `click` event, it is just the following:

```
@click='someAction'
```

So, in our `ControlsComponent.vue`, we import the `mapActions` object, map it to the component's `methods` property, and apply it to the corresponding button's clicks. That's all! The `<script>` tag of `ControlsComponent` will thus look like the following:

```
//ControlsComponent.vue
<script>
  import { mapGetters, mapActions } from 'vuex'

  export default {
    computed: mapGetters(['isStarted', 'isPaused', 'isStopped']),
```

```
    methods: mapActions(['start', 'stop', 'pause'])
  }
</script>
```

Now call these functions inside the event handler directives within the template so that the `<template>` tag of the `ControlsComponent` looks like the following:

```
//ControlsComponent.vue
<template>
  <span>
    <button  :disabled='isStarted && !isPaused'
    @click="start">
      <i class="glyphicon glyphicon-play"></i>
    </button>
    <button  :disabled='!isStarted || isPaused'
    @click="pause">
      <i class="glyphicon glyphicon-pause"></i>
    </button>
    <button  :disabled='!isStarted' @click="stop">
      <i class="glyphicon glyphicon-stop"></i>
    </button>
  </span>
</template>
```

Try to click the buttons. They do exactly what we need them to do. Nice work! Check it out in the `chapter5/pomodoro2` folder. However, we are not done yet. We still have to make our Pomodoro timer into an actual timer and not just some page that allows you to click some buttons and watch them changing their states from disabled to enabled.

Binding Pomodoro minutes and seconds

In the previous section, we were able to define three different states of the Pomodoro application: `started`, `paused`, and `stopped`. However, let's not forget about what the Pomodoro application should be used for. It must countdown some given time for work and then switch to the break count down timer, and then come back to work, and so on.

This leads us to realize that there is one more very important Pomodoro application's state: the binary state that toggles between *working* and *resting* periods of time. This state cannot be toggled by buttons; it should somehow be managed by our application's internal logic.

Let's start by defining two state properties: one for the counter that will be decreased with the time and the other one to distinguish between the working and not-working states. Let's assume that when we start our Pomodoro, we start our working day, so the working state should be set to true and the countdown counter should be set to the amount of time that we define for our working Pomodoro period. For the sake of modularity and maintainability, let's define the amount of time for work and for rest in an external file. Let's call it, for example, `config.js`. Create the `config.js` file in the project's root directory and add the following content:

```
//config.js
export const WORKING_TIME = 20 * 60
export const RESTING_TIME = 5 * 60
```

By these initializations I mean that our Pomodoro should count down *20* minutes for the working Pomodoro interval and *5* minutes for breaks. Of course, you are free to define your own values that are most suitable for you. Let's now export `config.js` in our store and reuse the `WORKING_TIME` value to initialize our counter. Let's also create a property that toggles between work/break and call it `isWorking`. Let's initialize it to `true`.

So, our new state will look like the following:

```
//store.js
<...>
import { WORKING_TIME } from '../config'

const state = {
  started: false,
  paused: false,
  stopped: false,
  isWorking: true,
  counter: WORKING_TIME
}
```

So, we have these two nice new properties. Before starting to create methods, actions, mutations, and other things that decrease the counter and toggle the `isWorking` property, let's think of the visual elements that rely on these properties.

We don't have so many elements, so it's easy to define.

- The `isWorking` state is affecting the title: we should display **Work!** when it's time to work and **Rest!** when it's time to have a rest.
- The `isWorking` state is also affecting the kittens component visibility: it should be displayed only when `isWorking` is `false`.

- The `counter` property affects `minute` and `second`: each time it decreases, the `second` should also decrease its value, and every 60 decreases, the `minute` should also decrease its value.

Let's define getters functions for the `isWorking` state and for the `minute` and the `second`. After defining these getters, we can reuse them in our components instead of using the hardcoded values. Let's start by defining a getter for the `isWorking` property:

```
//getters.js
export default {
  isStarted: state => state.started,
  isPaused: state => state.paused,
  isStopped: state => state.stopped,
  isWorking: state => state.isWorking
}
```

Let's reuse this getter in the components that were using hardcoded `isworking` defined in the `App.vue` component. Open `App.vue`, remove all the references to the `isworking` hardcoded variable, import the `mapGetters` object, and map the `isworking` property to the `isWorking` method inside the `computed` property as follows:

```
//App.vue
<script>
<...>
import { mapGetters } from 'vuex'

export default {
  <...>
  computed: mapGetters({
    isworking: 'isWorking'
  }),
  store
}
</script>
```

Repeat the same steps in `StateTitleComponent`. Import `mapGetters` and replace `props` with mapped `computed` property:

```
//StateTitleComponent.vue
<script>
  import { mapGetters } from 'vuex'

  export default {
    data () {
      return {
        workingtitle: 'Work!',
```

```
                    restingtitle: 'Rest!'
            }
        },
        computed: mapGetters({
            isworking: 'isWorking'
        })
    }
</script>
```

The rest is left untouched in both the components! Inside the templates, the `isworking` property is used. This property continues to exist; it's just imported from the reactive Vuex store and not from the hardcoded data!

Now we must define getters for minutes and seconds. This part is trickier because in these getters, we have to apply some computation to the counter state's property. This is not difficult at all. Our counter represents a total number of seconds. This means that we can easily extract minutes by dividing the counter by 60 and rounding to the lowest integer (`Math.floor`). The seconds can be extracted by taking the remainder of the division by 60. Thus, we can write our getters for minutes and seconds in the following way:

```
//getters.js
export default {
  <...>
  getMinutes: state => Math.floor(state.counter / 60),
  getSeconds: state => state.counter % 60
}
```

That's it! Let's now reuse these getters in the `CountdownComponent`. Import `mapGetters` and map its corresponding methods to the `min` and `sec` properties inside the `computed` property. Do not forget to remove the hardcoded data. Our `script` tag of the `CountdownComponent.vue` will thus look like the following:

```
//CountdownComponent.vue
<script>
  import { mapGetters } from 'vuex'

  export default {
    computed: mapGetters({
      min: 'getMinutes',
      sec: 'getSeconds'
    })
  }
</script>
```

The rest is left completely untouched! The template was referencing the `min` and `sec` properties, and they continue to exist. The code as it was until now can be found in the `chapter5/pomodoro3` folder. Look at the page; now the displayed minutes and seconds correspond to the amount of working time we've defined in our configuration file! If you change it, it will change as well:

Changing the configuration for the amount of working time will immediately affect the Pomodoro application view

Creating the Pomodoro timer

Okay, now everything is ready to actually start to count down our working time so we can finally have some rest! Let's define two auxiliary functions, `togglePomodoro` and `tick`.

The first one will just toggle the `isWorking` property. It will also redefine the state's counter. When the state `isWorking`, the counter should correspond to the working time, and when the state is not working, the counter should correspond to the resting time.

The `tick` function will just decrease the counter and check if it has reached "0" value, and in this case, will toggle the Pomodoro state. The rest is already being taken care of. So, the `togglePomodoro` function will look like the following:

```
//mutations.js
function togglePomodoro (state, toggle) {
  if (_.isBoolean(toggle) === false) {
    toggle = !state.isWorking
  }
  state.isWorking = toggle
  state.counter = state.isWorking ? WORKING_TIME : RESTING_TIME
}
```

Ah, and do not forget to import WORKING_TIME and RESTING_TIME from our config! Also, do not forget to import underscore since we are using it for the _.isBoolean check:

```
//mutations.js
import _ from 'underscore'
import { WORKING_TIME, RESTING_TIME } from './config'
```

Then, the tick function will just decrease the counter and check if it has reached the "0" value:

```
//mutations.js
function tick (state) {
  if (state.counter === 0) {
    togglePomodoro(state)
  }
  state.counter--
}
```

Fine! It's still not enough. We need to set the interval that would call the tick function for each second. Where should it be set? Well, it is more than clear that it should be done when we start our Pomodoro, in the START mutation!

But if we set the interval in the START mutation and it calls the tick function each second, how will it be stopped or paused on hitting the pause or stop button? That's why the setInterval and clearInterval JavaScript functions exist and that's why we have a store where we can save the initial state for the interval value! Let's start by defining interval as null in the store's state:

```
//store.js
const state = {
  <...>
  interval: null
}
```

Now, in our START mutation, let's add the following code that initializes the interval:

```
//mutations.js
export default {
  [types.START] (state) {
    state.started = true
    state.paused = false
    state.stopped = false
    state.interval = setInterval(() => tick(state), 1000)
  },
  <...>
}
```

We just set an interval that will call the `tick` function each second. In turn, the `tick` function will decrease the counter. The values that rely on the counter's value—minute and second—will change and reactively propagate these changes to the view.

If you click on the start button now, you will set the countdown in action! Yay! It's almost done. We just need to add the `clearInterval` function on the `pause` and `stop` mutation methods. Apart from this, on the `stop` method, let's call the `togglePomodoro` function with `true`, which will reset the Pomodoro timer to the working state:

```
//mutations.js
export default {
  [types.START] (state) {
    state.started = true
    state.paused = false
    state.stopped = false
    state.interval = setInterval(() => tick(state), 1000)
  },
  [types.PAUSE] (state) {
    state.paused = true
    state.started = true
    state.stopped = false
    clearInterval(state.interval)
  },
  [types.STOP] (state) {
    state.stopped = true
    state.paused = false
    state.started = false
    togglePomodoro(state, true)
  }
}
```

Changing the kitten

I hope you worked a lot and your resting time has finally come! If not and if you can't wait for it, just change the WORKING_TIME value in the config.js file for something considerably small and wait for it. I think I finally deserve some rest, so I've been staring at this nice image for some minutes already:

I am staring at the image, the cat is staring at me

Wouldn't you like the displayed image to change sometimes? Of course, you would! In order to achieve this, we must just append something to the image source so that it changes with time and delivers a non-cached image to us.

 One of the best practices to deliver non-cached things is to append the *timestamp* to the requested URL.

We could, for example, have another property in our store, let's say, timestamp, which would be updated with each counter decrease and its value would be appended to the image-source URL. Let's do it! Let's start by defining a timestamp property in our store's state as follows:

```
//store.js
const state = {
  <...>
  timestamp: 0
}
```

Tell the `tick` function to update this value on each tick:

```
//mutations.js
function tick(state) {
  <...>
  state.timestamp = new Date().getTime()
}
```

Create the getter for this value in `getters.js` and use it inside the `KittensComponent` by accessing the `this.$store.getters.getTimestamp` method inside the `computed` property:

```
//getters.js
export default {
  <...>
  getTimestamp: state => state.timestamp
}

//KittensComponent.vue
<script>
  export default {
    computed: {
      catimgsrc () {
        return 'http://thecatapi.com/api/images/get?size=med&ts='
          + this.$store.getters.getTimestamp
      }
    }
  }
</script>
```

Now it's a little bit too fast, right? Let's define a time to show each kitten. It's not difficult at all. For example, if we decide to show each kitten for 3 seconds, before changing the state of the timestamp inside the `tick` function, we just have to check if the counter value is divisible by 3. Let's also make the amount of seconds to show the kitten configurable. Add the following to `config.js`:

```
//config.js
export const WORKING_TIME = 0.1 * 60
export const RESTING_TIME = 5 * 60
export const KITTEN_TIME = 5 //each kitten is visible for 5 seconds
```

Now import it to the `mutations.js` file and use it in the `tick` function to check if it's time to change the timestamp's value:

```
//mutations.js
import { WORKING_TIME, RESTING_TIME, KITTEN_TIME } from './config'
<...>
function tick(state) {
  <...>
  if (state.counter % KITTEN_TIME === 0) {
    state.timestamp = new Date().getTime()
  }
}
```

We are done! You can check the final code for this section in the `chapter5/pomodoro4` folder. Yes, I've set the working time to 6 seconds so that you can have a break and enjoy some really nice kittens from `thecatapi.com`.

So, before reading the summary of this chapter and starting the next one, take a break! Just like this wonderful species:

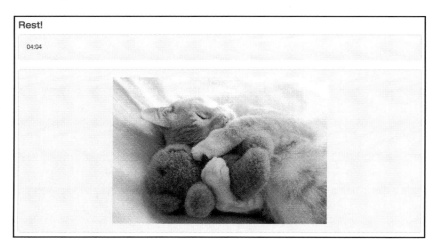

Wonderful thing having its break. Be like him. Take a break.

Summary

In this chapter, you saw how to use the events handling and triggering mechanism to propagate the components' data changes to their parents.

Most importantly, you used the power of Vuex architecture to be able to establish the data flow between the components. You saw how the store is created, and its main parts, mutations, and states. You learned how to structure the application that uses the store so that it becomes modular and maintainable. You also learned how to create the store's getters and how to define actions that dispatch the store state's mutations. We applied all the learned mechanisms to our applications and saw the data flow in action.

At this point, we are able to use any data exchanging mechanism in Vue applications, starting from simple local data binding inside the components and going further to global state management. At this point, we know all the bases to operate data inside our Vue application. We're almost done!

In the next chapter, we will go deep into the plugins system for Vue applications. You will learn how to use existing plugins and create your own plugin to enrich your applications with custom behavior.

6

Plugins – Building Your House with Your Own Bricks

In the previous chapter, you learned how to manage the global application store using the Vuex architecture. You learned a lot of new concepts and applied them. You also learned how to create a store, how to define its state and mutations, and how to use actions and getters. We brought our shopping list and Pomodoro applications to life using the knowledge acquired during the chapter.

In this chapter, we will revisit Vue plugins, see how they work, and how they must be created. We will use some existing plugins and create our own.

Summing it up, in this chapter, we are going to do the following:

- Understand the nature of Vue plugins
- Use the resource plugin in the shopping lists application
- Create a plugin that produces white, pink, and brown noises and apply it to our Pomodoro application

The nature of Vue plugins

Plugins in Vue.js are used for exactly the same purpose as they are used in any other scope: to add some nice functionality that, due to its nature, cannot be achieved with the core functionality of the system. Plugins written for Vue can provide various functionalities, starting from the definition of some global Vue methods or even the instance methods and moving toward providing some new directives, filters, or transitions.

In order to be able to use an existing plugin, you must first install it:

```
npm install some-plugin --save-dev
```

And then, tell Vue to use it in your application:

```
var Vue = require('vue')
var SomePlugin = require('some-plugin')

Vue.use(SomePlugin)
```

We can also create our own plugins. This is also easy. Your plugin must provide an `install` method where you define any global or instance methods, or custom directives:

```
MyPlugin.install = function (Vue, options) {
  // 1. add global method or property
  Vue.myGlobalMethod = ...
  // 2. add a global asset
  Vue.directive('my-directive', {})
  // 3. add an instance method
  Vue.prototype.$myMethod = ...
}
```

Then it can be used just like any other existing plugin. In this chapter, we will use the existing `resource` plugin for Vue (`https://github.com/vuejs/vue-resource`) and create our own plugin that generates white, pink, and brown noises.

Using the vue-resource plugin in the shopping list application

Open the shopping list application (the `chapter6/shopping-list` folder) and run `npm install` and `npm run dev`. It's nice and clean, but it still uses the hardcoded list of the shopping lists. It would be really nice if we were able to add new shopping lists, delete them, and store the information on updated shopping lists so that when we restart the application, the displayed information corresponds to the last we saw before restarting. In order to be able to do that, we will use the `resource` plugin, which allows us to easily create REST resources and call REST methods on them. Before starting, let's summarize everything that we need to do in order to achieve this:

- First of all, we need to have a simple server that contains some storage from where we can retrieve and where we can store our shopping lists. This server must provide the needed endpoints for all this functionality.

- After creating our server and all needed endpoints, we should install and use the `vue-resource` plugin to create a resource and actions that will call the methods on the provided endpoints.
- In order to guarantee the data integrity, we should call actions that update server's state on each shopping lists update.
- On the application start, we should fetch shopping lists from the server and assign them to our store's state.
- We should also provide a mechanism to create new shopping lists and delete the existing ones.

Doesn't sound too difficult, right? Let's start then!

Creating a simple server

For the sake of simplicity, we will use a very basic and easy-to-use HTTP server that stores data inside a regular JSON file. It is called `json-server` and it is hosted at `https://github.com/typicode/json-server`. Install it in the shopping list application's directory:

```
cd shopping-list
npm install --save-dev json-server
```

Create a `server` folder with the `db.json` file inside it with the following content:

```
//shopping-list/server/db.json
{
  "shoppinglists": [
  ]
}
```

This will be our database. Let's add the script entry to our `package.json` file so that we can easily start our server:

```
"scripts": {
  "dev": "node build/dev-server.js ",
  "server": "node_modules/json-server/bin/index.js --watch
  server/db.json",
  <...>
},
```

Now, to start a server, just run the following:

```
cd shopping-list
npm run server
```

Open the browser page at `http://localhost:3000/shoppinglists`. You will see an empty array as a result. This is because our database is still empty. Try to insert some data using `curl`:

```
curl -H "Content-Type:application/json" -d '{"title":"new","items":[]}'
http://localhost:3000/shoppinglists
```

If you refresh the page now, you will see your new inserted value.

Now that we have our simple REST server up and running, let's use it in our shopping list application with the help of the `vue-resource` plugin!

Installing vue-resource, creating resources, and its methods

Before going deeper into the usage of the `vue-resource` plugin, check out its documentation at `https://github.com/vuejs/vue-resource/blob/master/docs/resource.md`. Basically, the documentation provides an easy way of creating resources based on the given URL (in our case, it will be `http://localhost:3000/shoppinglists`). After the resource is created, we can call `get`, `delete`, `post`, and `update` methods on it.

Install it in the project's folder:

```
cd shopping-list
npm install vue-resource --save-dev
```

Now let's create the entry point for our API. Inside an `src` folder of the shopping list application, create a subfolder and call it `api`. Create an `index.js` file inside it. In this file, we will import the `vue-resource` plugin and tell `Vue` to use it:

```
//api/index.js
import Vue from 'vue'
import VueResource from 'vue-resource'

Vue.use(VueResource)
```

Nice! Now we are ready to create `ShoppingListsResource` and attach some methods to it. To create a resource using the `vue-resource` plugin, we just call a `resource` method on `Vue` and pass the URL to it:

```
const ShoppingListsResource = Vue.resource('http://localhost:3000/' +
'shoppinglists{/id}')
```

The `ShoppingListsResource` constant now exposes all the methods needed for the implementation of **CRUD (Create, Read, Update, and Delete)** operations. It is so easy to use that we could basically export the resource itself. But let's export nice methods for each of the CRUD operations:

```
export default {
  fetchShoppingLists: () => {
    return ShoppingListsResource.get()
  },
  addNewShoppingList: (data) => {
    return ShoppingListsResource.save(data)
  },
  updateShoppingList: (data) => {
    return ShoppingListsResource.update({ id: data.id }, data)
  },
  deleteShoppingList: (id) => {
    return ShoppingListsResource.remove({ id: id })
  }
}
```

The full code for the `api/index.js` file can be seen in this gist at `https://gist.github.co m/chudaol/d5176b88ba2c5799c0b7b0dd33ac0426`.

That's it! Our API is ready to be used and to populate our reactive Vue data!

Fetching all the shopping lists the application starts

Let's start by creating an action that will fetch and populate store's `shoppinglists` state. After its creation, we can call it on the main `App.vue` ready state.

Define a constant in the `mutation_types.js` file as follows:

```
//mutation_types.js
export const POPULATE_SHOPPING_LISTS = 'POPULATE_SHOPPING_LISTS'
```

Now create a mutation. This mutation will just receive an array of `shoppinglists` and assign it to the `shoppinglists` state:

```
//mutations.js
export default {
  [types.CHANGE_TITLE] (state, data) {
    findById(state, data.id).title = data.title
  },
```

```
  [types.POPULATE_SHOPPING_LISTS] (state, lists) {
    state.shoppinglists = lists
  }
}
```

Ok then! Now we just need an action that will use the API's `get` method and dispatch the populating mutation. Import the API in the `actions.js` file and create a corresponding action method:

```
import { CHANGE_TITLE, POPULATE_SHOPPING_LISTS } from './mutation_types'
import api from '../api'

export default {
  changeTitle: ({ commit }, data) => {
    commit(CHANGE_TITLE, data)
  },
  populateShoppingLists: ({ commit }) => {
    api.fetchShoppingLists().then(response => {
      commit(POPULATE_SHOPPING_LISTS, response.data)
    })
  }
}
```

In the preceding lines of code, we perform a very simple task—we call the `fetchShoppingLists` API's method that, in turn, calls the `get` method of the resource. This method performs an `http` `GET` call and returns a promise that is resolved when the data is back from the server.

This data is then used to dispatch the populating mutation with it. This method will assign this data to the store's state `shoppinglists` property. This property is reactive; do you remember? This means that all the views that rely on the `shoppinglists` property getter will be updated. Let's now use this action in the main `App.vue` component on its `mounted` state. Check more about `mounted` state hook in the official Vue documentation page at `https://vuejs.org/v2/api/#mounted`.

Open the `App.vue` component, import the `mapActions` object, map the `populateShoppingLists` action inside the component's `methods` property, and call it inside the `mounted` handler. So, after the changes, the `script` tag of `App.vue` looks like the following:

```
<script>
  import ShoppingListComponent from './components/ShoppingListComponent'
  import ShoppingListTitleComponent from
  './components/ShoppingListTitleComponent'
  import store from './vuex/store'
```

```
import { mapGetters, mapActions } from 'vuex'

export default {
  components: {
    ShoppingListComponent,
    ShoppingListTitleComponent
  },
  computed: mapGetters({
    shoppinglists: 'getLists'
  }),
  methods: mapActions(['populateShoppingLists']),
  store,
  mounted () {
    this.populateShoppingLists()
  }
}
</script>
```

If you open the page now, you will see the only shopping list that we created using `curl`, as shown in the following screenshot:

The displayed shopping lists are being served by our simple server!

Try to insert more items using `curl` or even directly modifying the `db.json` file. Refresh the page and look how it works like a charm!

Updating server status on changes

Very well, now we have our shopping lists being served by our REST API and everything works and looks nice. Try to add some shopping list items or change the titles of the shopping lists and check or uncheck items. After all these interactions, refresh the page. Whoops, the lists are empty, nothing happened. That's absolutely correct, we have an API method for updating the given shopping list but we don't call it anywhere, so our server is not aware of the applied changes.

Let's start by defining what components do something with our shopping lists so that these changes are sent to the server. The following three things can happen to the shopping lists and their items:

- The title of the list can be changed in `ChangeTitleComponent`
- The new item can be added to the shopping list in `AddItemComponent`
- The item of the shopping list can be checked or unchecked in `ItemComponent`

We must create an action that must be triggered on all these changes. Within this action, we should call the `update` API's method. Have a close look at the update method inside the `api/index.js` module; it must receive the whole shopping list object as a parameter:

```
//api/index.js
updateShoppingList: (data) => {
  return ShoppingListsResource.update({ id: data.id }, data)
}
```

Let's create an action that receives an `id` as a parameter, retrieves the shopping list by its ID, and calls the API's method. Before doing this, create a `getListById` method in the `getters.js` file and import it into the actions:

```
//getters.js
import _ from 'underscore'

export default {
  getLists: state => state.shoppinglists,
  getListById: (state, id) => {
    return _.findWhere(state.shoppinglists, { id: id })
  }
}

//actions.js
import getters from './getters'
```

Now we are ready to define the action for updating the shopping list:

```
//actions.js
<...>
export default {
  <...>
  updateList: (store, id) => {
    let shoppingList = getters.getListById(store.state, id)

    api.updateShoppingList(shoppingList)
  }
}
```

Actually, we can now delete the findById method from mutations.js and just reuse this one from getters.js:

```
//mutations.js
import * as types from './mutation_types'
import getters from './getters'

export default {
  [types.CHANGE_TITLE] (state, data) {
    getters.getListById(state, data.id).title = data.title
  },
  [types.POPULATE_SHOPPING_LISTS] (state, lists) {
    state.shoppinglists = lists
  }
}
```

Well, now we have defined the action that calls the updateList method of our API. Now we just have to call the action on each change that happens inside the components!

Let's start with AddItemComponent. We must dispatch the updateList action inside the addItem method using the this.$store.dispatch method with the action's name. However, there's a small problem—we must pass the list item ID to the updateList method and we do not have a reference to it inside this component. But it's actually an easy fix. Just add the ID inside the component's props and bind it to the component on its invocation inside ShoppingListComponent. So our AddItemComponent component's script tag looks like the following:

```
//AddItemComponent.vue
<script>
  export default {
    props: ['id'],
    data () {
      return {
```

```
        newItem: ''
      }
    },
    methods: {
      addItem () {
        var text

        text = this.newItem.trim()
        if (text) {
          this.$emit('add', this.newItem)
          this.newItem = ''
          this.$store.dispatch('updateList', this.id)
        }
      }
    }
  }
}
</script>
```

And, inside `ShoppingListComponent`, on the `add-item-component` invocation, bind the ID to it:

```
//ShoppingListComponent.vue
<template>
  <...>
    <add-item-component :id="id" @add="addItem"></add-item-component>
  <...>
</template>
```

Now, if you try to add items to the shopping lists and refresh the page, the newly added items appear in the list!

Now we should do the same for `ChangeTitleComponent`. Open the `ChangeTitleComponent.vue` file and check the code. Right now, it calls the `changeTitle` action on input:

```
//ChangeTitleComponent.vue
<template>
  <div>
    <em>Change the title of your shopping list here</em>
    <input :value="title" @input="onInput({ title:
      $event.target.value, id: id })"/>
  </div>
</template>

<script>
  import { mapActions } from 'vuex'

  export default {
```

```
    props: ['title', 'id'],
    methods: mapActions({
      onInput: 'changeTitle'
    })
  }
</script>
```

We could, of course, import the `updateList` action and call it right after calling the `changeTitle` action. But it might be easier to do it inside the action itself. You may remember that in order to dispatch the store's action, we should call the `dispatch` method applied to the store with the action's name as a parameter. So we can do it inside the `changeTitle` action. Just open the `action.js` file, find our `changeTitle` action, and add the call to `updateList`:

```
//actions.js
export default {
  changeTitle: (store, data) => {
    store.commit(CHANGE_TITLE, data)
    store.dispatch('updateList', data.id)
  },
  <...>
}
```

It's done! Open the page, modify the titles of the pages, and refresh the page. The titles should maintain their modified state!

The last change that we need to guarantee to be persisted is the change in the shopping list's items `checked` property. Let's look at `ItemComponent` and decide where we should call the `updateList` action.

Let's start by adding the ID inside the `props` attribute, just like we did with `AddItemComponent`:

```
//ItemComponent.vue
<script>
  export default {
    props: ['item', 'id']
  }
</script>
```

We must also bind the `id` property to the component's invocation, which is done inside `ItemsComponent`:

```
//ItemsComponent.vue
<template>
  <ul>
    <item-component v-for="item in items" :item="item" :id="id">
    </item-component>
  </ul>
</template>

<script>
  import ItemComponent from './ItemComponent'

  export default {
    components: {
      ItemComponent
    },
    props: ['items', 'id']
  }
</script>
```

This also means that we must bind the `id` property to `item-component` inside `ShoppingListComponent`:

```
//ShoppingListComponent.vue
<template>
  <...>
    <items-component :items="items" :id="id"></items-component>
  <...>
</template>
```

We should also import the `mapActions` object inside `ItemComponent` and export the `updateList` method inside the `methods` property:

```
//ItemComponent.vue
<script>
  import { mapActions } from 'vuex'

  export default {
    props: ['item', 'id'],
    methods: mapActions(['updateList'])
  }
</script>
```

Okay then, everything is bound to everything; now we just have to find the right place inside `ItemComponent` to call the `updateList` action.

And this turns out to be not such as easy task, because unlike in the other components where we had event handlers dealing with changes and calling the corresponding functions, here we just have class and model bindings attached to the checkbox element. Luckily for us, Vue provides a `watch` option that allows us to attach listeners to any of the component's data and bind the handlers to them. In our case, we want to watch the `item.checked` property and call the action. So, just add the `watch` attribute to the components options as follows:

```
//ItemComponent.vue
<script>
  import { mapActions } from 'vuex'

  export default {
    props: ['item', 'id'],
    methods: mapActions(['updateList']),
    watch: {
      'item.checked': function () {
        this.updateList(this.id)
      }
    }
  }
</script>
```

And...we are done! Try to add items to the shopping lists, check, uncheck, and check them again. Refresh the page. Everything looks like it was before refreshing!

Creating a new shopping list

Okay then, we are already fetching the shopping lists from the server; we also store applied changes, so we are fine. But wouldn't it also be nice if we could create the shopping lists using the user interface of our application instead of modifying the db.json file or using curl post requests? Of course, it would be nice. And, of course, we can do it with few lines of code!

Let's start by adding the action that calls the corresponding API method, as follows:

```
//actions.js
export default {
  <...>
  createShoppingList: ({ commit }, shoppinglist) => {
    api.addNewShoppingList(shoppinglist)
  }
}
```

Now we have to provide a visual mechanism for calling this action. For that, we can create an extra tab in the tab list with the plus button, which will call the action when it is clicked. We will do it inside the App.vue component. We have already imported the mapActions object. Let's just add the createShoppingList method to the exported methods property:

```
//App.vue
<script>
  import ShoppingListComponent from './components/ShoppingListComponent'
  import ShoppingListTitleComponent from
  './components/ShoppingListTitleComponent'
  import store from './vuex/store'
  import { mapGetters, mapActions } from 'vuex'

  export default {
    components: {
      ShoppingListComponent,
      ShoppingListTitleComponent
    },
    computed: mapGetters({
      shoppinglists: 'getLists'
    }),
    methods: mapActions(['populateShoppingLists',
    'createShoppingList']),
    store,
    mounted () {
      this.populateShoppingLists()
    }
  }
</script>
```

At this moment, our App.vue component has access to the createShoppingList action and can call it on an event handler. The question is—with what data? The createShoppingList method is waiting to receive an object that will then be sent to the server. Let's create a method that will generate a new list with a hardcoded title, and within this method, call the action with this new object. But where should it put this method? The methods property of the component is already occupied by the invocation of the mapActions helper. Well, the mapActions method returns a map of methods. We can simply *extend* this map with our local method:

```
//App.vue
methods: _.extend({},
    mapActions(['populateShoppingLists', 'createShoppingList']),
    {
      addShoppingList () {
        let list = {
          title: 'New Shopping List',
```

```
        items: []
    }

    this.createShoppingList(list)
  }
}),
```

Now we just need to add a button and bind the `addShoppingList` method to its `click` event. You can create your own button anywhere on the page. My button's code looks like the following:

```
App.vue
<template>
  <div id="app" class="container">
    <ul class="nav nav-tabs" role="tablist">
      <li :class="index===0 ? 'active' : ''" v-for="(list, index) in
        shoppinglists" role="presentation">
        <shopping-list-title-component :id="list.id"
          :title="list.title"></shopping-list-title-component>
      </li>
      <li>
        <a href="#" @click="addShoppingList">
          <i class="glyphicon glyphicon-plus-sign"></i>
        </a>
      </li>
    </ul>
    <div class="tab-content">
      <div :class="index===0 ? 'active' : ''" v-for="(list, index) in
        shoppinglists" class="tab-pane" role="tabpanel" :id="list.id">
        <shopping-list-component :id="list.id" :title="list.title"
          :items="list.items"></shopping-list-component>
      </div>
    </div>
  </div>
</template>
```

Look at the page; now we have a nice plus button on the last tab, which clearly indicates that there is a possibility of adding a new shopping list, as shown in the following screenshot:

Now we can add new shopping lists using this nice plus button

Try to click on the button. Whoops, nothing happens! However, if we look at the Network panel, we can see the request was actually performed and that succeeded:

The creation request was performed successfully; however, nothing changed on the page

Actually, this makes perfect sense. We updated the information on the server, but the client side is not aware of these changes. If we could populate shopping lists after the successful shopping list creation, it would be nice, wouldn't it? Did I say "if we could"? Of course we can! Just go back to `actions.js` and call the `populateShoppingLists` action on the promise's `then` callback using the `store.dispatch` method:

```
//actions.js
createShoppingList: (store, shoppinglist) => {
  api.addNewShoppingList(shoppinglist).then(() => {
    store.dispatch('populateShoppingLists')
  })
}
```

Now, if you click on the plus button, you will immediately see the newly created list appearing in the tab pane, as shown in the following screenshot:

Newly added shopping list after repopulating our lists

You can now click on the new shopping list, change its name, add its items, and check and uncheck them. When you refresh the page, everything is just like it was before the refreshing. Amazing work!

Deleting existing shopping lists

We are already able to create and update our shopping lists. Now we just need to be able to delete them. After all the things that we have learned in this chapter, this will be the easiest part. We should add the action that will call the `deleteShoppingList` method of our API, add the remove button to each of the shopping list, and call the action on the button click.

Let's start by adding the action. Similarly, as we did with the creation of shopping lists, we will call the `populate` method right after removing the shopping list, so our action will look like the following:

```
//action.js
deleteShoppingList: (store, id) => {
  api.deleteShoppingList(id).then(() => {
    store.dispatch('populateShoppingLists')
  })
}
```

Now let's think where we should add the remove button. I would like to see it near the shopping list title in the tab header. This is the component called `ShoppingListTitleComponent`. Open it and import the `mapActions` helper. Export it in the `methods` property. So, the code inside the `script` tag of this component looks like the following:

```
//ShoppingListTitleComponent.vue
<script>
  import { mapActions } from 'vuex'

  export default{
    props: ['id', 'title'],
    computed: {
      href () {
        return '#' + this.id
      }
    },
    methods: mapActions(['deleteShoppingList'])
  }
</script>
```

Now let's add the remove button and bind the `deleteShoppingList` method to its `click` event listener. We should pass the ID to this method. We can do it directly inside the template:

```
//ShoppingListTitleComponent.vue
<template>
  <a :href="href" :aria-controls="id" role="tab" data-toggle="tab">
    {{ title }}
    <i class="glyphicon glyphicon-remove"
      @click="deleteShoppingList(id)"></i>
  </a>
</template>
```

I also added a little bit of styling to the remove icon so that it looks a bit smaller and a bit more elegant:

```
<style scoped>
  i {
    font-size: x-small;
    padding-left: 3px;
    cursor: pointer;
  }
</style>
```

That's it! Open the page and you'll see a tiny **x** button near each shopping list title. Try clicking on it and you will immediately see the changes, as shown in the following screenshot:

Shopping lists with the remove X button that allows us to delete unused shopping lists

Congratulations! Now we have a fully functional application that allows us to create shopping lists for any occasion, remove them, and manage the items on each of them! Good work! The final code for this section can be found in the `chapter6/shopping-list2` folder.

Exercise

Our shopping lists are all very similar to each other. I would like to propose a small styling exercise in which you should attach coloring to your lists in order to make them differ one from another. It will require you to add one more field for the background color on the shopping list creation and to use it inside the component to paint your lists with the given color.

Creating and using a plugin in the Pomodoro application

Now that we know how to use existing plugins with our Vue application, why not create our own plugin? We already have a little bit of animation in our Pomodoro application, and the screen changes completely when the state is changed from the working Pomodoro interval to the resting interval. However, if we are not looking at the tab, we have no idea if we should work or rest. It would be nice to add some sounds to our Pomodoro!

When thinking about sounds in a time management application, I would like to think about the sound that is nice for working. Every one of us has our own favorite playlist for work. Of course, it differs according to each person's musical preferences. That's why I decided to add some neutral sound to our application during the working period of time. It was proven by some studies that different noises (white, pink, brown, and so on) are good for the kind of work where a high level of concentration is required. The Wikipedia entry about these studies can be found at `https://en.wikipedia.org/wiki/Sound_masking`. And some Quora experts talking about this can be found at `http://bit.ly/2cmRVW2`.

In this section, we will use the Web Audio API (`https://developer.mozilla.org/en-US/docs/Web/API/Web_Audio_API`) to create a plugin for Vue that generates white, pink, and brown noises. We will provide a mechanism to instantiate one noise or another using Vue directives and we will also provide global Vue methods that will start and pause these sounds. After that, we will use this plugin to switch between a silent state while resting and looking at cats and a noisy state while working. Does it sound challenging and interesting? I really hope it does! Let's start then!

Creating the NoiseGenerator plugin

Our plugin will be stored in a single JavaScript file. It will contain three methods, one for the generation of each noise and provide a `Vue.install` method where the directives and needed Vue methods will be defined. Use the `chapter6/pomodoro` folder as a starting point. Start by creating a `plugins` subfolder in the `src` folder and adding the `VueNoiseGeneratorPlugin.js` file there. Now let's create the following three methods:

- `generateWhiteNoise`
- `generatePinkNoise`
- `generateBrownNoise`

I will not reinvent the wheel and will just copy and paste the already existing code that I found on the Internet. Of course, I would like to give huge credit to the great resource that I found at `http://noisehack.com/generate-noise-web-audio-api/`. That being said, our plugin after copying the code and organizing it in the functions should look like the following:

```
// plugins/VueNoiseGenerator.js
import _ from 'underscore'

// Thanks to this great tutorial:
//http://noisehack.com/generate-noise-web-audio-api/
var audioContext, bufferSize, noise
audioContext = new (window.AudioContext || window.webkitAudioContext)()

function generateWhiteNoise () {
  var noiseBuffer, output

  bufferSize = 2 * audioContext.sampleRate
  noiseBuffer = audioContext.createBuffer(1, bufferSize,
    audioContext.sampleRate)

  output = noiseBuffer.getChannelData(0)
  _.times(bufferSize, i => {
    output[i] = Math.random() * 2 - 1
  })

  noise = audioContext.createBufferSource()
  noise.buffer = noiseBuffer
  noise.loop = true
  noise.start(0)

  return noise
}

function generatePinkNoise () {
  bufferSize = 4096
  noise = (function () {
    var b0, b1, b2, b3, b4, b5, b6, node
    b0 = b1 = b2 = b3 = b4 = b5 = b6 = 0.0
    node = audioContext.createScriptProcessor(bufferSize, 1, 1)
    node.onaudioprocess = function (e) {
      var output

      output = e.outputBuffer.getChannelData(0)
      _.times(bufferSize, i => {
        var white = Math.random() * 2 - 1
        b0 = 0.99886 * b0 + white * 0.0555179
```

```
            b1 = 0.99332 * b1 + white * 0.0750759
            b2 = 0.96900 * b2 + white * 0.1538520
            b3 = 0.86650 * b3 + white * 0.3104856
            b4 = 0.55000 * b4 + white * 0.5329522
            b5 = -0.7616 * b5 - white * 0.0168980
            output[i] = b0 + b1 + b2 + b3 + b4 + b5 + b6 + white * 0.5362
            output[i] *= 0.11 // (roughly) compensate for gain
            b6 = white * 0.115926
        })
      }
      return node
    })()

    return noise
}

function generateBrownNoise () {
    bufferSize = 4096

    noise = (function () {
      var lastOut, node

      lastOut = 0.0
      node = audioContext.createScriptProcessor(bufferSize, 1, 1)
      node.onaudioprocess = function (e) {
        var output = e.outputBuffer.getChannelData(0)
        _.times(bufferSize, i => {
          var white = Math.random() * 2 - 1
          output[i] = (lastOut + (0.02 * white)) / 1.02
          lastOut = output[i]
          output[i] *= 3.5 // (roughly) compensate for gain
        })
      }
      return node
    })()

    return noise
}
```

You can test all these noises in the JSFiddle at `https://jsfiddle.net/chudaol/7tuewm5z/`.

Okay, so we have all the three noises implemented. Now we must export the `install` method that will be called by `Vue`. This method receives the `Vue` instance and can create directives and methods on it. Let's create a directive and call it `noise`. This directive can have one of three values, `white`, `pink`, or `brown`, and according to the received value will instantiate the `noise` variable by calling the corresponding noise creation method. So, our directive creation within an `install` method will look like the following:

```
// plugins/VueNoiseGeneratorPlugin.js
export default {
  install: function (Vue) {
    Vue.directive('noise', (value) => {
      var noise

      switch (value) {
        case 'white':
          noise = generateWhiteNoise()
          break
        case 'pink':
          noise = generatePinkNoise()
          break
        case 'brown':
          noise = generateBrownNoise()
          break
        default:
          noise = generateWhiteNoise()
      }
      noise.connect(audioContext.destination)
      audioContext.suspend()
    })
  }
}
```

After the instantiation, we connect the `noise` to the already instantiated `audioContext` and `suspend` it because we don't want it to start producing the noise right on the directive binding. We want it to be instantiated on some events (for example, clicking on the start button) and paused on other events (for example, when someone clicks on the pause button). For that, let's provide methods for starting, pausing, and stopping our `audioContext`. We will put these three methods on the global Vue property called `noise`. We will call these methods `start`, `pause`, and `stop`. Within the `start` method, we want to resume `audioContext` and suspend it on both the `pause` and `stop` methods. So, our methods will look like the following:

```
// plugins/VueNoiseGeneratorPlugin.js
export default {
  install: function (Vue) {
    Vue.directive('noise', (value) => {
      <...>
    })
    Vue.noise = {
      start () {
        audioContext.resume()
      },
      pause () {
        audioContext.suspend()
```

```
      },
      stop () {
        audioContext.suspend()
      }
    }
  }
}
```

That's it! Our plugin is completely ready to be used. It's not perfect, of course, because we only have one `audioContext`, which is being instantiated once and then populated by one of the chosen noises, meaning we will not be able to use the `noise` directive more than once on the page, but again, this is just a prototype and you are more than welcome to enhance it and make it perfect and public!

Using the plugin in the Pomodoro application

Fine then, now we have our nice noise-producing plugin, and the only thing that is missing is using it! You already know how to do it. Open the `main.js` file, import `VueNoiseGeneratorPlugin`, and tell `Vue` to use it:

```
import VueNoiseGeneratorPlugin from
'./plugins/VueNoiseGeneratorPlugin'

Vue.use(VueNoiseGeneratorPlugin)
```

From now on, we can attach the `noise` directive and use the `Vue.noise` method in any part of our Pomodoro application. Let's bind it to our main template inside the `App.vue` component:

```
//App.vue
<template>
  <div id="app" class="container" v-noise="'brown'">
    <...>
  </div>
</template>
```

Note that we use `v-noise` in the name of the directive and not just `noise`. We already talked about it when we learned custom directives. To use a directive, we should always prepend the `v-` prefix to its name. Also note that we used double quotes inside the single quotes to wrap the `brown` string. If we didn't do it, Vue would search for the data property called `brown`, because that's how the Vue works. As we can write any JavaScript statement inside the directive binding assignment, we must pass the string with double quotes. You can go further and create a data property called `noise` and assign to it the value you want (`white`, `brown`, or `pink`) and reuse it inside the directive binding syntax.

After that being done, let's call the `Vue.noise.start` method in our `start` mutation:

```
//mutations.js
import Vue from 'vue'
<...>

export default {
  [types.START] (state) {
    <...>
    if (state.isWorking) {
      Vue.noise.start()
    }
  },
<...>
```

Check the page and click on the start button. You will listen to a nice brown noise. Be careful, however, to not to wake up your coworkers nor to scare your family (or vice versa). Try changing the value of the noise directive and choose your favorite noise to work with.

Still, we are not done. We created a mechanism so that the noise is started, but it's turning out to be a never-ending noise. Let's call the `Vue.noise.pause` and `Vue.noise.stop` methods on the `pause` and `stop` mutations, respectively:

```
//mutations.js
export default {
  <...>
  [types.PAUSE] (state) {
    <...>
    Vue.noise.pause()
  },
  [types.STOP] (state) {
    <...>
    Vue.noise.stop()
  }
}
```

Look at the page. Now if you click on the pause or stop button, the noise is suspended! We are still not done yet. Remember that our purpose was to have the noise only during working time and not during resting time. So, let's have a look at the `tooglePomodoro` method inside `mutations.js` and add a mechanism that starts or stops the noise according to the Pomodoro's current state:

```
//mutations.js
function tooglePomodoro (state, toggle) {
  if (_.isBoolean(toggle) === false) {
    toggle = !state.isWorking
  }
  state.isWorking = toggle
  if (state.isWorking) {
    Vue.noise.start()
  } else {
    Vue.noise.pause()
  }
  state.counter = state.isWorking ? WORKING_TIME : RESTING_TIME
}
```

The code of the Pomodoro application after all these modifications can be found in the `chapter6/pomodoro2` folder. Check how the noise is started when we start the application, how it's pausing when the working Pomodoro is completed, and how it restarted again when we should be back to work. Check also how the start, pause, and stop buttons trigger the noise as well. Nice work!

Creating a button to toggle the sound

It's really nice that we have the noise sound bound to the working state of the Pomodoro application. It's also nice that the sound is paused when we pause the application. However, it might be also useful to be able to pause the sound without having to pause the whole application. Think about those situations when you want to work in complete silence, or you might want to receive a Skype call. In these situations, having a noise in background, even if it's nice and pink, is not nice at all. Let's add a button to our application to toggle the sound. Start by declaring a store property called `soundEnabled` and initialize it with `true`. Also, create `getter` for this property. So `store.js` and `getters.js` start looking like the following:

```
//store.js
<...>
const state = {
  <...>
  soundEnabled: true
}
```

```
//getters.js
export default {
  <...>
  isSoundEnabled: state => state.soundEnabled
}
```

Now we must provide a mechanism to toggle the sound. Let's create a mutation method for this and add an action that dispatches this mutation. Start by declaring a mutation type called TOGGLE_SOUND:

```
//mutation_types.js
<...>
export const TOGGLE_SOUND = 'TOGGLE_SOUND'
```

Now let's open mutations.js and add the mutation method that toggles the soundEnabled store property:

```
//mutations.js
[types.TOGGLE_SOUND] (state) {
  state.soundEnabled = !state.soundEnabled
  if (state.soundEnabled) {
    Vue.noise.start()
  } else {
    Vue.noise.pause()
  }
}
```

Now let's add the action that dispatches this mutation:

```
//actions.js
export default {
  <...>
  toggleSound: ({ commit }) => {
    commit(types.TOGGLE_SOUND)
  }
}
```

Okay then, now we have everything we need to create a toggle sound button! Let's do it in our ControlsComponent. Start by adding a necessary getter and action to the map of methods:

```
//ControlsComponent.vue
<script>
  import { mapGetters, mapActions } from 'vuex'

  export default {
    computed: mapGetters(['isStarted', 'isPaused', 'isStopped',
    'isSoundEnabled']),
```

```
    methods: mapActions(['start', 'stop', 'pause', 'toggleSound'])
  }
</script>
```

Now we can add the button to our template. I suggest that it will be the icon with the `glyphicon` class that will be aligned to the right.

Let's only show this icon when the application is `started` and `not paused`, and only when the Pomodoro state *is* `working` so that we don't mess up the toggle sound button in a state where it is not supposed to have sound at all. This means that our `v-show` directive on this element will look like the following:

```
v-show="isStarted && !isPaused && isWorking"
```

Note that we are using the `isWorking` property here, which has not yet been imported. Add it to the map of `methods`:

```
//ControlsComponents.vue
<script>
  import { mapGetters, mapActions } from 'vuex'

  export default {
    computed: mapGetters(['isStarted', 'isPaused', 'isStopped',
    'isWorking', 'isSoundEnabled']),
    methods: mapActions(['start', 'stop', 'pause', 'toggleSound'])
  }
</script>
```

Let's also use the `glyphicon-volume-off` and `glyphicon-volume-on` classes on this element. They will indicate calling for the action to toggle the sound's state. This means that the `glyphicon-volume-off` class should be applied when the sound is *enabled* and the `glyphicon-volume-on` class should be applied when the sound is *disabled*. Putting it in the code, our class directive should look like the following:

```
:class="{ 'glyphicon-volume-off': isSoundEnabled, 'glyphicon-volume-up':
!isSoundEnabled }"
```

Last but not least, we should call the `toggleSound` action when the button is clicked. This means that we should also bind the `click` event listener to this element, which will look like the following:

```
@click='toggleSound'
```

So, the whole jade markup code for this button will be like the following:

```
//ControlsComponent.vue
<template>
  <span>
    <...>
    <i class="toggle-volume glyphicon" v-show="isStarted &&
    !isPaused && isWorking" :class="{ 'glyphicon-volume-off':
    isSoundEnabled, 'glyphicon-volume-up': !isSoundEnabled }"
    @click="toggleSound"></i>
  </span>
</template>
```

Let's just add a bit of styling to this button so that it appears aligned to the right:

```
<style scoped>
  <...>
  .toggle-volume {
    float: right;
    cursor: pointer;
  }
</style>
```

Open the page and start the Pomodoro application. Now you can see this nice button on the top-right corner that will allow you to turn the sound off, as shown in the following screenshot:

Now we can turn the sound off while working!

If you click on this button, it will transform into another button, whose purpose is to turn the sound on again, as shown in the following screenshot:

And we can turn it on again!

Now consider the following scenario: we start the application, turn off the sound, pause the application, and resume the application. Our current logic suggests that the sound is started each time the application is started. We will be in an inconsistent state—the application has started, the sound is playing, but the toggling sound button is suggesting to turn the sound on. That's not right, is it? But this has an easy fix—just add one more condition to the start mutation, not only it should check if `isWorking` is `true`, but also that the sound is enabled:

```
//mutations.js
[types.START](state) {
  <...>
  if (state.isWorking && state.soundEnabled) {
    Vue.noise.start()
  }
},
```

Now we are fine. The code after all these modifications can be found in the `chapter6/pomodoro3` folder.

Check the code, run the application, enjoy the sound, and do not forget to have a break!

Exercise

It would be nice if during our Pomodoro intervals we could also enjoy some happy nice music while looking at cats. Create a plugin that plays a chosen mp3 file and use it on the Pomodoro intervals.

Summary

While I was writing the last lines of code for this chapter and checking the page, at one point I got stuck looking at this picture:

A lot of cats looking at me and asking: will this chapter get to its end at some point?

I even paused the application to have a better look at this picture (yes, when you pause the Pomodoro application during resting time, the picture will pause as well because the cache-buster timestamp is not being updated anymore). Doesn't it seem like these cats are asking us to get some rest? Also, the amount of them is pretty close to the number of things that we've learned in this chapter!

In this chapter, you learned how the plugins system work with Vue.js. We used an existing `resource` plugin to attach the server-side behavior to our shopping list application. Now we can create, delete, and update our shopping lists.

We have also created our own plugin! Our plugin is able to produce sound that can help in concentrating during the working period. Not only have we created it, but we have also used it in our Pomodoro application! Now we can concentrate better while Pomodoro is working and toggle the sound at any time!

Now we have two really nice applications in our hands. Do you know what is better than a nice application?

The only thing that is better than a nice application is a nicely tested application!

With that in mind, it's about time we tested our applications. In the next chapter, we will check and apply some testing techniques. We will write unit tests using Karma test runner and Jasmine as an assertion library. We will also write end-to-end tests using Nightwatch. I love to test applications and I hope that you will love it as well. Let's go!

7
Testing – Time to Test What We Have Done So Far!

In the previous chapter, you learned how to use and create Vue plugins. We used the existing `resource` plugin for Vue and created our own `NoiseGenerator` plugin.

In this chapter, we will ensure the quality of both the Pomodoro and shopping list applications. We will test these applications applying different testing techniques. First, we will perform a classic unit test on Vue components and on Vuex-related code such as actions, mutations, and getters. After that, we will learn how to perform end-to-end testing using Nightwatch. So, in this chapter, we will do the following:

- Talk about the importance of unit and end-to-end tests
- Implement unit tests for the Pomodoro and shopping list applications
- Learn how to mock server responses in unit tests
- Implement end-to-end tests for both applications using Nightwatch

Why unit tests?

Before we start writing unit tests, let's try to understand what we're trying to achieve by writing them. Why is unit testing so important? Sometimes when I write my tests, the only thing I can think about is my code coverage; I want to achieve a level of 100%.

Code coverage is a very important metric and helps a lot to understand the code flow and what needs to be tested. But it is not a metric of unit test quality. This is not a metric of a good code quality. You can have your code 100% covered just because you call all your functions in your testing code, but if your assertions are wrong, the code might be wrong as well. Writing good unit tests is an art that requires time and patience. But when your unit tests are good enough and when you are concentrating on making good assertions, with regard to corner cases and branch coverage, they provide the following:

- Help us to identify failures in algorithms and logic
- Help us to improve the code quality
- Make us write code that is easy to test
- Prevent future changes from breaking the functionality
- Help us to have more predictable deadlines and estimations

Code that is easy to cover with unit tests is at the same time code that is easy to read. Code that is easy to read is less error-prone and more maintainable. Maintainability is one of the main pillars of an application's quality.

 Check more about unit testing in the presentation at `https://chudaol.gi thub.io/presentation-unit-testing`.

Let's write some unit tests for our applications.

We will use the Karma test runner, Mocha test framework, Chai expectations library, and Sinon for mocks.

For more information about these tools, refer to the following:

- **Karma**: `http://karma-runner.github.io/`
- **Mocha**: `https://mochajs.org`
- **Chaijs**: `http://chaijs.com/`
- **Sinon**: `http://sinonjs.org/`

If we hadn't bootstrapped our application using `vue-cli webpack` scaffolding, we would have to install all these tools via `npm`. But in our case, we don't need this installation. Check your `package.json` file and you can see that all these things are already there:

```
"devDependencies": {
  <...>
  "chai": "^3.5.0",
  <...>
  "karma": "^0.13.15",
  "karma-chrome-launcher": "^2.0.0",
  "karma-coverage": "^0.5.5",
  "karma-mocha": "^0.2.2",
  "karma-phantomjs-launcher": "^1.0.0",
  "karma-sinon-chai": "^1.2.0",
  "mocha": "^2.4.5",
  <...>
}
```

You certainly know how simple it is to write unit tests for simple functions. It's almost like speaking human language. It (this function) should return *X* if the input is *Y*. I expect it to be *X*.

So if we have a module that exports, let's say, a function that returns the sum of two arguments, the unit test for this function must call the function with different arguments and expect some output. So, let's assume we have a function such as the following:

```
function sum(a, b) {
  return a + b
}
```

Then our unit test might look like the following:

```
it('should follow commutative law', () => {
  let a = 2;
  let b = 3;

  expect(sum(a, b)).to.equal(5);
  expect(sum(b, a)).to.equal(5);
})
```

We should never be shy when we think about the possible inputs to functions that are being unit tested. Empty inputs, negative inputs, string inputs, everything counts! Have you seen this famous tweet (`https://twitter.com/sempf/status/514473420277694465`)?

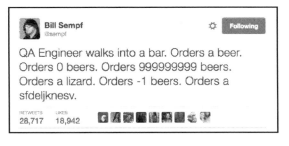

Viral tweet about QA Engineer's mindset

Think about all the possible inputs and adequate outputs. Express this in expectations and assertions. Run the tests. See what is failing. Fix your code.

Unit tests for Vue application

First, let's check on some particularities of unit testing our Vue application and its components. In order to be able to write tests for the component instance, first of all, it should be instantiated! Quite logical, right? The thing is, how do we instantiate the Vue component so that its methods become accessible and easily testable? To test basic assertions of the initial state of the component, you must just import them and assert their properties. If you want to test dynamic properties—things that change once the component is bound to DOM—you must do just the following three things:

1. Import a component.
2. Instantiate it by passing it to the Vue function.
3. Mount it.

When the instance is bound to the physical DOM, once instantiated, the compilation is started immediately. In our case, we are not binding the instance to any real physical DOM element, and thus we have to explicitly make it compile it by invoking manually the mount method (`$mount`).

Now you can use the created instance and access its methods. In pseudo-code, it looks something like the following

```
import MyComponent from <path to my component>
var vm = new Vue(MyComponent).$mount()
```

Now we can access all `vm` instance methods and test them. The rest of the things, such as `data`, `props`, and so on we can just fake. There is no problem with faking things because it offers us the possibility of trying all sorts of input easily and testing all the viable outputs for each of them.

If you want to have a more real scenario while testing components that use `props`, which come bound to the component by its parent, or access to the `vuex` store, and so on, you can use the `ref` attribute to bind the component to the `Vue` instance. This `Vue` instance, in its turn, instantiates the store and data and binds the data items to the component in a usual way. After that, you access the component instance by using the `$refs` Vue property. This kind of binding will look like the following:

```
import store from <path to store>
import MyComponent from <path to my component>
// load the component with a vue instance
var vm = new Vue({
  template: '<div><test :items="items" :id="id"
ref=testcomponent></test></div>',
  components: {
    'test': MyComponent
  },
  data() {
    return {
      items: [],
      id: 'myId'
    }
  },
  store
}).$mount();

var myComponent = vm.$refs.testcomponent;
```

Now you can test all the methods of `myComponent` without being worried about overriding its `props`, `methods`, and other instance-related things. This is a good part of this approach; however, as you can see, it is not the easiest setup and you should think about everything. For example, if your component calls some store's action that calls some API's methods, you should be ready to have to fake the server responses.

I personally like to keep things as simple as possible, fake all the data inputs, and concentrate on testing the functions' possible outputs and all the possible edge cases. But it is just my personal point of view, and also, we should try everything in our lives, so in this chapter, we will try different approaches.

Writing unit tests for the shopping list application

Before starting the actual writing of our unit tests, let's establish some rules. For each of our `.js` or `.vue` files, there will exist a corresponding test spec file, which will have the same name and a `.spec.js` extension. The structure of these specs will follow this approach:

- It will describe the file we are testing
- It will have a `describe` method for each of the methods that is being tested
- It will have an `it` method for each of the cases we are describing

So, if we had a `myBeautifulThing.js` file and spec for it, it might look like the following:

```
// myBeautifulThing.js
export myBeautifulMethod1() {
  return 'hello beauty'
}

export myBeautifulMethod2() {
  return 'hello again'
}
```

```
// myBeautifulThing.spec.js
import myBeautifulThing from <path to myBeautifulThing>

describe('myBeautifulThing', () => {
  //define needed variables

  describe('myBeautifulMethod1', () => {
    it('should return hello beauty', () {
      expect(myBeautifulThing.myBeautifulMethod1()).to.equal('hello
        beauty')
    })
  })
})
```

Let's start by covering with unit tests all the things that are inside the `vuex` folder.

Testing actions, getters, and mutations

For this section, use the code inside the `chapter7/shopping-list` folder. Do not forget to run the `npm install` command. Note that there are two new mutations: `ADD_SHOPPING_LIST` and `DELETE_SHOPPING_LIST`. These mutations add new shopping list to the list and remove the list by its ID. They are used inside the `createShoppingList` and `deleteShoppingList` actions inside the promise failure handlers:

```
//actions.js
createShoppingList: (store, shoppinglist) => {
  api.addNewShoppingList(shoppinglist).then(() => {
    store.dispatch('populateShoppingLists')
  }, () => {
    store.commit(ADD_SHOPPING_LIST, shoppinglist)
  })
},
deleteShoppingList: (store, id) => {
  api.deleteShoppingList(id).then(() => {
    store.dispatch('populateShoppingLists')
  }, () => {
    store.commit(DELETE_SHOPPING_LIST, id)
  })
}
```

Thus, even if our backend server is down, we still are not losing this functionality.

If you check your project's structure, you will see that there is already an existing directory named `test`. Inside this directory, there are two directories, `unit` and `e2e`. For now, we should go to the `unit` folder. Here, you will see another directory called `specs`. This is where all our unit test specifications will reside. Let's start by creating a directory called `vuex` inside `specs`. Here is where all our specs for Vuex-related JavaScript files will live.

Let's start by testing the `mutations.js` method.

Create a `mutations.spec.js` file. In this file, we should import `mutations.js` and mutation types so that we can easily invoke mutations. Have a look at mutations declared in `mutations.js`. All of them receive `state` and some other parameters. Let's also create a fake `state` object with the `shoppinglist` array inside it so we can use it in our tests.

Let's also reset it before each test to an empty array.

So, after all the preparations, the bootstrapped spec for `mutations.js` looks like the following:

```
// mutations.spec.js
import mutations from 'src/vuex/mutations'
import { ADD_SHOPPING_LIST, DELETE_SHOPPING_LIST, POPULATE_SHOPPING_LISTS,
CHANGE_TITLE } from 'src/vuex/mutation_types'

describe('mutations.js', () => {
  var state

  beforeEach(() => {
    state = {
      shoppinglists: []
    }
  })
})
```

Let's now add tests for the `ADD_SHOPPING_LIST` mutation.

Check again what it is doing:

```
[types.ADD_SHOPPING_LIST] (state, newList) {
  state.shoppinglists.push(newList)
},
```

This mutation just pushes the received object to the `shoppinglists` array. Pretty straightforward and easy to test.

Start by creating a `describe` statement with the name of the function:

```
describe('ADD_SHOPPING_LIST', () => {
})
```

Now, inside this `describe` callback, we can add `it` statements with the needed assertions. Let's think what should happen when we add a new shopping list to the `shoppinglists` array. First of all, the array's length will increase, and it will also contain the newly added shopping list object. This is the most basic thing to test. Our `it` function with the needed assertions will look like the following:

```
it('should add item to the shopping list array and increase its
  length', () => {
//call the add_shopping_list mutations
mutations[ADD_SHOPPING_LIST](state, {id: '1'})
//check that the array now equals array with new object
expect(state.shoppinglists).to.eql([{id: '1'}])
//check that array's length had increased
```

```
   expect(state.shoppinglists).to.have.length(1)
})
```

After creating this function, the whole spec's code should look like the following:

```javascript
// mutations.spec.js
import mutations from 'src/vuex/mutations'
import { ADD_SHOPPING_LIST, DELETE_SHOPPING_LIST, POPULATE_SHOPPING_LISTS,
CHANGE_TITLE } from 'src/vuex/mutation_types'

describe('mutations.js', () => {
  var state

  beforeEach(() => {
    state = {
      shoppinglists: []
    }
  })

  describe('ADD_SHOPPING_LIST', () => {
    it('should add item to the shopping list array and increase its
      length', () => {
      mutations[ADD_SHOPPING_LIST](state, {id: '1'})
      expect(state.shoppinglists).to.eql([{id: '1'}])
      expect(state.shoppinglists).to.have.length(1)
    })
  })
})
```

Let's run the tests! Open the console in the project's directory and run the following:

```
npm run unit
```

You should see the following output:

The output of running our test

Remember the joke about a QA engineer? We can test the `add_shopping_list` function for all possible inputs. What should happen, for example, if we call it without passing any object? In theory, it should not add it to the shopping list array, right? Let's test it. Create a new `it` statement and try to call the function without the second parameter. Assert for an empty list.

This test will look something like the following:

```
it('should not add the item if item is empty', () => {
  mutations[ADD_SHOPPING_LIST](state)
  expect(state.shoppinglists).to.have.length(0)
})
```

Run the tests with the `npm run unit` command. Oh, snap! It failed! The error is as follows:

```
expected [ undefined ] to have a length of 0 but got 1
```

Why? Have a look at the corresponding mutation. It just pushes the received parameter to the array without any checks. That's why we are able to add any garbage, any undefined, and any other inappropriate value! Do you remember when I said that writing good unit tests helps us to create less error-prone code? This is the case. Now we realize that we should probably run some checks before pushing the new item to the array. Let's add the check that the received item is an object. Open the `ADD_SHOPPING_LIST` mutation in the `mutations.js` file and rewrite it as follows:

```
//mutations.js
[types.ADD_SHOPPING_LIST](state, newList) {
  if (_.isObject(newList)) {
    state.shoppinglists.push(newList)
  }
}
```

Run the tests now. They are all passing!

Of course, we could be even more precise. We could check and test for empty objects and we could also run some validations for this object to contain properties such as `id`, `items`, and `title`. I will leave it to you as a small exercise. Try to think about all possible inputs and all possible outputs, write all the possible assertions, and make the code to correspond to them.

Good test criteria

A good unit test is one that would fail when you change your code. Imagine, for example, that we decide to assign a default title to the new shopping list before pushing it to the array. So, the mutation would look like the following:

```
[types.ADD_SHOPPING_LIST](state, newList) {
  if (_.isObject(newList)) {
    newList.title = 'New Shopping List'
    state.shoppinglists.push(newList)
  }
}
```

If you run the tests, they will fail:

Unit test fails when the code changes

And this is very good. When your tests fail after the changes in the code, the possible outcome is that you fix the test because the code is performing the intended behavior, or you fix your code.

Code coverage

I am sure that you have noticed some test statistics in the console output after running the tests. These statistics display different types of coverage that our tests achieved at the time of running. Right now, it looks like the following:

Code coverage of mutations.js after writing two tests for the ADD_SHOPPING_LIST mutation

Do you remember when I said that good code coverage doesn't mean that our tests and code are perfect? We actually have somewhat nice statements, branches, and lines coverage, but we still just tested only one function of only one file, and we haven't even covered all possible inputs of this function. But numbers do not lie. We have almost 100% branches coverage because we almost do not have branches in our code.

If you want to see a more detailed report, just open the `index.html` file from the `test/unit/coverage/lcov-report` directory in your browser. It will give you a complete and full picture of your code and what exactly is covered and how. Currently, it looks like the following:

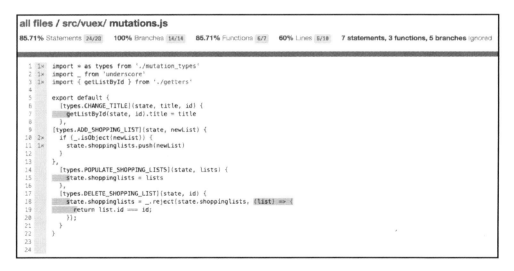

The whole picture of our codebase coverage

You can drill down to the folders, open the files, and check how exactly our code is covered. Let's check `mutations.js`:

```
all files / src/vuex/ mutations.js
85.71% Statements 24/28    100% Branches 14/14    85.71% Functions 6/7    60% Lines 5/10    7 statements, 3 functions, 5 branches ignored

 1  1x   import * as types from './mutation_types'
 2  1x   import _ from 'underscore'
 3  1x   import { getListById } from './getters'
 4
 5       export default {
 6          [types.CHANGE_TITLE](state, title, id) {
 7             getListById(state, id).title = title
 8          },
 9          [types.ADD_SHOPPING_LIST](state, newList) {
10  2x        if (_.isObject(newList)) {
11  1x           state.shoppinglists.push(newList)
12             }
13          },
14          [types.POPULATE_SHOPPING_LISTS](state, lists) {
15             state.shoppinglists = lists
16          },
17          [types.DELETE_SHOPPING_LIST](state, id) {
18             state.shoppinglists = _.reject(state.shoppinglists, (list) => {
19                return list.id === id;
20             });
21          }
22       }
23
24
```

Coverage report for actions.js show exactly which code was covered and which was not

Now you see what still has to be tested. Do you want to see how it reports the `if...else` missing branch coverage? Just skip our second test:

```
it.skip('should not add the item if item is empty', () => {
  mutations[ADD_SHOPPING_LIST](state)
  expect(state.shoppinglists).to.have.length(0)
})
```

Run the tests and refresh the report for `actions.js`. You will see an **E** icon on the left of the `if` statement:

The E icon near the if statement indicates that the else branch was not covered by tests

This indicates that we haven't covered the `else` branch. If you skip the first test and leave the one with the empty object, you will see the **I** icon that is indicating that we have skipped the `if` branch:

The I icon near the if statement indicates that the if branch was not covered by tests

Write tests for the rest of the mutations. Perform at least the following checks:

- For the `DELETE_SHOPPING_LIST` mutation, check that the list with the ID we pass is actually deleted if it existed before in the list, and that calling the mutation with the ID that doesn't exist in the list will not cause any change
- For the `POPULATE_SHOPPING_LISTS` mutation, check that the `shoppinglist` array is overridden with the array we pass when call this mutation
- For the `CHANGE_TITLE` mutation, check that when we pass the new title and the ID, exactly this object's title is changed

In the end, your `mutation.spec.js` file will probably look like the gist at `https://gist.g ithub.com/chudaol/befd9fc5701ff72dff7fb68ef1c7f06a`.

After these tests, the coverage of `mutation.js` looks pretty nice, actually:

```
all files / src/vuex/ mutations.js

100% Statements 28/28    100% Branches 14/14    100% Functions 7/7    100% Lines 10/10    7 statements, 5 branches Ignored


 1  1x  import * as types from './mutation_types'
 2  1x  import _ from 'underscore'
 3  1x  import { getListById } from './getters'
 4
 5      export default {
 6        [types.CHANGE_TITLE](state, title, id) {
 7  1x      getListById(state, id).title = title
 8        },
 9        [types.ADD_SHOPPING_LIST](state, newList) {
10  2x      if (_.isObject(newList)) {
11  1x        state.shoppinglists.push(newList)
12          }
13        },
14        [types.POPULATE_SHOPPING_LISTS](state, lists) {
15  1x      state.shoppinglists = lists
16        },
17        [types.DELETE_SHOPPING_LIST](state, id) {
18  1x      state.shoppinglists = _.reject(state.shoppinglists, (list) => {
19  3x        return list.id === id;
20          });
21        }
22      }
23
24
```

100% coverage for mutations.js after writing unit tests for all the mutations

In the exact same way, we can test our `getters.js`. Create a `getters.spec.js` file and fill it with tests to test our two getters functions. In the end, it might look like the gist at `https://gist.github.com/chudaol/e89dd0f77b1563366d5eec16bd6ae4a9`.

The only important store component that is missing in unit testing is `actions.js`. But our `actions.js` uses extensively the API that, in turn, performs HTTP requests. Its functions are also asynchronous. Can this kind of thing be unit tested in the same flexible and easy way as we just tested getters and actions? Yes, it can! Let's see how can we fake server responses using `sinon.js` and how can we write asynchronous tests with `mocha.js`.

Faking server responses and writing asynchronous tests

Open the `actions.js` file and check the very first action method:

```
//actions.js
populateShoppingLists: ({ commit }) => {
  api.fetchShoppingLists().then(response => {
    commit(POPULATE_SHOPPING_LISTS, response.data)
  })
}
```

First of all, let's add a `return` statement to this function to make it return a promise. We do it to enable us to call the `.then` method once the promise resolves so that we can test everything that happens in the meantime. So, our function looks like the following:

```
//actions.js
populateShoppingLists: ({ commit }) => {
  return api.fetchShoppingLists().then(response => {
    commit(POPULATE_SHOPPING_LISTS, response.data)
  })
}
```

Now, check what is happening here:

1. This function receives `store` with its `dispatch` method.
2. It performs a call to the API. The API, in turn, calls the resource `get` method that just performs an HTTP request to our server.
3. After the API's `fetchShoppingLists` promise is resolved, our method is calling the store's `commit` method with two parameters: a `POPULATE_SHOPPING_LISTS` string and the data that came in response.

How can we unit test this workflow? If we were able to catch the request and mock the response, we could check if the `commit` method (passed by us, which means that it can also be mocked) is called with the response that we provide in our server's mock. Sounds confusing? Not at all! The steps are the following:

1. Create a mock for the `store` and its `commit` method.
2. Create a mock for the hypothetical server response.
3. Create a fake server that will intercept the GET request and return the mocked response.
4. Check the `commit` method is called with our mocked response and the `POPULATE_SHOPPING_LISTS` string.

It means that our test could look something like the following:

```
it('should test that commit is called with correct parameters', () => {
  actions.populateShoppingLists({ commit }).then(() => {
    expect(commit).to.have.been.calledWith(<...>)
  })
})
```

The problem here is that our tests are synchronous, meaning the code will never reach what is inside our .then callback. Luckily for us, mocha.js provides support for asynchronous testing. Check it out at https://mochajs.org/#asynchronous-code. The only thing you have to do is to pass done callback to it() and call it when the test is complete. In this way, our pseudo-code for this test would look the following:

```
it('should test that commit is called with correct parameters',
(done) => {
  actions.populateShoppingLists({ commit }).then(() => {
    expect(commit).to.have.been.calledWith(<...>)
    done()
  })
})
```

Let's code now! Create a test spec and call it actions.spec.js, and write all the needed bootstrapping code:

```
// actions.spec.js
import actions from 'src/vuex/actions'
import { CHANGE_TITLE, POPULATE_SHOPPING_LISTS } from
'src/vuex/mutation_types'

describe('actions.js', () => {
  describe('populateShoppingLists', () => {
    //here we will add our test case
  })
})
```

Now let's follow our steps. First of all, let's mock the server response. Just create the lists variable and initialize it in the beforeEach method:

```
//actions.spec.js
describe('actions.js', () => {
  var lists
  beforeEach(() => {
    // mock shopping lists
    lists = [{
      id: '1',
      title: 'Groceries'
    }, {
      id: '2',
      title: 'Clothes'
    }]
  })
  describe('populateShoppingLists', () => {
  })
})
```

Now, let's mock the store's `commit` method:

```
// actions.spec.js
describe('actions.js', () => {
  var lists, store

  beforeEach(() => {
    <...>
    //mock store commit method
    store = {
      commit: (method, data) => {},
      state: {
        shoppinglists: lists
      }
    }
  })
  <...>
})
```

Now, we have to spy on this `commit` method in order to be able to assert that it was called with the required parameters. We will use the `sinon.stub` method for this. Check the documentation on `sinon.js` on this matter at `http://sinonjs.org/docs/#stubs`. Creating a stub on a given function is very easy. Just call the `sinon.stub` method and pass to it the object and its method that we want to spy on:

```
sinon.stub(store, 'commit')
```

So, our `beforeEach` function will look like the following:

```
beforeEach(() => {
    <...>
    // mock store commit method
    store = {
      commit: (method, data) => {},
      state: {
        shoppinglists: lists
      }
    }
    sinon.stub(store, 'commit')
})
```

It's very important that after each method, we *restore* the stub so that each testing method runs in a clean environment that is not affected by other tests. For this, create an `afterEach` method and add the following line:

```
afterEach(function () {
  //restore stub
```

```
      store.commit.restore()
  })
```

Now the only thing we need to do is fake our server response with our mocked data. Let's use Sinon's `fakeServer` for this purpose. Check sinon's documentation at `http://sinonjs.org/docs/#fakeServer`. We just need to create `fakeServer` and tell it to respond with our mocked response to the GET request:

```
describe('actions.js', () => {
  var lists, store, server

  beforeEach(() => {
    <...>
    //mock server
    server = sinon.fakeServer.create()
    server.respondWith('GET', /shoppinglists/, xhr => {
      xhr.respond(200, {'Content-Type': 'application/json'},
      JSON.stringify(lists))
    })
  })
  <...>
})
```

After these preparations, each test that will somehow perform a request should call the server's `respond` method in order to invoke the server's functionality.

However, we can simplify this by just telling the server to auto-respond each caught request:

```
server.autoRespond = true
```

So, our code for mocking the server will look like the following:

```
beforeEach(() => {
    <...>
    //mock server
    server = sinon.fakeServer.create()
    server.respondWith('GET', /shoppinglists/, xhr => {
      xhr.respond(200, {'Content-Type': 'application/json'},
      JSON.stringify(lists)
    })
    server.autoRespond = true
})
```

It is very important that after each test, we restore our fake server so that no other test is affected by our mocks in this test. So add the following line to the `afterEach` method:

```
afterEach(() => {
  //restore stubs and server mock
  store.commit.restore()
  server.restore()
})
```

Now that we have mocked everything that it was possible to mock, we can finally write our test case! So, you remember, we create an `it()` statement with `done` callback, call our `populateShoppingLists` method, and check that the resolved response is the same as our mocked `list` object. Step into the `describe` method and just translate into the code what we've just described:

```
it('should call commit method with POPULATE_SHOPPING_LIST and with mocked lists', done => {
  actions.populateShoppingLists(store).then(() => {
    expect(store.commit).to.have.been.calledWith(POPULATE_SHOPPING_LISTS,
    lists)
    done()
  }).catch(done)
})
```

Our whole test spec now looks like the gist at `https://gist.github.com/chudaol/addb 6657095406234bc6f659970f3eb8`.

Run the tests with `npm run unit`. It works!

Now we just have to mock the server's responses for the PUT, POST, and DELETE methods. These methods do not return any data; however, in order to be able to test the responses, let's return faked success messages, and in each test, check that the returned data corresponds to these responses. Add the following variables on top of the spec:

```
var server, store, lists, successPut, successPost, successDelete

successDelete = {'delete': true}
successPost = {'post': true}
successPut = {'put': true}
```

And add the following fake responses methods to our server:

```
server.respondWith('POST', /shoppinglists/, xhr => {
  xhr.respond(200, {'Content-Type': 'application/json'},
    JSON.stringify(successPost))
})
server.respondWith('PUT', /shoppinglists/, xhr => {
```

```
    xhr.respond(200, {'Content-Type': 'application/json'},
      JSON.stringify(successPut))
  })
  server.respondWith('DELETE', /shoppinglists/, xhr => {
    xhr.respond(200, {'Content-Type': 'application/json'},
      JSON.stringify(successDelete))
  })
```

Let's see how it'll work, for example, for the changeTitle method. In this test, we want to test that the commit method will be called with the given ID and title. Our test, therefore will look like the following:

```
describe('changeTitle', () => {
  it('should call commit method with CHANGE_TITLE string', (done) => {
    let title = 'new title'

    actions.changeTitle(store, {title: title, id: '1'}).then(() => {
      expect(store.commit).to.have.been.calledWith(CHANGE_TITLE,
      {title: title, id: '1'})
      done()
    }).catch(done)
  })
})
```

For this to work properly, we should also mock the store's dispatch method since it's being used inside the changeTitle action. Just add the dispatch property to our store's mock and return a resolved promise:

```
// mock store commit and dispatch methods
store = {
  commit: (method, data) => {},
  dispatch: () => {
    return Promise.resolve()
  },
  state: {
    shoppinglists: lists
  }
}
```

Check the final code for unit tests at this moment at https://gist.github.com/chudaol /1405dff6a46b84c284b0eae731974050.

Finish the testing for actions.js by adding unit tests for the updateList, createShoppingList, and deleteShoppingList methods. Check the whole code for unit tests until now in the chapter7/shopping-list2 folder.

Testing components

Now that all our Vuex-related functions are unit tested, it is time to apply specific Vue components testing techniques to test components of our shopping list application.

You remember from the first section of this chapter that in order to prepare the `Vue` instance to be unit tested, we must import, initiate (passing it to new `Vue` instance), and mount it. Let's do it! Create a `components` folder inside the `test/unit/specs` directory. Let's start by testing the `AddItemComponent` component. Create an `AddItemComponent.spec.js` file and import `Vue` and `AddItemComponent`:

```
//AddItemComponent.spec.js
import Vue from 'vue'
import AddItemComponent from 'src/components/AddItemComponent'

describe('AddItemComponent.vue', () => {
})
```

The variable `AddItemComponent` can be used to access directly all the component's initial data. So we can assert, for example, that the component data is initialized with a `newItem` property that equals to empty string:

```
describe('initialization', () => {
  it('should initialize the component with empty string newItem', () => {
    expect(AddItemComponent.data()).to.eql({
      newItem: ''
    })
  })
})
```

Let's now check which methods of this component we can cover with unit tests.

This component has only one method, which is `addItem` method. Let's check what this method does:

```
//AddItemComponent.vue
addItem () {
  var text

  text = this.newItem.trim()
  if (text) {
    this.$emit('add', this.newItem)
    this.newItem = ''
    this.$store.dispatch('updateList', this.id)
  }
}
```

This method access to the store, so, we have to use another strategy of initializing the component rather than just directly using the imported value. In this case, we should initialize Vue main component with `AddItemComponent` as a child, pass all the necessary attributes to it, and access it using the `$refs` attribute. So, the component's initialization inside the test method will look like the following:

```
var vm, addItemComponent;

vm = new Vue({
  template: '<add-item-component :items="items" :id="id"
  ref="additemcomponent">' +
  '</add-item-component>',
  components: {
    AddItemComponent
  },
  data() {
    return {
      items: [],
      id: 'niceId'
    }
  },
  store
}).$mount();

addItemComponent = vm.$refs.additemcomponent
```

Back to the method's functionality. So, the `addItem` method grabs the instance's `newItem` property, trims it, checks if it's not falsy and, if not, emits the custom event `add`, resets the `newItem` property, and dispatches the `updateList` action on store. We can test this method by assigning different values `component.newItem`, `component.id` and checking if the output corresponds to what we are expecting of it.

 Positive testing means testing a system by giving it valid data. **Negative testing** means testing a system by giving it invalid data.

In our positive test, we should initialize the `component.newItem` property with a valid string. After calling the method, we should ensure various things:

- The `$emit` method of the component has been called with `add` and the text we assigned to the `newItem` property
- `component.newItem` was reset to the empty string

- The store's `dispatch` method has been called with the `id` property of the component

Let's go! Let's start by adding the describe method for the `addItem` function:

```
describe('addItem', () => {

})
```

Now we can add the `it()` method where we will assign a value to `component.newItem`, call the `addItem` method, and check everything we need to check:

```
//AddItemComponent.spec.js
it('should call $emit method', () => {
  let newItem = 'Learning Vue JS'
  // stub $emit method
  sinon.stub(component, '$emit')
  // stub store's dispatch method
  sinon.stub(store, 'dispatch')
  // set a new item
  component.newItem = newItem
  component.addItem()
  // newItem should be reset
  expect(component.newItem).to.eql('')
  // $emit should be called with custom event 'add' and a newItem value
  expect(component.$emit).to.have.been.calledWith('add', newItem)
  // dispatch should be called with updateList and the id of the list
  expect(store.dispatch).to.have.been.calledWith('updateList',
  'niceId')
  store.dispatch.restore()
  component.$emit.restore()
})
```

Run the tests and check that they are passing and everything is okay. Check the final code for `AddItemComponent` in the `chapter7/shopping-list3` folder.

Try to write unit tests for the rest of the components of the shopping list application. Remember to write unit tests to cover your code so that it breaks if you change it.

Writing unit tests for our Pomodoro application

Ok! Let's move to our Pomodoro application! By the way, when was the last time you took a break? Probably, it is time to open the application in your browser, wait a few minutes of the Pomodoro working period timer, and check for some kittens.

I just did it and it made me feel really nice and cute:

I'm not your clothes... please have some rest

Let's start with mutations. Open the code in the `chapter7/pomodoro` folder. Open the `mutations.js` file and check what is happening out there. There are four mutations happening: `START`, `STOP`, `PAUSE`, and `TOGGLE_SOUND`. Guess which one we will start with. Yes, you are right, we will start with the `start` method. Create a `vuex` subfolder inside the `test/unit/specs` folder and add the `mutations.spec.js` file. Let's bootstrap it to be ready for tests:

```
// mutations.spec.js
import Vue from 'vue'
import mutations from 'src/vuex/mutations'
import * as types from 'src/vuex/mutation_types'

describe('mutations', () => {
  var state

  beforeEach(() => {
```

```
      state = {}
      // let's mock Vue noise plugin
      //to be able to listen on its methods
      Vue.noise = {
        start: () => {},
        stop: () => {},
        pause: () => {}
      }
      sinon.spy(Vue.noise, 'start')
      sinon.spy(Vue.noise, 'pause')
      sinon.spy(Vue.noise, 'stop')
    })

  afterEach(() => {
    Vue.noise.start.restore()
    Vue.noise.pause.restore()
    Vue.noise.stop.restore()
  })

  describe('START', () => {
  })
})
```

Note that I mocked all the methods of the noise generator plugin. This is because in this spec, we don't need to test the plugin's functionality (in fact, we must do it in the scope of the plugin itself before publishing it). For the scope of this test, we should test that the plugin's methods are called when they need to be called.

In order to be able to test the start method, let's think what should happen. After the start button is clicked, we know that the application's started, paused, and stopped states must gain some specific values (actually, true, false, and false, respectively). We also know the application's interval should be started. We also know that if the Pomodoro's state is working and if the sound is enabled, the start method of the noise generator plugin should be called. In fact, this is what our method is actually doing:

```
  [types.START] (state) {
    state.started = true
    state.paused = false
    state.stopped = false
    state.interval = setInterval(() => tick(state), 1000)
    if (state.isWorking && state.soundEnabled) {
      Vue.noise.start()
    }
  },
```

But even if it didn't do all these things and we have written the test to test it, we would immediately understand that something is missing in our code and fix it. Let's then write our test. Let's start by defining the it() method that tests that all the properties were correctly set. In order to be sure that they are not already set before calling the method, let's also assert that all these properties are not defined at the start of the test:

```
it('should set all the state properties correctly after start', () => {
  // ensure that all the properties are undefined
  // before calling the start method
  expect(state.started).to.be.undefined
  expect(state.stopped).to.be.undefined
  expect(state.paused).to.be.undefined
  expect(state.interval).to.be.undefined
  // call the start method
  mutations[types.START](state)
  // check that all the properties were correctly set
  expect(state.started).to.be.true
  expect(state.paused).to.be.false
  expect(state.stopped).to.be.false
  expect(state.interval).not.to.be.undefined
})
```

Let's now check on the Vue.noise.start method. We know that it should only be called if state.isWorking is true and state.soundEnabled is true. Let's write a positive test. In this test, we would initialize both Boolean states to true and check that the noise.start method is called:

```
it('should call Vue.noise.start method if both state.isWorking and
state.soundEnabled are true', () => {
  state.isWorking = true
  state.soundEnabled = true
  mutations[types.START](state)
  expect(Vue.noise.start).to.have.been.called
})
```

Let's add two negative tests for each of the states, with isWorking and soundEnabled being false:

```
it('should not call Vue.noise.start method if state.isWorking is not true',
() => {
  state.isWorking = false
  state.soundEnabled = true
  mutations[types.START](state)
  expect(Vue.noise.start).to.not.have.been.called
})

it('should not call Vue.noise.start method if state.soundEnabled is not
```

```
true', () => {
  state.isWorking = true
  state.soundEnabled = false
  mutations[types.START](state)
  expect(Vue.noise.start).to.not.have.been.called
})
```

Our `start` mutation is nicely tested! Check the final state of the code in the `chapter7/pomodoro2` folder. I suggest that you now write the rest of the unit tests not only for the mutations, but also for all the store-related functions that reside in getters and actions. After that, apply the techniques to test Vue components that we just learned and test some of the components of our Pomodoro application.

At this point, we are done with unit testing!

What is end- to-end testing?

End-to-end (e2e) testing is a technique in which the whole flow of the application is being tested. In this kind of testing, neither mocks nor stubs are used, and the real system is being under the test. Performing e2e testing allows us to test all the aspects of the application—APIs, frontend, backend, databases, server load, assuring thus the quality of the system integration.

In the case of web applications, these tests are performed via UI testing. Each test describes all the steps from opening the browser until closing it. All the steps needed to perform in order to achieve some system's functionality must be described. In fact, this is the same as you clicking and doing some operations on your application's page, but is automated and fast. In this section, we will see what a Selenium webdriver is, and what Nightwatch is, and how they can be used to create e2e tests for our applications.

Nightwatch for e2e

If you have already worked with test automation or if you have worked with someone who has worked with test automation, for sure, you have already heard the magic word Selenium—Selenium opens the browser, clicks, writes, does everything like a human, in a parallel, nicely distributed, multiplatform, and cross-browser way. In fact, Selenium is just a JAR file that contains an API to perform different operations on a browser (click, type, scroll, and so on).

Check out Selenium's documentation at `http://www.seleniumhq.org/`.

When this JAR file is executed, it connects to the specified browser, opens the API, and waits for the commands to be performed on the browser. The commands sent to the Selenium server can be performed in tons of different ways and languages.

There are a lot of existing implementations and frameworks that allow you to call selenium commands with couple lines of code:

- You can use the native Selenium's framework for Java (`http://seleniumhq.gith ub.io/selenium/docs/api/java/`)
- You can use the Firefox plugin for browsers (`https://addons.mozilla.org/en-us/firefox/addon/selenium-ide/`)
- You can use **Selenide**, which is yet another implementation for Java but a lot easier to use than Selenium's framework (`http://selenide.org/`)
- If you are an AngularJS developer, you can use Protractor, which is a very nice e2e test framework for AngularJS applications that also uses the Selenium webdriver (`http://www.protractortest.org/`)

In our case, we will use Nightwatch, which is a nice and very easy-to-use testing framework to call Selenium's commands using JavaScript.

Check Nightwatch's documentation at `http://nightwatchjs.org/`.

Vue applications, when bootstrapped using the `vue-cli webpack` method, already contains support for writing Nightwatch tests right away without the need to install anything. Basically, each test spec will look somewhat like the following:

```
module.exports = {
  'e2e test': function (browser) {
    browser
    .url('http://localhost:8080')
      .waitForElementVisible('#app', 5000)
      .assert.elementPresent('.logo')
      .assert.containsText('h1', 'Hello World!')
      .assert.elementCount('p', 3)
      .end()
  }
}
```

The syntax is nice and easy to understand. Each of the highlighted methods is a Nightwatch command that behind the scenes is transformed into the Selenium command and invoked as such. Check the full list of the Nightwatch commands in the official documentation page at `http://nightwatchjs.org/api#commands`.

Writing e2e tests for the Pomodoro application

So, now that we know all the theory behind the UI testing, we can create our first end-to-end test for our Pomodoro application. Let's define the steps that we will perform and the things that we should test. So, first of all, we should open the browser. Then, we should probably check that our container (that has the `#app` ID) is on the page.

We can also try to check that the pause and stop buttons are disabled and that the sound toggle button does not exist on the page.

Then we can click on the start button and check that the sound toggle button has appeared, the start button has become disabled, and the pause and stop buttons have become enabled. There is an innumerous number of possibilities of further clicking and checking, but let's perform at least the described steps. Let's just write them in the form of bullet points:

1. Open the browser at `http://localhost:8080`.
2. Check that the `#app` element is on the page.
3. Check that the `.toggle-volume` icon is not visible.
4. Check that the `'[title=pause]'` and `'[title=stop]'` buttons are disabled and the `'[title=start]'` button is enabled.
5. Click on the `'[title=start]'` button.
6. Check that the `'[title=pause]'` and `'[title=stop]'` buttons are now enabled and the `'[title=start]'` button is disabled.
7. Check that the `.toggle-volume` icon is now visible.

Let's do it! Just open the `test.js` file inside the `tests/e2e/specs` folder, delete its content, and add the following code:

```
module.exports = {
  'default e2e tests': (browser) => {
    // open the browser and check that #app is on the page
    browser.url('http://localhost:8080')
      .waitForElementVisible('#app', 5000);
```

```
      // check that toggle-volume icon is not visible
      browser.expect.element('.toggle-volume')
        .to.not.be.visible
      // check that pause button is disabled
      browser.expect.element('[title=pause]')
        .to.have.attribute('disabled')
      // check that stop button is disabled
      browser.expect.element('[title=stop]')
        .to.have.attribute('disabled')
      // check that start button is not disabled
      browser.expect.element('[title=start]')
        .to.not.have.attribute('disabled')
      // click on start button, check that toggle volume
      // button is visible
      browser.click('[title=start]')
        .waitForElementVisible('.toggle-volume', 5000)
      // check that pause button is not disabled
      browser.expect.element('[title=pause]')
        .to.not.have.attribute('disabled')
      // check that stop button is not disabled
      browser.expect.element('[title=stop]')
        .to.not.have.attribute('disabled')
      // check that stop button is disabled
      browser.expect.element('[title=start]')
        .to.have.attribute('disabled')
      browser.end()
  }
}
```

Do you see how super human-friendly this language is? Let's now perform a check to see whether, after the period of working time, the kitten element appears on the screen. In order to make the test shorter and not wait for a long time for test to pass, let's establish the working period as 6 seconds. Change this value in our `config.js` file:

```
//config.js
export const WORKING_TIME = 0.1 * 60
```

The element that contains the cat images has a `'div.well.kittens'` selector, so we will check whether it is visible. Let's also check in this test that after the kitten element appears, the source of the image contains the `'thecatapi'` string. This test will be as simple as the following:

```
'wait for kitten test': (browser) => {
  browser.url('http://localhost:8080')
    .waitForElementVisible('#app', 5000)
  // initially the kitten element is not visible
  browser.expect.element('.well.kittens')
```

```
        .to.not.be.visible
    // click on the start button and wait for 7s for
    //kitten element to appear
    browser.click('[title=start]')
        .waitForElementVisible('.well.kittens', 7000)
    // check that the image contains the src element
    //that matches thecatapi string
    browser.expect.element('.well.kittens img')
        .to.have.attribute('src')
        .which.matches(/thecatapi/);
    browser.end()
}
```

Run the tests. In order to do that, invoke the e2e npm command:

```
npm run e2e
```

You will see how the browser opens and performs all the operations by itself.

It's a kind of magic!

All our tests have passed and all expectations are fulfilled; check out the console:

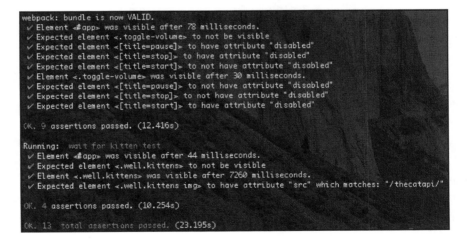

All tests are passing!

Congratulations! You've just learned how to use Nightwatch to write e2e tests. Check the code in the `chapter7/pomodoro3` folder. Write more test cases for our Pomodoro application. Do not forget about our shopping list application, which might have even more scenarios for UI tests. Write them all and check how Selenium does the work for you. If you decide to enhance the code, not only is your code quality protected by unit tests, but it also now has regression testing applied to it. Each time you change the code, run both types of tests just with one command:

```
npm test
```

Now you certainly deserve some rest. Take a cup of coffee or tea, open your browser on the Pomodoro application page, wait for 6 seconds, and appreciate our little fluffy friends:

Actually, this is not a kitten from thecatapi. This is my cat Patuscas wishing you all to have a good rest time!

Summary

In this chapter, we've tested both of our applications. We have written unit tests for Vuex methods and Vue components. We have used simple unit tests and asynchronous unit tests and we got familiar with Sinon mocking techniques such as spying on methods and faking server responses. We also learned how to create UI tests using Nightwatch. Our applications are now tested and prepared to be deployed to production! We will discover how to deploy them in the next chapter, which will be devoted to deploying applications using the Heroku cloud application platform.

8
Deploying – Time to Go Live!

In the previous chapter, you learned how to test your Vue applications. We tested them applying different testing techniques. In the beginning, we have performed classic unit testing on Vue components and on Vuex-related modules, such as actions, mutations, and getters. After that, we learned how to apply end-to-end testing techniques using Nightwatch.

In this chapter, we will make our applications go live by deploying them to a server and making them available to the world. We will also guarantee continuous integration and continuous deployment of our applications. This means that every time we commit changes performed on the applications, they will automatically be tested and deployed.

With this in mind, in this chapter, we are going to do the following:

- Set up a continuous integration process using Travis
- Set up a continuous deployment using Heroku

Software deployment

Before starting to deploy our applications, let's first try to define what it actually means:

"Software deployment is all of the activities that make a software system available for use."
– Wikipedia: https://en.wikipedia.org/wiki/Software_deployment

This definition means that after we perform all the necessary activities, our software will be accessible to the public. In our case, as we are deploying web applications, it means that there will be a public URL, and any person will be able to type this URL on their browser and access the application. How can this be achieved? The simplest way is to provide your own IP address to your friends and run the application. Thus, people inside your private network will be able to access the application on their browser. So, run, for example, the Pomodoro application:

```
> cd <path to pomodoro>
> npm run dev
```

And then check your IP:

```
ifconfig
```

Checking the IP address with the ifconfig command

And then share the address with your friends on the same private network. In my case, it would be `http://192.168.1.6:8080`.

However, only your friends who are inside your network will be able to access the application, and there's obviously not that much fun in it.

You can use some software that will create a publicly accessible address and thus transform your computer into a hosting provider, for example, ngrok (`https://ngrok.com/`). Run the application and then run the following command:

```
ngrok http 8080
```

This will create an address that will be accessible from anywhere, just like a regular website:

Using ngrok to provide a tunnel to your localhost

In my case, it would be `http://5dcb8d46.ngrok.io`. I can share this address on my social networks and everybody will be able to access it and try the Pomodoro application! But stop ... I can leave my laptop on for the whole night, but I can't leave it on forever. Once I switch it off, the network connection is lost and there is no access to my application anymore. Also, even if I could leave it on forever, I don't like this website address. It's a bunch of letters and numbers, and I want it to be something meaningful.

There are more robust ways. I can buy, for example, a virtual instance on **AWS (Amazon Web Services)**, copy my application to this instance, buy a domain at a domain provider such as GoDaddy, associate this domain to the bought instance's IP, and run the application there and it will be accessible, maintained, backed up, and taken care of by the Amaz(on)ing service. Amazing, but ... expensive as hell. Let's think of this solution when our applications reach the corresponding size and payback level.

For now, for this chapter, we want our deployment solution to be cheap (where cheap means free), robust, and simple. That is why we will deploy our application to Heroku, a cloud-application platform. In order to do that, we will first host our application on GitHub. Do you remember that deployment is something that makes our applications ready to use? I consider an application to be ready to use when it's tested and when tests are not failing. That is why we will also use Travis to guarantee the quality of our applications before their actual deployment. So, our necessary activities to deploy the application will be the following:

1. Create GitHub repositories for the applications and move the applications into the repositories.
2. Set up continuous integration with Travis.

3. Connect applications to Heroku, and set up and configure them in order for Heroku to run them and to expose them to the world.

In the next three subsections, I will give a small introduction to GitHub, Travis, and Heroku.

What is GitHub?

GitHub is a hosting provider for Git-based projects.

It can be used at a small, personal scale for individual private and public projects. It can also be used for big corporate projects and all development-related activities, such as code reviews, continuous integration, and so on.

Everyone who lives in the world of open source software knows GitHub. If you are reading this book about Vue, which is hosted on GitHub (`https://github.com/vuejs/`), I am sure that you are skipping this subsection, so probably I can write some stupid jokes about you here and you will never notice them! Just kidding!

What is Travis?

Travis is a tool for GitHub that allows us to connect GitHub projects to it and ensure their quality. It runs tests in your projects and tells you that build has passed, or warns you that build has failed. Check more about Travis and how to use it at `https://travis-ci.org/`.

What is Heroku?

Heroku is a cloud platform for deploying your apps. It is extremely easy to use. You just create an application, give it a nice meaningful name, connect it to your GitHub project, and voilà! Each time you push to a given branch (for example, to the `master` branch), Heroku will just run a script provided by you as an entry point script of your app and redeploy it.

It is highly configurable and also provides a command-line interface so that you can access all your applications from your local command line without having to check your Heroku dashboard website. Let's then start and learn everything by doing it ourselves.

Moving the application to the GitHub repository

Let's start by creating the GitHub repositories for our applications.

Please use the code from the `chapter8/pomodoro` and `chapter8/shopping-list` directories.

If you still don't have an account at GitHub, create it. Now log in to your GitHub account and create two repositories, `Pomodoro` and `ShoppingList`:

Create a repository at GitHub

Once you hit the **Create repository** button, a page with different instructions appears. We are particularly interested in the second paragraph, which says **...or create a new repository on the command line**. Copy it, paste it to the command line while in the Pomodoro application directory, remove the first line (because we already have the README file) and modify the third line to add everything inside the directory, and hit the *Enter* button:

```
git init
git add
git commit -m "first commit"
git remote add origin https://github.com/chudaol/Pomodoro.git
git push -u origin master
```

Refresh your GitHub project page, and you will see that all the code is there! In my case, it is at https://github.com/chudaol/Pomodoro.

Do the same for the shopping list application. I just did it and here I am: https://github.com/chudaol/ShoppingList.

If you don't want to create your own repositories, you can just fork mine. Open source is open!

Setting continuous integration with Travis

In order to be able to set up continuous integration with Travis, first of all you have to connect your Travis account with your GitHub account. Open https://travis-ci.org/ and click on the **Sign in with GitHub** button:

Click on the Sign in with GitHub button

Now you can add repositories that will be tracked with Travis. Click on the plus sign (+):

Click on the plus sign to add your GitHub project

After you click on the plus button, the whole list of your GitHub project appears. Choose the projects you want to track:

Choose the projects you want to track with Travis

Now that we have our projects connected to the Travis build system that listens to every commit and push to the `master` branch, we need to tell it somehow what it has to do once it detects changes. All the configuration for Travis should be stored in the `.travis.yml` file. Add the `.travis.yml` file to both the projects. We have at least to tell which node version should be used. Check the Node version of your system (this is the one that you are completely sure that works with our projects). Just run the following command:

```
node --version
```

In my case, it is `v5.11.0`. So I will add it to the `.travis.yml` file:

```
// .travis.yml
language: node_js
node_js:
  - "5.11.0"
```

If you commit and push now, you will see that Travis automatically starts running tests. By default, it calls the `npm test` command on the project. Wait for a few minutes and observe the result. Unfortunately, it will fail while performing end-to-end (Selenium) tests. Why does this happen?

By default, virtual images of the Travis building and testing environment do not have the Chrome browser installed. And our Selenium tests are trying to run on the Chrome browser. But fortunately for us, Travis provides a mechanism of performing some commands before building. It should be done in the `before_script` section of the YML file. Let's invoke the necessary commands to install Chrome and export the `CHROME_BIN` variable. Add the following to your `.travis.yml` files:

```
before_script:
  - export CHROME_BIN=/usr/bin/google-chrome
  - sudo apt-get update
  - sudo apt-get install -y libappindicator1 fonts-liberation
  - wget https://dl.google.com/linux/direct/google-chrome-
    stable_current_amd64.deb
  - sudo dpkg -i google-chrome*.deb
```

As you can see, in order to perform the installation and system update, we must invoke commands with `sudo`. By default, Travis does not let you execute `sudo` commands in order to prevent accidental damage by non-trustworthy scripts. But you can tell Travis explicitly that your script uses `sudo`, which means that you are aware of what are you doing. Just add the following lines to your `.travis.yml` files:

```
sudo: required
dist: trusty
```

Now your whole `.travis.yml` file should look like the following:

```
//.travis.yml
language: node_js
sudo: required
dist: trusty
node_js:
  - "5.11.0"

before_script:
  - export CHROME_BIN=/usr/bin/google-chrome
  - sudo apt-get update
  - sudo apt-get install -y libappindicator1 fonts-liberation
  - wget https://dl.google.com/linux/direct/google-chrome-
    stable_current_amd64.deb
  - sudo dpkg -i google-chrome*.deb
```

Try to commit it and check your Travis dashboard.

Oh no! It fails again. This time, it seems to be timeout issue:

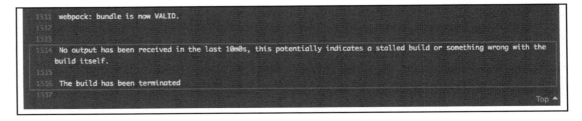

Even after installing Chrome, tests silently fail due to the timeout

Why did it happen? Let's recall what actually happens when we run our end-to-end tests. Each test opens the browser and then performs clicks, inputs, and other things to test our UI. The keyword of the last sentence is *UI*. If we need to test a UI, we need a **graphical user interface (GUI)**. Travis virtual images do not have graphical displays. Thus, there is no way that they can open the browser and display our UIs in it. Fortunately for us, there is a nice thing called *Xvfb – X virtual framebuffer*.

Xvfb is a display server that implements the protocol used by the physical displays. All needed graphical operations are performed in memory; thus, there is no need of having physical displays. Therefore, we can run an Xvfb server that will provide a virtual graphical environment to our tests. And if you carefully read the Travis documentation, you will find that this is exactly what it suggests as a way of running tests that require GUI: `https://doc s.travis-ci.com/user/gui-and-headless-browsers/#Using-xvfb-to-Run-Tests-That -Require-a-GUI`. So open the `.travis.yml` files and add the following to the `before_script` section:

```
- export DISPLAY=:99.0
- sh -e /etc/init.d/xvfb start
```

The whole YML file now looks like the following:

```
//.travis.yml
language: node_js
sudo: required
dist: trusty
node_js:
  - "5.11.0"

before_script:
  - export CHROME_BIN=/usr/bin/google-chrome
  - sudo apt-get update
  - sudo apt-get install -y libappindicator1 fonts-liberation
  - wget https://dl.google.com/linux/direct/google-chrome-
    stable_current_amd64.deb
  - sudo dpkg -i google-chrome*.deb
  - export DISPLAY=:99.0
  - sh -e /etc/init.d/xvfb start
```

Commit it and check your Travis dashboard. The Pomodoro application was built successfully!

The Pomodoro application built with success!

However, the shopping list application's build has failed. Note that Travis even changes the tab's title color for each of the build states:

Travis changes the icon on the tab's title according to the build state

So what is happening with the shopping list application build? There's a step in the end-to-end test that checks for the **Groceries** title being present on the page. The thing is that this title comes from our backend server that should be run with the npm run server command. Do you remember we implemented it in Chapter 6, *Plugins – Building Your House with Your Own Bricks*, using the vue-resource plugin? This means that before building the application, we need to tell Travis to run our small server. Just add the following line to the .travis.yml file of the shopping list application:

```
- nohup npm run server &
```

Commit your changes and check Travis dashboard. The build passed! Everything is green and we are happy (at least I am, and I hope that successful build makes you happy as well). Now it would be nice if we could tell the world that our builds are passing. We can do it by adding the Travis button to our README.md files. This will allow us to immediately see the build status on the project's GitHub page.

Click on the **build passing** button on the Travis page of your application, check the **Markdown** option from the second drop-down list, and copy the generated text to the README.md file:

Click on the build passing button, select option Markdown from the second drop-down, and copy the text to the README.md file

Look how nice it looks in the README file on the GitHub page of our project:

The Travis button looks really fancy in the README file of the project on its GitHub page

Now that our applications are being checked on each commit and therefore we have for sure guaranteed their quality, we can finally deploy them to the publicly accessible place.

Before starting the process of deployment, please create an account at Heroku (https://signup.heroku.com/dc) and install Heroku Toolbelt (https://devcenter.heroku.com/articles/getting-started-with-nodejs#set-up).

Now we are ready to deploy our projects.

Deploying the Pomodoro application

Let's start by adding new application to our Heroku account. Click on the **Create New App** button on the Heroku dashboard. You can create your own name or leave the name input field blank, and Heroku will create a name for you. I will call my application *catodoro* because it is Pomodoro that has cats!

Creating a new app with Heroku

Click on the **Create App** button and you will proceed to the page, choosing a deployment pipeline for your application. Choose the GitHub method, and then from the proposed drop-down of your GitHub projects, choose the project that we want to deploy:

Choose the GitHub method of deployment and select the corresponding project from your GitHub projects

After clicking on the **Connect** button, two things that you might probably want to check are the **Automatic deploys from master are enabled** and **Wait for CI to pass before deploy** options:

Check the Wait for CI to pass before deploy checkbox and click on the Enable Automatic Deploys button

Everything is ready to perform a first deployment and you can even click on the **Deploy Branch** button, and Heroku will try to perform a build, but then, if you try to open the application in the browser, it will not work. If you wonder why, you should always look at the running log while performing such operations.

Checking logs

I hope you have successfully installed the Heroku CLI (or Heroku toolbelt), so now you can run `heroku` commands in your command line. Let's check the logs. Run the `heroku logs` command in your shell:

```
heroku logs --app catodoro --tail
```

You will see a continuously running log while Heroku tries to perform a build. And the error is `npm ERR! missing script: start`. We don't have a `start` script in our `package.json` file.

This is entirely true. In order to create a start script, let's first try to understand how to build and run a Vue application for production. The README file tells us that we need to run the `npm run build` command. Let's run it locally and check what happens:

The output of the npm run build command

So we know that the result of the build command goes to the `dist` folder. And we also know that we have to serve the `index.html` file from this folder using an HTTP server. We also know that we have to create a `start` script in the `scripts` section of the `package.json` file, so Heroku knows how to run our application.

Preparing the application to run on Heroku

We were able to gather a lot of information by checking the log file. Let's also summarize here Heroku's pipeline for running the application before proceeding to the steps for deploying the application.

So, Heroku does the following:

- Runs the `npm install` script to install all the needed dependencies (it checks the dependencies in the `dependencies` section of the `package.json` file)
- Runs the `npm start` script from the `package.json` and serves the result of it on the known web address

So, given this information and the information we gathered from the logs and running the `npm build` script, we need to do the following:

- Tell Heroku to install all the needed dependencies; for that, we need to move project dependencies from the `devDependencies` section to the `dependencies` section in the `package.json` file so that Heroku installs them all

- Tell Heroku to run a build script after performing `npm install`; for that, we need to create a `postinstall` script in the `package.json` file where we will call the `npm run build` command.
- Create a `server.js` file that serves the `index.html` file from the `dist` folder
- Provide a way for Heroku to run the `server.js` script; for this, we need to create a `start` script in the `package.json` file that runs the `server.js` script

Start by moving all the dependencies, except the ones that have to do with testing, from the `devDependencies` section to the `dependencies` section of our `package.json` file:

```
"dependencies": {
  "autoprefixer": "^6.4.0",
  "babel-core": "^6.0.0",
  "babel-eslint": "^7.0.0",
  "babel-loader": "^6.0.0",
  "babel-plugin-transform-runtime": "^6.0.0",
  "babel-polyfill": "^6.16.0",
  "babel-preset-es2015": "^6.0.0",
  "babel-preset-stage-2": "^6.0.0",
  "babel-register": "^6.0.0",
  "chalk": "^1.1.3",
  "connect-history-api-fallback": "^1.1.0",
  "cross-spawn": "^4.0.2",
  "css-loader": "^0.25.0",
  "es6-promise": "^4.0.5",
  "eslint": "^3.7.1",
  "eslint-config-standard": "^6.1.0",
  "eslint-friendly-formatter": "^2.0.5",
  "eslint-loader": "^1.5.0",
  "eslint-plugin-html": "^1.3.0",
  "eslint-plugin-promise": "^2.0.1",
  "eslint-plugin-standard": "^2.0.1",
  "eventsource-polyfill": "^0.9.6",
  "express": "^4.13.3",
  "extract-text-webpack-plugin": "^1.0.1",
  "file-loader": "^0.9.0",
  "function-bind": "^1.0.2",
  "html-webpack-plugin": "^2.8.1",
  "http-proxy-middleware": "^0.17.2",
  "inject-loader": "^2.0.1",
  "isparta-loader": "^2.0.0",
  "json-loader": "^0.5.4",
  "lolex": "^1.4.0",
  "opn": "^4.0.2",
  "ora": "^0.3.0",
  "semver": "^5.3.0",
```

```
    "shelljs": "^0.7.4",
    "url-loader": "^0.5.7",
    "vue": "^2.0.1",
    "vuex": "^2.0.0",
    "vue-loader": "^9.4.0",
    "vue-style-loader": "^1.0.0",
    "webpack": "^1.13.2",
    "webpack-dev-middleware": "^1.8.3",
    "webpack-hot-middleware": "^2.12.2",
    "webpack-merge": "^0.14.1"
},
"devDependencies": {
    "chai": "^3.5.0",
    "chromedriver": "^2.21.2",
    "karma": "^1.3.0",
    "karma-coverage": "^1.1.1",
    "karma-mocha": "^1.2.0",
    "karma-phantomjs-launcher": "^1.0.0",
    "karma-sinon-chai": "^1.2.0",
    "karma-sourcemap-loader": "^0.3.7",
    "karma-spec-reporter": "0.0.26",
    "karma-webpack": "^1.7.0",
    "mocha": "^3.1.0",
    "nightwatch": "^0.9.8",
    "phantomjs-prebuilt": "^2.1.3",
    "selenium-server": "2.53.1",
    "sinon": "^1.17.3",
    "sinon-chai": "^2.8.0"
}
```

Now let's create a `postinstall` script in which we will tell Heroku to run the `npm run build` script. In the `scripts` section, add the `postinstall` script:

```
"scripts": {
    <...>
    "postinstall": "npm run build"
},
```

Now let's create a `server.js` file in which we will serve the `index.html` file from the `dist` directory. Create a `server.js file` in the project's folder and add the following content:

```
// server.js
var express = require('express');
var serveStatic = require('serve-static');
var app = express();
app.use(serveStatic(__dirname + '/dist'));
var port = process.env.PORT || 5000;
```

```
app.listen(port);
console.log('server started '+ port);
```

Okay, now we just need to create a `start` script in the `scripts` section of our `package.json` file and we are done! Our `start` script should just run `node server.js`, so let's do it:

```
"scripts": {
  <...>
  "postinstall": "npm run build",
  "start": "node server.js"
},
```

Commit your changes, go to the Heroku dashboard, and click on the **Deploy Branch** button. Do not forget to check running logs!

And yippee! The build was successful! After a successful build, you are invited to click the **View** button; don't be shy, click on it and you will see your application in action!

The Pomodoro application is successfully deployed to Heroku

Now you can use your Pomodoro application everywhere. Now you can ask your friends to use it as well by simply providing them the Heroku link.

Well, congratulations! You've just deployed your Vue application, and it can be used by everyone. How nice is it?

Deploying the shopping list application

In order to deploy our shopping list application, we need to perform exactly the same steps as we have done with the Pomodoro application.

Create a new application on your Heroku dashboard and connect it to your GitHub shopping list project. After that, copy the `server.js` file from the Pomodoro application, deal with the dependencies in the `package.json` file, and create `postinstall` and `start` scripts.

However, we still have one step left. Do not forget about our backend server that serves the REST API for the shopping lists. We need to run it as well.

Or even better, why do we need to run two servers if we can have just one server that does everything? We can integrate our JSON server with our express server by providing it the routing path to serve the shopping list endpoint, let's say `api`. Open the `server.js` file, import the `jsonServer` dependency there, and tell the express app to use it. So, your `server.js` file will look like the following:

```
//server.js
var express = require('express');
var jsonServer = require('json-server');
var serveStatic = require('serve-static');
var app = express();

app.use(serveStatic(__dirname + '/dist'));
app.use('/api', jsonServer.router('server/db.json'));
var port = process.env.PORT || 5000;
app.listen(port);
console.log('server started '+ port);
```

With the preceding line, we tell our express app to use `jsonServer` and serve the `db.json` file over the `/api/` endpoint.

We should also change the endpoint's address in our `Vue` resource. Open `index.js` in the API folder and replace `localhost:3000` with an `api` prefix:

```
const ShoppingListsResource = Vue.resource('api/' + 'shoppinglists{/id}')
```

We should also add JSON server support to `dev-server.js`; otherwise, we will not be able to run the application in development mode. So, open the `build/dev-server.js` file, import `jsonServer`, and tell the express app to use it:

```
//dev-server.js
var path = require('path')
var express = require('express')
var jsonServer = require('json-server')
<...>
// compilation error display
app.use(hotMiddleware)
```

```
// use json server
app.use('/api', jsonServer.router('server/db.json'));
<...>
```

Try to run the application in dev mode (npm run dev). Everything works fine.

You can now also remove the server running command (– nohup npm run server &) from the travis.yml file. You can also remove the server script from package.json.

Run tests locally and check that they are not failing.

We are almost done. Let's try our application locally.

Trying Heroku locally

Sometimes it gets a lot of try-fail iterations to get things work. We try something, commit, push, try to deploy, see whether it works. We realize that we have forgotten about something, commit, push, try to deploy, see the error log. Do it again and again. It might be really time-consuming because things over the network take time! Fortunately for us, the Heroku CLI provides a way to run the application locally as it was already deployed to the Heroku server. You just need to run the heroku local web command right after building the application:

```
npm run build
heroku local web
```

Try it.

Open http://localhost:5000 in your browser. Yes, it works!

Running the application locally with the Heroku local web command. It works!

Let's now commit and push the changes.

Now you can wait for the successful Travis build and automatic deploy by Heroku after that, or you can just open your Heroku dashboard and click on the **Deploy Branch** button. Wait a bit. And ... it works! Here is the result of two deployments we performed today:

- **Pomodoro application**: `https://catodoro.herokuapp.com/`
- **Shopping list application**: `https://shopping-list-vue.herokuapp.com/`

The respective GitHub repositories can be found at `https://github.com/chudaol/Pomodoro` and `https://github.com/chudaol/ShoppingList`.

Fork, play, test, deploy. At this moment, you have all the instruments needed to enhance, improve, and show these applications to the whole world. Thank you for being with me through this exciting journey!

Summary

In this chapter, you learned how to make our applications available for everyone. You also learned how to deploy them using Heroku integration with the GitHub repository. You also learned how to do it automatically on each commit and push. We also used Travis for automatic builds on each deployment. Now our applications are being fully tested and automatically redeployed each time we commit a change. Congratulations!

You probably think that this is the end of the journey. No, it is not. This is just the beginning. In the next chapter, we will see what you can learn and what nice things you can do next with both the Pomodoro and shopping list applications. Stay with me!

9
What Is Next?

In the previous chapter, we made our applications go live by deploying them to a server and making them available to the world. We have also guaranteed continuous integration and continuous deployment of our applications. This means that every time we commit changes performed on the applications, they will automatically be tested and deployed.

It seems that our journey in this book has finished. But, in fact, it has just started. After all we have discovered and learned, there is still so much to do! In this chapter, we will wrap up everything we have learned so far and see what we still have to learn and what nice things we still can do to reach the level of awesomeness of our applications. So, in this chapter, we will do the following:

- Wrap up everything we have learned so far
- Make a list of follow up things

The journey so far

We have been on a big journey so far, and it's time to sum up what we have done and what we have learned.

In Chapter 1, *Going Shopping with Vue.js*, we had our first date with Vue.js. We talked about what Vue.js is, how it was created, and what it does and saw some basic examples.

In Chapter 2, *Fundamentals – Installing and Using*, we went deep into behind the scenes of Vue.js. We learned about MVVM architectural pattern, we saw how does Vue.js work, and we touched different aspects of Vue.js such as *components*, *directives*, *plugins*, and application *state*. We learned different ways of installing Vue.js, starting from using a simple standalone compiled script, passing by using the CDN version, NPM version, and going toward using the development version of Vue.js being able to not only use it but also contribute to its codebase . We learned how to debug and how to scaffold Vue.js application using Vue-cli. We have even created a really simple Chrome application using CSP-compliant version of Vue.

In Chapter 3, *Components – Understanding and Using*, we put our hands deep inside the component's system. We learned how to define Vue components, how component's scope works, and how do components relate to each other, and we started using single-file components in the applications that we have bootstrapped before.

In Chapter 4, *Reactivity – Binding Data to Your Application*, we went deep into data binding and reactivity with Vue.js. We learned how to use directives, expressions, and filters. We brought data binding to the applications developed in the initial chapters and made them interactive, thanks to the reactivity fashion of Vue.js.

In Chapter 5, *Vuex – Managing State in Your Application*, we learned how to manage global state in Vue applications using the Vuex store system. We learned how to use state, actions, getters, and mutations in order to create a modular and nice application structure where the components can easily communicate with each other. We applied this new knowledge in our applications that we developed so far in the previous chapters.

In Chapter 6, *Plugins – Building Your House with Your Own Bricks*, we learned how Vue plugins cooperate with Vue applications. We used an existing plugin, vue-resource, which helped us to save the application's state between browser refreshes. We also created our own plugin for Vue applications that produces white, brown, and pink noises. At this point, we had fully functional applications with a quite nice set of working features.

In Chapter 7, *Testing – Time to Test What We Have Done So Far!*, we learned how to test our Vue applications. We learned how to write unit tests and how to create and run end-to-end tests with Selenium driver. We learned what code coverage is and how to fake server responses in unit tests. We covered almost 100% of our code with unit tests and we saw the Selenium driver in action running our end-to-end tests.

In `Chapter 8`, *Deploying – Time to Go Live!*, we finally exposed our applications to the whole world. We deployed them to the Heroku cloud system and now they can be accessed from everywhere where the Internet exists. More than that, we made our deployment process completely automated. Each time we push code changes to the `master` branch, the application is deployed! Even more than that. They are not only deployed on each push, but also automatically tested with the Travis continuous integration system.

Thus, in this book, we haven't just learned a new framework. We applied our knowledge to develop two simple, yet nice applications from scratch. We applied the most important Vue's concepts to make our applications reactive, fast, maintainable, and testable. However, this is not the end. During the writing of this book, Vue 2.0 has been launched. It brings some new possibilities and some new things to learn and use.

Vue 2.0

Vue 2.0 launched on the September 30, 2016. Check out this post of Evan You at `https://me dium.com/the-vue-point/vue-2-0-is-here-ef1f26acf4b8#.ifpgtjlek`.

Across this book, we used the newest version; however, I tried to reference the way of doing things in the first generation of Vue whenever it was necessary. Actually, the API is almost the same; there are some slight changes, some deprecated attributes, but the whole interface provided to the final user remains almost untouched.

Nevertheless, it was almost rewritten from scratch! Of course, there are some parts of code that were almost 100% reused, but overall, it was a major refactor and some of the concepts were completely changed. For example, the rendering layer was completely rewritten. If, earlier, the rendering engine was using the real DOM, now it uses a lightweight virtual DOM structure (`https://github.com/snabbdom/snabbdom`). Its performance beats everything! Check out the benchmark figure in the following:

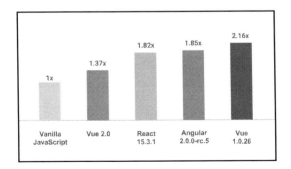

Performance benchmark (the lower is better) taken from https://medium.com/the-vue-point/vue-2-0-is-here-ef1f26acf4b8#.fjxegtv98

There is another interesting point in this new version. If you have already used the first generation of Vue, and read about it and listened to podcasts, you probably know that one of the major differences between, let's say, Vue and React was React Native (the framework that allows us to build native apps based on React). Evan You was always claiming that Vue was just a tiny layer for web interfaces. Now, we have the emerging **Weex**, a framework that renders Vue-inspired components into native apps (`https://github.com/alibaba/we ex`). According to Evan You, very soon, "Vue-inspired" will become "Vue-powered"! Just wait for it. Just stay tuned. I would like to recommend this amazing Full Stack Radio podcast, where Evan You talks about the new version of Vue: `http://www.fullstackradio .com/50`.

> *Vue has evolved a lot since its humble beginning as a side project. Today it is community funded, widely adopted in the real world, and boasts one of the strongest growth trends among all JavaScript libraries according to stats.js.org. We believe 2.0 is going to push it even further. It's the biggest update to Vue since its inception, and we are excited to see what you build with it.*
> *- Evan You, https://medium.com/the-vue-point/vue-2-0-is-here-ef1f26acf4b8#.fjxegtv98)*

With this in mind, if you are coming from the Vue 1.0 generation, it will not be hard for you to upgrade your applications. Check the migration guide, `http://vuejs.org/guide/migra tion.html`, install the migration helper, `https://github.com/vuejs/vue-migration-help er`, apply all needed changes, and see how your applications perform after that.

Revisiting our applications

Let's check again what have we done so far. We have developed two applications using Vue.js. Let's revisit them.

Shopping list application

The shopping list application that we have developed in this book's chapters is a web application that allows the following:

- Create different shopping lists
- Add new items to the shopping lists and check them once they are bought
- Rename shopping lists and remove them

Our shopping list application resides on the Heroku cloud platform: `https://shopping-li st-vue.herokuapp.com/`.

Its code is hosted on GitHub: `https://github.com/chudaol/ShoppingList`.

It is continuously integrated with Travis: `https://travis-ci.org/chudaol/ShoppingList`

Its interface is simple and easy to understand:

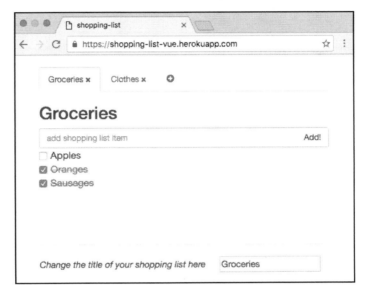

The interface of the shopping list application developed using Vue.js

It is still far from something that you would use every time you go shopping, isn't it?

The Pomodoro application

The Pomodoro application that we have developed in this book is a web application that implements a Pomodoro timer with white noise during the working Pomodoros and nice pictures of cats during the interval time. It allows the following:

- Start, pause, and stop the application
- Listen to white noise while working, noise that helps concentrating
- Mute and unmute the white noise sound
- Stare at the kittens during spare time

Our Pomodoro application is also hosted on the Heroku cloud platform: `https://catodoro`
`.herokuapp.com/`.

Its code is also hosted at GitHub: `https://github.com/chudaol/Pomodoro`.

And it is also built and tested on each push using the Travis continuous integration
platform: `https://travis-ci.org/chudaol/Pomodoro`.

Its interface is clean and easy to use. Here is what it shows for the 20-minute working
Pomodoro interval:

The Pomodoro application during the working Pomodoro

And here's what appears when the time for a 5-minute break comes:

The Pomodoro application during its interval time

It is actually pretty usable, but also still far from perfect.

Why is it just the beginning?

In the previous section, we summarized what the applications that we have developed throughout the book are doing. We have also agreed (I hope) that they are still far from perfect. Things that are far from perfect are things that we want to improve and therefore they give us challenges and purpose. There is actually still a lot of work to be done. Our applications are nice, but they lack features, style, identity, UX patterns, extension to other platforms, and so on. Let's check what we can still do.

Adding features to our applications

Our applications already have some pretty nice features, but they can have even more. They can be more configurable. They can be more flexible. They can be more UI/UX friendly. Let's look at each of them and write a list of features that can be added. It will be your homework.

Shopping list application

Open our shopping list application in the browser and look at it. You can add your lists and items to them. You can delete items and lists. But every person who opens the application in the browser will be able to do the same. It means that we have to provide a way of every person having their own shopping list application, which is only possible with an authentication mechanism.

There are also some UX issues. Why should we change the name of the shopping list using the input field in the footer if we can change it, let's say, inline? Well, actually, shopping list's name editing in the input field was the first thing we implemented when we were learning how to achieve data binding in Vue applications. So, it made sense at the time, but now it can and should be improved.

Another thing has to do with deleted items. There is no way of clearing them up. If we have a long list of items, even when we delete them, they stay forever unless we remove the whole shopping list. There should be a way of clearing up checked items on the list.

Another cosmetic change that we can apply has to do with styling. Different lists might have a different background colors, different font colors, and probably even different font styles and sizes. With that, here's the list of improvements for the shopping list application:

- Implement an authentication mechanism
- Implement inline name editing

- Implement clearing up checked items
- Implement a mechanism of configuring different shopping lists' styling, such as background color, text color, font size, and style

You can also implement categories for the items and icons for each of the categories. As an inspiration, you can have a look at the Splitwise application at `https://www.splitwise.com/`. When you start adding items, the icon of the item is generic. Once you type in something meaningful, the icon changes, as shown in the following screenshot:

The screenshot of the Splitwise application for the inspiration for the icon categories: it adapts to what you type in the input field

Try to implement this kind of categorization for our shopping list application. It would be a really nice and powerful bonus!

The Pomodoro application

Open our Pomodoro application in your browser and try using it. It's nice, without any doubt. It is simple and easy to use. However, some extra configuration might bring some extra power to it. For example, why should I work for 20 minutes? Maybe I would like to have 15-minute periods of working Pomodoros. Or maybe I want to have bigger working Pomodoros, let's say 25 or 30 minutes. It should definitely be configurable.

Let's thoroughly check the description of the Pomodoro technique in Wikipedia to see if we are missing something: `https://en.wikipedia.org/wiki/Pomodoro_Technique`.

I'm pretty sure we are. Check this point at the underlying principles:

> *"After four pomodoros, take a longer break (15-30 minutes), reset your checkmark count to zero, then go to step 1."*
>
> *- https://en.wikipedia.org/wiki/Pomodoro_Technique*

Aha! Something should happen after four Pomodoros. Bigger interval, more time staring at cats (or doing whatever you want to do). Hmm, probably it would be nice to be able to configure this period of time as well!

There's another important thing. As any human being, after working hard, I would like to see some progress. Wouldn't it be nice if our Pomodoro application could display some statistics about the amount of time we were able to concentrate on ourselves and to do our work? For this, we could collect some statistics and display them in our Pomodoro timer.

Also, wouldn't it be nice to store these statistics to be able to visualize them during some period of time, let's say, one week, one month, one year? This leads us to the need to implement a storage mechanism. This store should store statistics for each user, so again, an authentication mechanism is needed as well.

Let's think about our nice white, brown, and pink noises. Currently, we just play the brown noise that is hardcoded in our App.vue:

```
<template>
 <div id="app" class="container" v-noise="'brown'">
 </div>
</template>
```

Shouldn't we be able to switch between noises and choose our favorite one? Hence, we have identified one more item to add to the application's configuration. That's enough for now; let's put all this in the list:

- Implement the authentication mechanism
- Implement a storage mechanism—it should collect the statistics about working times and store them in some persistence layer
- Implement the statistics displaying mechanism—it should grab the stored statistical data and display it in a nice and clean way (for example, charts)

- Add a configuration mechanism to the Pomodoro application. This configuration should allow the following:
    - Configure the Pomodoro working period of time
    - Configure the resting intervals of times
    - Configure a big resting time after a configurable amount of working Pomodoros (4 by default)
    - Configure the preferred noise to play during the working intervals

As you can see, you still have some work to do. It's a good thing, you have already a working Pomodoro timer application to use while you are working on its improvements!

Beautifying our applications

Both applications are currently pretty gray. Only the Pomodoro timer application becomes a little bit more colorful when a cat appears on the screen. It would be nice to add some design to them. Make them unique, give them their identity; you worked so hard on them, they clearly deserve some nice clothes. Let's think about what we can do with styling.

Logotype

Start with the logotype. A good logo defines your product and makes it unique. I can help you with the Pomodoro application's logo, at least with the idea for it. I have a very good friend called Carina who designed a tomato for me and I have just tried my best to add a little kitten to it. Check it out. You can use it as is or use just as an idea to develop your own. Even the sky is not the limit for your imagination, really!

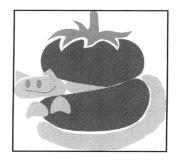

The idea for a logotype for the Pomodoro application

Think about a nice logo for the shopping list app. What can it be? A bag for the groceries? A checkbox? Just initials—SL? Again, no limits. I hope to see your nice logos in the repositories forks. Can't wait for it!

Identity and design

Our applications definitely need some unique design. Use some UX techniques to develop a nice identity guide for them. Think about colors, fonts, and how the elements should be composed on the page so that they provide a unique user-friendly experience to our users.

Animations and transitions

Animations and transitions are powerful mechanisms that bring some life to an application. However, they cannot be abused. Think about where and how they make sense. For example, hovering on the shopping lists titles could end up in some highlighting, shopping list items can do some tiny bouncing when they are checked, the process of changing the title of the shopping list could also be highlighted in some way, and so on. The Pomodoro application can change its background color on each of the state's transitions. It can also be aware of the time of the day and color the background accordingly. The number of opportunities is endless. Use your creativity, use Vue's power to achieve your ideas.

Extending our applications to other devices

Both of our applications are web applications. While it might be okay for the Pomodoro application if we work the whole day on the computer and use the Web, it might be a little bit uncomfortable for the shopping list application. You don't bring your laptop when you go shopping. Of course, you can fill the shopping list with items at home and then open the mobile browser in the supermarket, but it might be slow and not so nice to use. Use Weex (h ttps://github.com/alibaba/weex) to bring our web applications to the mobile devices. Both the applications can also be extended to be used as a Google Chrome app, just as we learned in Chapter 2, *Fundamentals – Installing and Using*. Extend your work to each and every device you can. I am looking forward to checking your work.

Summary

This is the last chapter of this book. Honestly, I feel a little bit sad about it. I had a really fun time with you. I know that I don't know you, but I feel like I do. I talk to you and I feel that sometimes you talk to me. Everything that was developed so far, I cannot say at all that it was developed by me; I feel that we have been working together on it all this time.

It is a very funny feeling, actually, because I am at the same time in the present and in the future when you are reading this book (for me, it's the future). And you are now in your present and at the same time talking to me in the past. I love the way that books and technologies establish connections not only between people but also between different time intervals. This is amazing.

I really hope that you became a fan of Vue.js in the same way I am a fan of it.

I really hope that you will enhance at least one of the applications we have developed so far and show it to me. I will be really glad to help if you need my help. Do not hesitate to drop me a message at `chudaol@gmail.com`.

Thank you for being with me all this time, and I hope to meet you soon in the next book!

Solutions to Exercises

Exercise for chapter 1

In the end of the first chapter, there was the following exercise:

 The Pomodoro timer that we have built in the previous chapters is, without any doubt, great, but it still lacks some nice features. A really nice thing that it could provide would be showing random kittens from `http://thecatapi.com/` during resting time. Can you implement this? Of course you can! But please do not confuse resting with working time! I am almost sure that your project manager will not like much if you stare at the kittens instead of working :)

Let's solve it.

Check the code for Pomodoro at `https://jsfiddle.net/chudaol/b6vmtzq1/`.

Check `http://thecatapi.com/` website.

Let's start by adding the well Bootstrap element with an image whose source points to the cat API:

```
<div id="app" class="container">
  <...>
  <div class="well">
    <img :src="' http://thecatapi.com/api/images/get?
      type=gif&size=med'" />
  <div>
</div>
```

If you open the page you will see that the image is always visible. This is not what we want, we want, it to only be visible when we are in our Pomodoro resting interval. You already know how to do it. There are several ways of achieving this; let's use the class binding method and bind a class that's hidden when the state is working:

```
<div class="well" :class="{ 'hidden': pomodoroState === 'work' }">
  <img :src="'http://thecatapi.com/api/
    images/get?type=gif&size=med'" />
</div>
```

Now, if you open the page you will see that the image only appears when the working Pomodoro is finished.

However, the problem is that for all the time that we rest, the image is the same. It would be great if we could update it every, let's say, 10 seconds.

Let's use a cache buster mechanism for this purpose. If we attach some property to our URL and change it each 10 seconds, the URL will change and therefore we will obtain another random cat. Let's add a `timestamp` variable to our Vue application and change it inside the `_tick` function:

```
<...>
new Vue({
  el: "#app",
  data: {
    <...>
    timestamp: 0
  },
  <...>
  methods: {
    <...>
    _tick: function () {
      //update timestamp that is used in image src
      if (this.second % 10 === 0) {
        this.timestamp = new Date().getTime();
      }
      <...>
    }
  }
});
```

After the timestamp is created and updated, we can use it in our image source URL:

```
<div class="well" :class="{ 'hidden': pomodoroState === 'work' }">
  <img :src="'http://thecatapi.com/api/images/get?
    type=gif&size=med&ts=' + timestamp" />
</div>
```

That's all! Check the whole code in this JSFiddle at `https://jsfiddle.net/chudaol/4hnbt0pd/2/`.

Exercises for chapter 2

Enhancing MathPlugin

Enhance our `MathPlugin` with trigonometrical functions (sine, cosine, and tangent).

Actually, it is just about adding the missing directives and using the `Math` object's functions in it. Open `VueMathPlugin.js` and add the following:

```
//VueMathPlugin.js
export default {
  install: function (Vue) {
    Vue.directive('square', function (el, binding) {
      el.innerHTML = Math.pow(binding.value, 2);
    });
    Vue.directive('sqrt', function (el, binding) {
      el.innerHTML = Math.sqrt(binding.value);
    });
    Vue.directive('sin', function (el, binding) {
      el.innerHTML = Math.sin(binding.value);
    });
    Vue.directive('cos', function (el, binding) {
      el.innerHTML = Math.cos(binding.value);
    });
    Vue.directive('tan', function (el, binding) {
      el.innerHTML = Math.tan(binding.value);
    });
  }
};
```

You can check how this directive works in the HTML file:

```
//index.html
<div id="app">
  <input v-model="item"/>
  <hr>
  <div><strong>Square:</strong> <span v-square="item"></span></div>
  <div><strong>Root:</strong> <span v-sqrt="item"></span></div>
  <div><strong>Sine:</strong> <span v-sin="item"></span></div>
  <div><strong>Cosine:</strong> <span v-cos="item"></span></div>
  <div><strong>Tangent:</strong> <span v-tan="item"></span></div>
</div>
```

That's it!

Creating a Chrome application of the Pomodoro timer

Please combine a solution of bootstrapping the application using a SCP-compliant version of Vue.js and the simple Pomodoro application that we created in Chapter 1, *Going Shopping with Vue.js*. Check the code in the chrome-app-pomodoro folder.

Exercises for chapter 3

Exercise 1

When we were rewriting the shopping list application using simple components, we lost the application's functionality. The exercise suggests using an events emitting system in order to bring the functionality back.

The code we ended up with in this section was looking similar to what is in the chapter3/vue-shopping-list-simple-components folder.

Why doesn't it work? Check the devtools error console. It states the following:

```
[Vue warn]: Property or method "addItem" is not defined on the instance but
referenced during render. Make sure to declare reactive data properties in
the data option.
(found in component <add-item-component>)
```

Aha! This happens because inside `add-item-template` we are calling the `addItem` method which does not belong to this component. This method belongs to the parent component, and of course, the child component does not have access to it. What should we do? Let's emit events! We already know how to do it. So, we don't have to do too much. Actually, we have to do three small things:

- Attach the `addItem` method to `add-item-component` in which we will emit an event and pass this component's `newItem` property to it.
- Modify/simplify the `addItem` method of the parent component. It should now just receive a text and add it to its `items` property.
- Attach the `v-on` modifier with the name of the event to the component's invocation inside the main markup that will call the `addItem` method each time the event is emitted.

Let's start by adding the `addItem` method to `add-item-component`. It is called each time the add button or *Enter* is hit. This method should check the `newItem` property, and if it contains a text, should emit an event. Let's call this event `add`. Thus, the JavaScript code of our component will now look the follows:

```
//add item component
Vue.component('add-item-component', {
  template: '#add-item-template',
  data: function () {
    return {
      newItem: ''
    }
  },
  methods: {
    addItem: function () {
      var text;


      text = this.newItem.trim();
      if (text) {
        this.$emit('add', this.newItem);
        this.newItem = '';
      }
    }
  }
});
```

When the `add` event is emitted, somehow the `addItem` method of the main component should be invoked. Let's bind the `add` event to `addItem` by attaching the `v-on:add` modifier to the `add-item-component` invocation:

```
<add-item-component v-on:add="addItem" :items="items">
</add-item-component>
```

Okay then. As you can see, this method does almost the same that the `addItem` method of the main component was doing before. It just doesn't push `newItem` to the `items` array. Let's modify the `addItem` method of the main component so it just receives already processed text and pushes it into the array of items:

```
new Vue({
  el: '#app',
  data: data,
  methods: {
    addItem: function (text) {
      this.items.push({
        text: text,
        checked: false
      });
    }
  }
});
```

We're done! The full solution of this exercise can be found in the `appendix/chapter3/vue-shopping-list-simple-components` folder.

Exercise 2

In the section called *Rewriting the shopping list application with single-file components* in `Chapter` 3, *Components – Understanding and Using*, we did quite a nice job of changing the shopping list application using single-file components, but there are still few things left. We have two missing functionalities: adding items to the items list, and changing the title.

In order to achieve the first functionality, we have to emit an event from `AddItemComponent` and attach the `v-on` modifier to the `add-item-component` invocation with the main `App.vue` component, exactly like we have done in the case of dealing with simple components. You can basically just copy and paste the code.

The same goes for the changing title functionality. We should also emit an `input` event, just like we did in the simple components example.

Do not forget to add the style to the `App.vue` component to make it look just as it was before.

Check the full code in the `appendix/chapter3/shopping-list-single-file-components` folder.

Index

W

X

78201846R00186

Made in the USA
San Bernardino, CA
02 June 2018